The Ultimate Sound Blaster™ Book

Martin L. Moore

The Ultimate Sound Blaster Book

Library of Congress Catalog No.: 93-85047

ISBN: 1-56529-298-7

95 94 93   4 3 2 1

Interpretation of the printing code: the rightmost double-digit number is the year of the book's printing; the rightmost single-digit number is the number of the book's printing. For example, a printing code of 93-1 shows that the first printing of the book occurred in 1993.

Screens reproduced in this book were created using Collage Plus from Inner Media, Inc., Hollis, NH.

Publisher: David P. Ewing

Associate Publisher: Rick Ranucci

Director of Publishing: Michael Miller

Managing Editor: Corinne Walls

Marketing Manager: Ray Robinson

Dedication

For my kids: Ann, Adam, and Colleen. Remember. . .

> *Men are never so likely to settle a question rightly as when they discuss it freely.*

Thomas Babington, Lord Macaulay
Southey's Colloquies on Society [1830]

and

> *Who built the seven gates of Thebes?*
> *In the books are listed the names of kings.*
> *Did the kings heave up the building blocks?*

Bertolt Brecht

Publishing Manager
Don Roche, Jr.

Acquisitions Editor
Thomas F. Godfrey, III

Product Director
Jim Minatel

Production Editor
Virginia Noble

Editors
Jodi Jensen
Cindy Morrow

Technical Editor
Michael Watson

Book Designer
Amy Peppler-Adams

Cover Designer
Jay Corpus
Kathy Hanley

Production Team

Angela Bannan	*Heather Kaufman*
Danielle Bird	*Bob LaRoche*
Ayrika Bryant	*Mike Mucha*
Charlotte Clapp	*Juli Pavey*
Dennis Clay Hager	*Dennis Wesner*
Carla Hall	*Donna Winter*

Indexer
Joy Dean Lee

Editorial Assistant
Jill L. Stanley

Composed in *ITC Century Light* and *MCPdigital* by Que Corporation

About the Author

Martin L. Moore is the President of MDP, Inc., a multimedia development company in Portland, Oregon. Most recently, he was the Director of Engineering for Que Software, a developer of language software tools, including RightWriter. He is the author of three books and more than a dozen magazine articles, and his focus is on the future of multimedia.

Acknowledgments

As much as a writer likes to think otherwise, no book is an individual effort. My thanks to Ginny Noble for her unflagging positive attitude while editing this book. My thanks also to Michael Watson for trying to keep me technically honest. All flaws are my own. This book would not have been possible had it not been for the quick and invaluable assistance of Theresa Palido at Creative Labs. Jim Minatel—what can I say? And to Rick Ranucci and Dave Ewing, thanks for giving me a shot.

Trademarks

Contents
at a Glance

Table of Contents

Introduction

This is a book about the Sound Blaster family of products for PCs. So? When people ask me what I'm working on these days and I tell them that I'm doing a book about a product that adds sound capability to a personal computer, I sometimes get a response that goes something like, "Sound, huh? What does that do?" Fortunately, those people are in the minority. The rest of the people I talk to immediately recognize some benefit, either to themselves or their company, to having sound capability in their computers.

Although first perceived as an interesting "gimmick," the capability to record and play back sound on a PC is now coming into its own. When you sit up and look around, it's clear that multimedia is the next big wave in the personal computer industry, and sound is an integral part of that wave. If you prefer more rustic analogies, multimedia is a three-legged stool, and sound is one of the legs. If you are thinking of upgrading your system to multimedia capability, you should read this book. Or, if you already own a Sound Blaster, you will find information within these pages not available from the documentation provided with your sound card. If you are interested in writing software that makes use of Sound Blaster, you will find file format information, as well as a description of how to use the Sound Blaster driver routines.

A number of sound systems are now available for personal computers. The Sound Blaster family from Creative Labs, Inc., is probably one of the best product lines available, and certainly the most popular. The Sound Blaster family satisfies a wide range of budgets and needs. This book covers the four mainstream Sound Blaster models currently available: Sound Blaster V2.0, Sound Blaster Pro, Sound Blaster 16, and Sound Blaster 16 ASP. The utility and application software provided by Creative Labs is also described.

Finally, a number of carefully selected shareware packages are included with this book—software that you should find very useful in getting the most from your Sound Blaster.

How This Book Is Organized

This book consists of 11 chapters and 4 appendixes.

Chapter 1, "A Look Back: A Short History of Electronic Music," provides a brief historical perspective of the art of electronic sound, from the heavyweight Teleharmonium at the turn of the century, through the Moog synthesizer, to today's PC-based synthesizer technology.

In Chapter 2, "What Is Sound, Anyway?" you find out how you hear, how what you hear can be turned into digital 1s and 0s, and how electrons can be shaped to imitate existing sounds or create sounds never heard before.

Chapter 3, "The Sound Blaster Family," describes the Sound Blaster family of products. Installation information, as well as a description of many of the utility programs that come with Sound Blaster, are provided.

Chapter 4, "Finding and Editing Sounds," shows you where to find sounds and how to create your own. Creative Labs' Voice Editor, VEDIT2, is described as well.

Many computers are able to create and save sound files. Chapter 5, "Saving Sounds," provides information on how to convert those files into a form that can be used by Sound Blaster. A number of conversion utilities provided by Creative Labs, as well as several shareware utilities, are covered.

Chapter 6, "Musical Instrument Digital Interface," describes MIDI, the Musical Instrument Digital Interface specification. Sound Blaster can serve as a MIDI instrument and can route MIDI instructions to other MIDI instruments through its MIDI/joystick connector.

MIDI sequencers are software programs that let you build and play songs on MIDI instruments like Sound Blaster. The Voyetra SP Pro is a DOS-based MIDI sequencer offered with some versions of the Sound Blaster MIDI kit. Chapter 7, "The Voyetra SP Pro MIDI Sequencer," covers this sequencer.

Cakewalk Apprentice from Twelve Tone Systems, Inc., is an outstanding Windows-based MIDI sequencer. Chapter 8, "Cakewalk Apprentice for Windows," describes Cakewalk Apprentice in full detail.

Chapter 9, "Windows and Sound Blaster," focuses on using Sound Blaster in a Windows environment. Included are tips on using the sometimes mysterious Windows MIDI Mapper, as well as the Windows-based applications provided by Creative Labs.

If you are a software programmer, Chapter 10, "Programming Sound Blaster," provides the information you need for accessing Sound Blaster's registers and using the Sound Blaster driver routines. This chapter is not for the faint of heart or nonprogrammers.

Chapter 11, "Sources and Shareware," directs you to sources of software, music, and sound files. The shareware applications provided with this book are also briefly described.

The appendixes provide information on frequencies of sound, the VOC sound file format, how Sound Blaster MIDI cables are constructed, and instructions on installing the shareware that comes with this book.

Conventions Used in This Book

Several typefaces are used in this book. Variables, new terms, and emphasized text appear in *italics*. Information that you type and hot keys for menu items appear in **boldface**. On-screen prompts and messages appear in a `special typeface`.

A Final Word

For this book, it is assumed that you already know how to use DOS and the Windows user interface. Very little introductory information is provided about working within those environments. Readers of Chapter 10 are assumed to be experienced software engineers, already familiar with the details of accessing driver routines to control hardware.

Otherwise, you should find it relatively easy to get around within these chapters.

CHAPTER 1

A Look Back:
A Short History of
Electronic Music

In 1972, while attending a small college in northern Idaho, a group of students and I followed a professor into the campus computer room. We watched as a computer operator loaded a card deck into the card reader (this was 1972!) and had the computer read the FORTRAN 66 program into core.

The operator then did a remarkable thing. He laid a transistorized FM radio on top of the cabinet holding the CPU. With a glint in his eye, he then punched the button to begin execution. To our surprise, out of the radio issued strains of "Lady of Spain."

Someone had noticed that different FORTRAN instructions caused the rather noisy circuitry inside the computer to switch on and off at different rates. By noting which instruction created which tone, some enterprising student was able to write a FORTRAN program that played the song.

That was my introduction to digital music.

In this chapter, you take a brief tour through the history of electronic sound. A little background will help you understand the genesis of Sound Blaster. You also see how electronics are used to generate speech, music, and sounds that have never been heard before.

That computer in 1972 was just one point in a rather long and stately history of creating sounds with electricity. Sounds have been generated with electricity for a century now, with a variety of interesting (and occasionally ludicrous) machines. Until the invention of the electronic oscillator and vacuum-tube amplifiers, most electronic sound was produced mechanically.

Two Hundred Tons of Sound

What must still hold the record as the world's largest musical instrument was a 200-ton behemoth called the Dynamophone or the Telharmonium, invented in 1906 by Thaddeus Cahill. The Dynamophone produced sounds by feeding the output of banks of dynamos into a telephone speaker.

The dynamo is a very simple generator of alternating current (AC) electricity. It's been around for a long time. You can use the alternating current generated by a dynamo to move the coil of a speaker back and forth, as shown in figure 1.1. The faster you turn the dynamo, the higher the frequency of AC generated, and the faster the speaker cone moves back and forth.

Fig. 1.1

Using a dynamo to create sine waves.

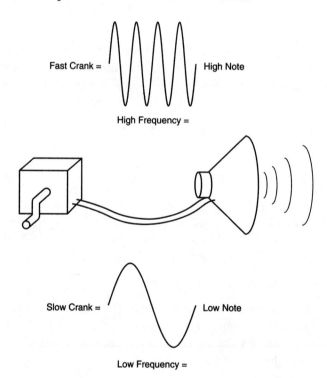

Fast Crank =   High Note

High Frequency =

Slow Crank =   Low Note

Low Frequency =

The dynamo generates *sine* waves, which are electrical signals that change polarity and voltage over time. The alternating current (AC) available from your wall socket is delivered to your house in the form of sine waves. Mr. Cahill took advantage of the fact that you can electrically add two or more pure tones generated by sine waves to create a third complex tone called an "overtone." His thinking was that he could build a machine with many different dynamos generating many different sine waves. Those sine waves could be routed to the speaker through switches mounted under a keyboard. All this before the days of tube-type amplifiers!

The Telharmonium even boasted a touch-sensitive keyboard in that as a key was pressed, one electrical coil of wire moved closer to another, dynamically changing the loudness of the note. None of this on-off stuff for Thaddeus Cahill.

The instrument required several railroad boxcars to move what was in essence a rolling power station, because the multiple dynamos were generating about 15,000 watts of power each.

The Telharmonium's day in the sun occurred in the summer of 1906, when a concert was held in the Hamilton Hotel in Holyoke. The signal that drove the speaker was sent over what must have been sizzling telephone lines from the main plant, about a mile away. Later that fall, the instrument was packed up and shipped to New York for a concert put on for the New York Electrical Society. At that time, the machinery had the power to send music out over the telephone lines, supplying nearly 20,000 subscribers. Plans were under way to provide four different circuits with four different kinds of music—an early day precursor to cablecasting.

Alas, the Telharmonium had a limited future. Aside from creating havoc with the local telephone service, the instrument apparently generated a rather constant and painful background noise that "in time grew highly irritating to the nerves," according to one of the keyboard artists.[1] The idea did crop up again, quite successfully, as it turned out.

Mr. Hammond's Organ

The once-dead technology used in the Telharmonium was dragged out of the attic and updated in 1935 by Laurens Hammond. But this time, instead of boxcars of dynamos producing thousands of watts of power, the Hammond Organ could actually fit into a living room. There were two significant advances

[1] *The Art of Electronic Music, compiled by Tom Darter and edited by Greg Ambruster (New York: William Morrow and Company, Inc., 1984).*

that made the early Hammond possible: the first was the use of a synchronous motor developed for the Hammond Company's first product, the electric clock; and the second was the development of the vacuum-tube amplifier. The synchronous motor is an AC motor capable of spinning at a very consistent rate as long as the AC power frequency is constant. Previous electric motors had trouble maintaining a constant rotation speed.

The principle, however, was the same. The new synchronous motor drove multiple dynamos that generated various frequencies. But this time, the 91 dynamos, called tone wheels, were iron disks about the size of an American silver dollar (before the Susan B. Anthony) and were turned at a very precise rate, giving the instrument greatly improved tonal stability. The smaller tone wheels were possible because the small signal generated by these minia-ture dynamos could be amplified with vacuum-tube amplifiers. Cahill's Telharmonium had shrunk from 200 tons of hair-raising power generation to a small console that nearly anyone could have. Thus began the long history of the Hammond Organ.

Pianos, Electrified

The electric piano had part of its origins in the desire to make pianos portable. Harold Rhodes invented the Air Corps Piano in the 1940s because he needed something cheap and portable to use to teach patients in the Army hospital how to play.

What Rhodes actually came up with was an electronic xylophone, but instead of striking the sound bars with a hammer, Rhodes built a keyboard that struck the bars for you. And instead of relying on the natural acoustic sound generated by the metal tubes, Rhodes built an amplifier that amplified the vibrations of the sound bars, which were made of 3/8-inch aluminum hydraulic tubing.

After the war, Rhodes developed a piano for in-home use. For $99.50 you, too, could own a Rhodes Pre-Piano. The three octave instrument had an amplifier and a 6-inch speaker built into the console. The tone bars were made of tines manufactured by a toy company.

But Rhodes wasn't the only player in the electric piano field. Benjamin Miessner, long a major figure in the development of electronics, was very interested in electronic instruments and spent a significant number of years working on the problem of electric pianos.

One of his early successes was an electric piano that had once been a standard piano. Standard pianos rely on the existence of a sound board to reflect and direct (and to some extent sustain) the vibrations of the piano strings outward. In fact, the sound board is very critical to the kind of tone a piano string or strings make. The sound board vibrates in sympathy with the piano strings, making very rich sounds with lots of harmonics and subharmonics.

What Miessner did was to cut the sound board out of the piano and place electrostatic pickups near the metal strings. As the string vibrated in proximity to the pickup, the resulting, varying electrical field was amplified. Voilà! An electric piano.

More important, however, was Miessner's research in placing pickups in a variety of places and in different orientations along the length of the string. This gave him the ability to select specific characteristics to be amplified: timbre, voicing, and even envelope control, all of which are discussed in the next chapter.

A number of stringless pianos were developed. My mother still has a portable electric piano built in the late 1950s that uses aluminum bars as the tone generator. Metal reeds, tubes, tuning forks, square bars, round bars—all have been tried with mixed success. It wasn't until the advent of the electronic oscillator that the purely electronic sound generator was possible.

Lee de Forest—The Father of Electronic Music

Two technological breakthroughs set the stage for development of all things electronic. Before 1906, the only way that mechanically or electrically produced sound could be amplified was through the use of large speaker horns.

Lee de Forest was one of the most influential people of this century. He was granted the first patent for an electronic oscillator using regenerative feedback. That was in 1915. Couple that with de Forest's earlier development in 1906 of the Audion, the triode vacuum-tube amplifier, and you can see that all electronically generated and amplified sound can be traced back to this one man.

De Forest recognized the potential of his inventions to create sound in a magazine article about his oscillating circuitry. Note the following excerpt:

> "The pitch of the notes is very easily regulated by changing the capacity or the inductance in the circuits, which can be easily effected by a sliding contact or simply by turning the knob of the condenser [capacitor]. In fact, the pitch of the notes can be changed by merely putting the finger on certain parts of the circuit or even by holding the hand close to parts of the circuit. In this way, very weird and beautiful effects can easily be obtained."[2]

Lee de Forest's observations did not go unnoticed.

Good Vibrations

Leon Theremin (or Termen) was a Russian physicist. In 1924, Theremin invented an electronic instrument called the Thereminvox or the Aetherphon, which ultimately came to be called, oddly enough, the "Theremin." Based on the principle that your body can have an influence on electronic circuits, Dr. Theremin's invention consisted of two capacitors, with a metal rod or wire being one side of the capacitor, and your body being the other. When you moved your right hand closer to or farther from the tone rod, the pitch went up and down. Your left hand controlled volume by changing its proximity to the volume rod. The artist never touches the Theremin—truly the first "air guitar."

Theremin's instrument used the principle of heterodyning, which works like this: When two generators of very high (inaudible in this case) frequencies are working precisely at the same frequency, only the original frequency is produced. However, if one of the generators is running slightly faster or slower than the other, a third "beat" frequency is generated, which can be a much lower audible frequency. What the player of the Theremin does is to detune one of the tone generators by moving her hand nearer to or farther from the tone rod, thus changing the frequency of the "beat" tone. Guitar players use the heterodyne principle when they tune their guitars by ear. A player listens for the "beat" of two strings that are out of tune. When the strings are in tune, no beat frequency is heard.

A more modern version of the Theremin was used by the Beach Boys in their song "Good Vibrations." The ephemeral sort of sliding sound used in that recording was generated by a transistorized version of the Theremin. The

---

[2]The Art of Electronic Music, *compiled by Tom Darter and edited by Greg Ambruster (New York: William Morrow and Company, Inc., 1984).*

player controlled the pitch by sliding his finger up and down the length of a copper wire embedded in the top of an electronic piano keyboard.

The Theremin soon died out as anything other than a novelty. But it did demonstrate heterodyning, which is used today in a number of electronic devices, including radios. As an interesting aside, the heterodyne effect used by Theremin was also used in the *Star Wars* movies to generate the low-pitched sound made by the two light sabers wielded by Luke Skywalker and Darth Vader. As the light sabers approached one another, the sound intensity rose. The sound was, as is nearly always the case in the movies, added on a sound stage after the films had been shot. A sound effects expert (called a "Foley") held a wired broom handle nearly the length of the light saber, and as the actors in the film swung at each other, the sound effects man would swing his broom handle toward a vertical rod. The proximity of the broom handle to the vertical rod would change the intensity of the sound generated. Thus, a little modern day movie magic was created by an invention from 1924.

Tubes, Tubes, Everywhere Tubes

What was simple becomes complex. In the inevitable march forward, the rather uncomplicated (though difficult to play) single-tone Theremin was replaced by keyboard instruments that generated hundreds of tones. The Coupleux-Givelet Organ developed in the 1930s used one oscillator tube for each note of the scale. The organ generated 70 notes, in 10 different timbres, and for each timbre used a series of oscillator tubes followed by an amplifier. The entire instrument contained *hundreds* of tubes.

The Hammond Novachord solved the problem of hundreds of tubes by taking advantage of the fact that octaves are a multiple of two. In other words, the C below middle C vibrates at half the frequency of middle C. Likewise, the next C above middle C vibrates at twice the frequency of middle C. Given the development of electronics that can divide frequencies in two, or even double them, Hammond was able to develop an organ that had only one tube for each fundamental frequency.

The Novachord could generate percussive notes (notes with a steep attack and long decay, sort of like striking one string of a guitar and letting the sound die away) as well as sustained tones. In addition, the Novachord was *poly-phonic*—that is, if you could press all the keys simultaneously, all the notes would sound simultaneously. This is unlike the FM Organ provided with your Sound Blaster card, which is *monophonic*—it can play only a single tone at a time from the PC keyboard.

It was the Novachord's control over envelope and timbre that made it a real breakthrough. For the first time, here was an electronic instrument that behaved like a synthesizer: the Novachord player could control the envelope of the sound. When we talk about sound, we can talk about its shape, or *envelope*, because its shape is a large part of how it sounds. If you were to do a simple graph of how a bell sounds over time when struck with a gong, the graph might look something like that in figure 1.2.

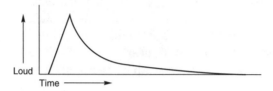

As you can visualize, when the bell is struck, the volume goes to maximum very quickly and then slowly decays over time. Hitting a lump of concrete, though, would produce an entirely different envelope, perhaps as shown in figure 1.3. This is the classic "thunk" sound, with no sustained tone at all. And the volume wouldn't be all that impressive, either.

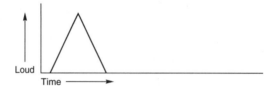

The Hammond Novachord was also able to attach a vibrato to the note. A *vibrato* is a slight variation in pitch or tone, sometimes coupled or even replaced with a slight variation in volume (which is really called *tremolo*). Finally, a number of filters allowed the player to control the tonal variations— did the note sound shrill and thin, or heavy, deep, and murky? Given these controls over how the note sounded, tasted, and felt, the Hammond Novachord was, in essence, a synthesizer in that it could produce sounds never heard before on the planet.

Digital Control

Remember the Coupleux-Givelet Organ mentioned earlier? Edouard E. Coupleux and Joseph A. Givelet introduced the first automated synthesizer at the Paris Exposition in 1929. Called an "Automatically Operating Musical Instrument of the Electric Oscillation Type," the instrument was controlled by what was really a five-track paper tape reader. The synthesizer had four electronic voices, and the paper tape controlled pitch, loudness, tremolo, articulation, and tone color.

The Coupleux-Givelet synthesizer was nearly as much a mechanical beast as an electronic instrument, but it did establish the use of a storage medium, although the player piano had been using the same medium for quite a bit longer. Milestones are milestones, however, and the Coupleux-Givelet was certainly that.

So here you are. A means exists to produce tones electronically and alter their pitch, timbre, and volume. A mechanism exists to control such alterations, called a paper tape reader. This must be the equivalent of Sound Blaster, right? Well, not far from it. Add the development of the transistor, integrated circuit, microprocessor, analog-to-digital converters, and a fair amount of software, and you're in the 1990s. It seems we've come a long way, and yet not very far at all.

Moving Forward Quickly

Bob Moog made a living while attending graduate school at Cornell by selling Theremins. After earning his Ph.D. in physics, he collaborated with Herb Deutsch to develop two key pieces of new technology for the electronic sound world: the voltage-controlled oscillator and the voltage-controlled amplifier. To these two components were added an envelope generator from Vladimir Ussachevsky and the low-pass filter from Gustav Ciamaga. Thus was born the Moog Synthesizer, probably the most widely known sound synthesizer of the 1960s, thanks to an album called *Switched-On Bach* by Wendy Carlos.

Donald Buchla developed what he called a "sequencer," which was in fact a way to program electronic instruments to play a short element repeatedly. You can thank Buchla for his early sequencer work when you ask Sound Blaster's FM Organ to play a little background rhythm. In 1975, Buchla introduced his 300 series, which used a computer to control sound generation.

Bell Labs developed a way to digitally sample sound, turning what is fundamentally an analog, or continuous, event into a series of 1s (ones) and 0s (zeros) that can be stored, manipulated, and played back. This development came out of the desire to use audible tones to dial telephones instead of using the old expensive and unreliable pulses of electricity, as well as research into digitizing speech.

Add to the mix high-speed personal computers and an affordable digital synthesizer like Sound Blaster, and you have an incredible sound laboratory in your own home! The efforts of many brilliant people and a lot of hard work and luck have culminated in products like Sound Blaster.[3]

Now that you've glimpsed a little of the history behind Sound Blaster, you are ready to move on and spend a little time learning about sound itself.

[3]*For more information on the background of electronic music, refer to* The Art of Electronic Music, *compiled by Tom Darter and edited by Greg Ambruster (New York: William Morrow and Company, Inc., 1984).*

CHAPTER 2

What Is Sound, Anyway?

The Sound Blaster is an electronic product that synthesizes—synthetically creates—sounds that may be very familiar to you, or even sounds that you've never heard before. The original synthesizer was probably a mockingbird, a natural mimic that shows some appreciation for the sounds of other birds, as well as sounds that don't come from birds at all. Parrots are another group of birds with the natural ability to synthesize a wide range of sounds, but they are particularly known for being able to synthesize human speech. Why do I say synthesize? Because a parrot simply does not have the mechanical ability to speak. A parrot's tongue, pallet, and vocal chords are not suited to forming words in the same way that we form words. Instead, the parrot recognizes human speech as a pattern of sounds that it can re-create, and it does have the equipment to make sounds that, to us, are very close to being speech. If the archaeologists are correct, and birds are direct descendents of dinosaurs, then organic synthesizers have probably been roaming the earth for a long time.

This chapter serves as an introduction to the synthetic creation of sound. Because our ears are rather critical to sound, the first part of the chapter covers how the ear functions. Then the difference between digitizing and synthesizing sound is discussed. The chapter ends with a discussion of the business of synthesis itself.

Drums, Hammers, Anvils

If you recall from your seventh-grade science class, you have a fair amount of hardware inside your head that lets you hear. It looks something like that shown in figure 2.1.

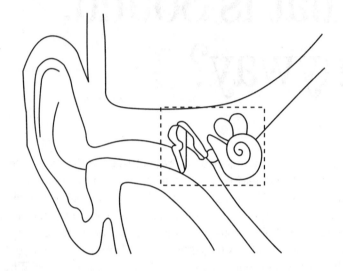

Figure 2.2 shows a close-up look at the inner ear.

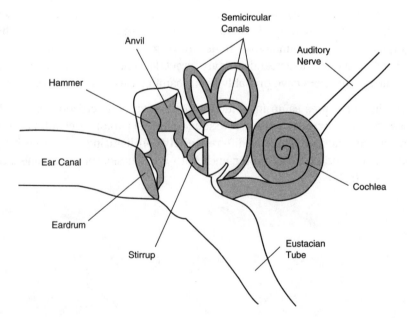

For the hearing, sound exists as rapid changes in air pressure. These changes in air pressure enter the ear canal in waves. The air pressure waves push and pull on the eardrum, which moves the hammer that moves the anvil that moves the stirrup—until the wave is ultimately transferred to the cochlea.

The inside of the cochlea is lined with thousands of tiny hairs. As the stirrup moves the cochlea, these little hairs are moved back and forth. At the root of each hair is a neurotransmitter that sends electrical impulses down the auditory nerve to your brain. Quiet sounds move the cochlear hairs just a little, and loud sounds move the hairs a great deal. Different frequencies move different hairs in different parts of the cochlea.

As an aside, certain hearing impairments are caused by damage to the eardrum, hammer, anvil, or stirrup, even while the cochlea is perfectly healthy. In some instances, cochlear implants are used to help the deaf person hear again (or even hear for the first time). A microphone and special amplifier are worn outside the body. The amplifier separates sound picked up by the microphone into several different channels. These are then fed to probes that are surgically implanted in the cochlea. In this way, external sounds directly stimulate the nerve bundles in the cochlea, thus bypassing the malfunctioning standard ear parts. Cochlear implants have had mixed success, but as we learn more about how humans hear, and how to break sound down into electrical impulses that are useful to the brain, this technology can only improve.

Hearing is a very complex thing. At first, you may think that sound is sound is sound, and that is true—but it doesn't come close to describing the complexities of what we hear. That bunch of organic hardware deep down in your ear canal, coupled with the wetware (to borrow a phrase from science fiction) between your ears, is capable of far more than you think.

Describing Sound

Before you can talk about sound, you have to be able to describe it in some common vocabulary. But first, consider how you can *see* sound.

Sound can be represented in a graphical manner. The air pressure changes that make up sound have three characteristics:

- They are made up of waves, and the size of the waves represents the volume.

- The time between the peaks in the wave represents the frequency of the sound.

- The sound happens over time.

Given these characteristics, you can graph the look of a sound. The graph in figure 2.3 represents the guitar's A string being struck.

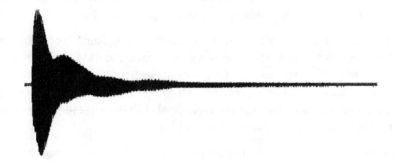

What you see here is a graphical representation of how a sound looks. The figure shows the shape of the sound of an A string being plucked on a guitar, and then after approximately 2 seconds, being dampened with a finger. Time flows from left to right. The amplitude, or volume, of the sound lines is indicated by the dark mass that moves up and down from the horizontal center line. The farther the mass is from the center horizontal line, the louder the sound. As you can see, there is hardly any sound just before the string was plucked; then the volume got loud very quickly and then started to taper off into quiet again.

The dark mass in figure 2.3 actually consists of a great amount of detail that you can't see unless you zoom in and look more closely, as shown in figure 2.4.

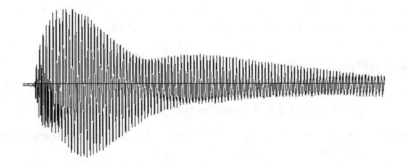

In figure 2.4, you can begin to see the waves that make sound. The *frequency*, or pitch, of the sound is measured by how many cycles there are per second. The distance between the two adjacent points on the graph indicates the time between cycles, which is very easy to convert into cycles per second. By zooming in a bit more, as shown in figure 2.5, you can see the individual waves.

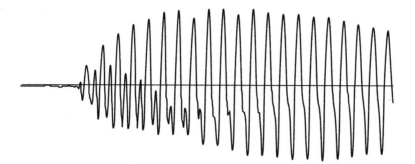

Fig. 2.5

The frequency at which sound waves occur determines the pitch of the sound.

It is the height of these waves, the distance between the peak of each wave, and the shape of the wave that make a sound unique.

Refer back to figure 2.3. This figure illustrates one other concept important to describing sound, and that is the envelope of the sound. The shape of the envelope is one of the ways that sound is described in terms of time, amplitude, and frequency. More on the envelope is provided later in this chapter.

How Does a Sound Sound?

The sine wave is a pure tone. In this case, *pure* refers to the result of the wave's shape, which is shown in figure 2.6. Unlike other wave forms, the sine wave's shape is such that only a single note can be heard, without any undertones or overtones. A tuning fork can produce a sine wave, as can an electronic oscillator. As discussed before, though, most organic sounds are much more complicated than a sine wave. These complications are what make up the timbre of a sound.

The *timbre* is the characteristic tonal quality of the sound. Timbre lets us tell the difference between the sound of a violin and that of a tenor saxophone. Timbre is made up of several elements, including the shape of the envelope and the complexity of the frequency pattern within the envelope.

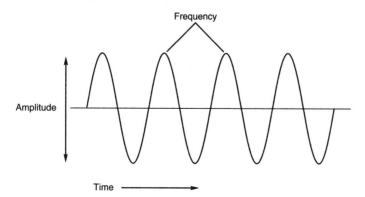

Fig. 2.6

The shape of a sine wave.

But when you compare the sine wave to the guitar waveform, shown in figure 2.7, the guitar waveform is much more complex.

Fig. 2.7

The shape of the guitar's sound.

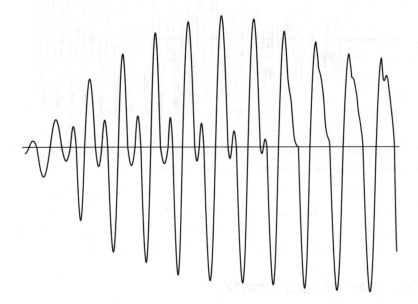

The little dips, spikes, and curves that are imposed on the pure sine wave are called *overtones*. Overtones are what add color or character to a sound. You can see that the *fundamental* sine wave is present, but it is modified and changed by harmonic overtones. *Harmonic* overtones are multiples of the fundamental frequency. For example, if the fundamental frequency is 440 Hz—the A above middle C—the second harmonic is 880 Hz, the third harmonic is 1,320 Hz, and so on. (Hz stands for hertz, which refers to cycles per second.)

To further illustrate overtones, figures 2.8 and 2.9 show two tones. The tone in figure 2.8 is an A note sine wave generated by a Casio MT-640 keyboard. The tone in figure 2.9 is also an A note but is generated by the A string on an acoustic guitar.

The Casio is trying to create a tone that sounds like a flute. As you can see, there isn't much going on beyond the generation of a slightly warped sine wave. Pure, but not very rich. An acoustic flute, by the way, generates a fair number of even-numbered harmonics (overtones that are two, four, or six times the fundamental frequency). Compare that wave to the guitar's A string shown in figure 2.9.

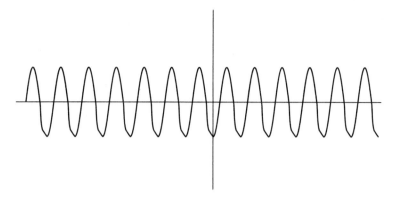

Fig. 2.8

An electronic flute
sound.

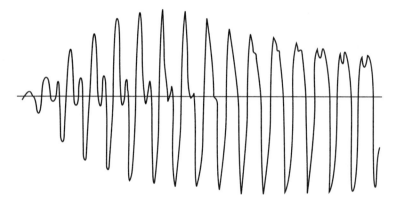

Fig. 2.9

An acoustic guitar
sound.

As you can see, the guitar note is fundamentally a sine wave but is much more
complex. Some interesting things are going on here. What makes the guitar
waveform look complex is also what makes it sound rich. The sound generated
by the A string is actually made up of a variety of factors:

- The sound of the A string moving back and forth

- The influence of any waves that are moving up and down the length of the
  string itself

- The sympathetic vibrations of the other strings on the guitar

- The vibrations of the wood in the guitar neck and box, both of which are
  influenced by the kind of wood used, the finish on the wood, the humidity
  and temperature, and so on

All these factors contribute to the rich sound—the timbre—of an acoustic
guitar. What makes the special sound of a Stradivarius violin is all the elements

working together. The glue Stradivari used, the age of the wood, the number of scales on the horse hair in the bow, the speed at which the bow is drawn across the strings—all these things make up the characteristic sound of the Stradivarius. All these physical elements are manifested in the sound you hear.

And this is the challenge for synthesizers like Sound Blaster. It's easy to make a pure sine wave. But if you want to synthesize standard instruments, it becomes much more difficult. To synthesize a Stradivarius, you have to understand how a Stradivarius makes those sounds in the first place. Science thinks it might know, and modern-day artisans come very close to re-creating the sound of a Stradivarius with custom violins, but the magic has not been captured just yet.

In summary, what you hear is much more than it might seem at first. Organic sound is a very complex thing, and our brains have come to appreciate and expect complex sounds. We demand that our electronic equipment be able to reproduce complex sounds with great fidelity. In the early days of electronic sound synthesis, it was thought that pure tones were a scientific curiosity and mildly entertaining, but certainly not music. They sounded "electronic" and never seemed to satisfy our needs. People want to hear sound with character and variety!

The Envelope, Please!

Look again at the guitar waveform, repeated in figure 2.10. It has some components you need to understand.

Fig. 2.10

The parts of a sound envelope.

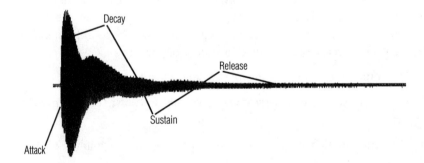

An envelope has four parts:

- *Attack.* The time from no sound to the maximum volume.
- *Decay.* The time from the moment the sound starts to decrease from the maximum until it reaches some level that can be called the sustaining level.

- *Sustain.* The time the sound lingers.

- *Release.* The time it takes for the sound to fade to nothing.

Each of these elements is different for every instrument. In fact, each element is different for each string on a guitar.

Figure 2.11 shows another waveform, with the fundamental and harmonic frequencies indicated.

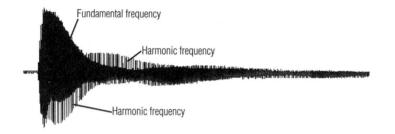

Fig. 2.11

The fundamental and harmonic frequencies.

The fundamental frequency is shown as a dark, solid band in this waveform. A harmonic frequency (some frequency less than the fundamental) is shown as a lighter waveform.

So, what do you do if you want to synthesize an acoustic guitar sound? You do a lot of analysis and head scratching. As you can see, synthesizing sound isn't as easy as it may seem. Next, look at what Sound Blaster is doing by examining how it samples and digitizes sound. Then you can see how it re-creates stored sound as well as synthesizes new sounds.

Sound Blaster as Digital Sampler

The Sound Blaster card is actually three separate electronic devices:

- A sound digitizer

- A sound synthesizer

- A MIDI (Musical Instrument Digital Interface) controller

The digitizer element is what lets you feed sounds into Sound Blaster by way of a microphone or line input, store the sounds on disk, and modify them or play them back unmodified. The synthesizer element is used to generate sounds electronically. Finally, the MIDI element lets Sound Blaster serve as a MIDI instrument and allows your computer to control other MIDI instruments. MIDI is described in greater detail in Chapter 6.

What Is Digitized Sound?

Now look at the simple sine wave again, as shown in figure 2.12.

Fig. 2.12

A simple sine
wave.

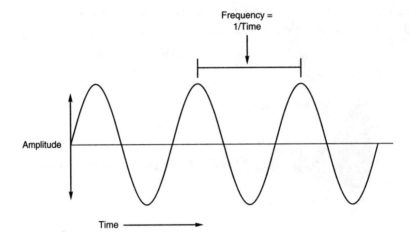

If your task were to look at this sine wave and try representing it with numbers, you would probably come up with something like this:

1. Let the center line equal zero amplitude.

2. Let time start at the beginning of the sound and stop at the end of the sound.

3. Write down a number that represents the amplitude at certain points of time during the length of the sound.

Suppose that the sine wave lasts exactly one second and that you want to measure its amplitude every 1/20 of a second. This means that you'll have 21 samples during the course of the second. As shown in figure 2.13, you would take a sample at the beginning of time (T_0), 1/20 of a second after the beginning of time (T_1), 1/20 of a second after that (T_2), and so on.

Now you can build a table of numbers that represents the sine wave:

Sample Number	0	1	2	3	4	5	6	7	8	9	10	11	12	13	14	15	16	17	18	19	20	21
Amplitude	0	+1	0	–1	0	+1	0	–1	0	+1	0	–1	0	+1	0	–1	0	+1	0	–1	0	+1

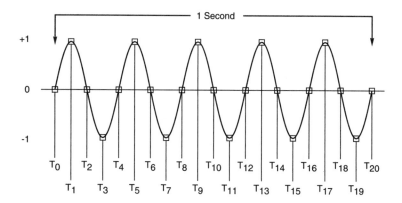

Fig. 2.13

Sampling a sine wave.

At time T_0, the amplitude is 0; in 1/20 of a second, at T_1, the amplitude is +1; and so on.

What you've done is *sampled* the sine wave at a *sample rate* of 1 sample every 1/20 of a second (a sample frequency of 20 Hz). And you've built a table of numbers that represents the sample. In other words, you have *digitized* the sine wave—turned an analog signal into a digital signal that can now be stored in a computer.

What you have done, in a limited way, is what every producer of compact disks does to transfer music onto a CD. This process is basically the same as that used by Sound Blaster to digitize and store your voice on your computer.

Sample Rates

If you look at how often the nearly perfect sine wave was sampled, and you compare the shape of the sine wave to the shape of the waveform from the guitar's A string, you'll begin to see a problem. The problem becomes even more apparent when you try to reconstruct the sine wave.

First consider the guitar. Figure 2.14 shows the imperfect sine wave created by the guitar.

It should be obvious that if you don't sample very often, you're going to miss a lot of information. That's why Sound Blaster Pro has a sampling rate of up to 44,000 Hz, instead of the paltry 20 Hz in the example used here. The more often you sample the incoming sound, the more accurately you can reproduce the sound later on. Suppose that you wanted to reproduce the simple sine wave from the table of data gathered at the 20 Hz sample rate. It would look something like the reconstruction shown in figure 2.15.

Fig. 2.14

The guitar
waveform.

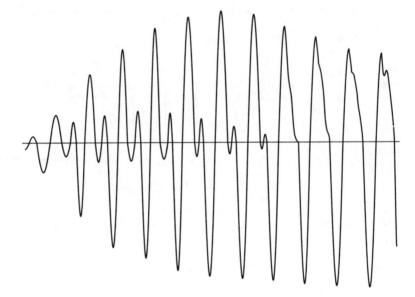

Fig. 2.15

The results of a
low sample rate.

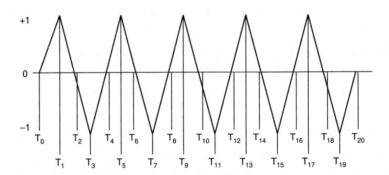

The extremely low sample rate sampled the sine wave only at its maximums
and as it was at 0 amplitude. Low sample rates result in poor reproduction of
the original sound. For best fidelity, you will sample at the highest rate
possible. If, for instance, you sampled one complete cycle of the sine wave at
a much higher sample rate, you would be able to reconstruct more of the
original shape, as shown in figure 2.16.

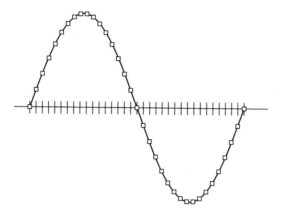

Fig. 2.16

Sampling at a higher rate.

In this case, you've sampled one cycle 34 times. As you can see, when it comes time to reconstruct this waveform, you will have something more closely resembling the original.

In short, that's how digital sampling is done. When you speak into Sound Blaster's microphone, Sound Blaster takes a measurement of your speech up to 44,000 times per second and stores that information as numbers in memory or on disk.

Synthesizing Sound

The next few pages explain how sound is synthesized. There are a number of approaches to consider quickly, and then you'll focus on the Sound Blaster approach.

Synthesizer—A Definition

A *synthesizer* is a set of electronics that can generate waveforms—that's the short definition, anyway. A synthesizer produces and modifies waveforms and then filters and merges those waveforms in a variety of clever ways, ultimately producing an electronic signal that can make a sound come out of your speaker. What comes out of your speaker can be a pretty fair imitation of a sound you recognize—a cello, for example—or a sound you've never heard before, such as the voice of a small robot called R2D2. When the synthesizer is inside a computer and can be controlled by software, you suddenly have command of a rather amazing piece of technology.

Synthesis always starts with the generation of a waveform.

Your PC Speaker as a Synthesizer

Your PC already contains a rudimentary synthesizer in the form of that little speaker which beeps at you when something goes wrong.

As just mentioned, synthesis starts with the generation of a waveform. Fortunately, your computer is full of waveforms; most, but not all, of them are square. Your computer contains an oscillator that oscillates at a fixed frequency, usually something like 8 MHz if you're stuck with an old AT system, or 16, 25, 33, 50, or 66 MHz for newer machines. (MHz stands for megahertz, or one million cycles per second.) Somewhere on the motherboard of your computer is an oscillator, creating a sine wave at the fundamental frequency. The sine wave is chopped at both the top and the bottom to create a square wave (see fig. 2.17).

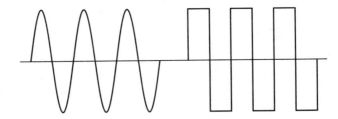

Why a square wave? Because this waveform is used to turn logic circuits within the computer on and off. The faster the computer and the more quickly you want the circuits turned on and off, the more square your wave must be.

So square waves are running around all over the inside of your computer. When the PC was first developed, the makers needed some way to alert the user that something was going on. They put a little three-inch speaker inside the PC cabinet and coupled it to the output of a gate (which either does or doesn't let the square wave through). When something happened and they wanted to buzz the user, the computer would open the gate (close the switch, as shown in fig. 2.18) and let a string of square waves through.

Of course, square waves don't sound very pretty, but they do make a sound. With a programmable divider circuit, your computer can generate a wide variety of frequencies, and most do. One of the software packages provided with this book lets Windows use the computer speaker circuitry, rather than the Sound Blaster card, as an output device. If you're interested, or if you haven't gotten your Sound Blaster card yet, take a look at the WinSpeak driver on the disk. WinSpeak is distributed by Microsoft.

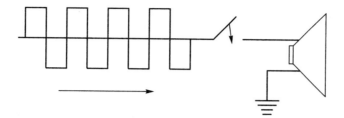

Fig. 2.18

The PC speaker driven by square waves.

The PC speaker and circuitry are only the crudest approximation of a synthesizer. You get just the barest hint of what the sound files really sound like; but if all you are interested in is attaching various beeps to events in the Windows environment, the PC speaker might be suitable.

Sound Blaster, however, is much more than that.

Modifying Waveforms

There are two approaches to synthesizing sound. The first is to generate a nice waveform, add it to another waveform, and then warp and modify the result with filters. The second approach is to generate a waveform that already has nearly the correct shape in the first place.

Interesting things happen when one waveform is used to modify another. As shown in figure 2.19, adding a slow sine wave to a faster sine wave results in a whole new waveform. In this instance, a *tremolo* effect results—the note stays the same, but the volume (amplitude) goes slightly up and down.

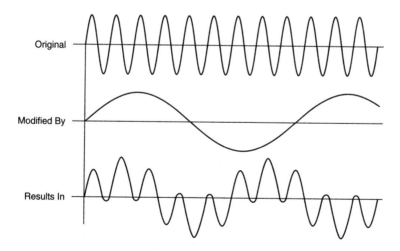

Original

Modified By

Results In

Fig. 2.19

Amplitude modulation with voltage-controlled oscillator.

The resulting waveform in figure 2.19 shows how the amplitude of the original wave can be modified—modulated—by letting a slower waveform be the controlling element. In a sense, the slower waveform has control of the volume knob and can change the shape of the faster waveform.

This control is made possible by an invention called the *voltage-controlled oscillator* (VCO). An oscillator creates the sine wave, but the frequency and amplitude of the sine wave can be controlled by another oscillator. In this instance, the original amplitude is being controlled by the slower sine wave to create a third signal.

The same voltage-controlled oscillators can be used to modify the frequency as well—even at the same time the amplitude is being modified. The VCO can shift the frequency of the waveform up and down while a sound is being played. In this way, a synthesizer can make very new waveform shapes, like that shown in figure 2.20, where both amplitude and frequency are being modified.

Fig. 2.20

Amplitude and frequency modulation.

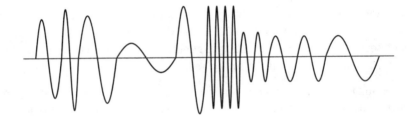

The waveform in figure 2.20 has a very strange and probably not very useful envelope. It is a synthesized waveform, however, and it gives you some idea of how synthesis works. As a small mind exercise, you might consider what would happen if you used a sawtooth wave to control the amplitude of the fast sine wave in figure 2.19. A sawtooth waveform is shown in figure 2.21.

Fig. 2.21

A sawtooth waveform.

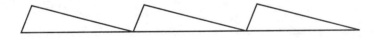

It's easy to see that the amplitude would grow very quickly and then taper off slowly to quiet. This is called a "repeat percussion" modulation waveform and is used to synthesize percussive types of sounds, such as the pluck of a banjo string. Percussive sounds typically have a very rapid attack and decay, like a drum stick hitting a drum head, as opposed to a note being held by a flute.

By now, you should have some idea of how voltage-controlled oscillators are used to modify waveforms in a wide variety of ways.

Look again at figure 2.19. More is happening than meets the eye in this rather simple rendition. If you were an audio expert and connected an oscilloscope to the output of the modulated oscillator (the last waveform in the figure), you would be able to detect four different frequencies being generated, because one frequency is actually being added to another:

- *Fundamental.* The original, or carrier, frequency (the fast sine wave in fig. 2.19).

- *Modulating.* The frequency used to modify the fundamental frequency (the slower sine wave in fig. 2.19).

- *Sum.* The sum of the fundamental and modulating frequencies.

- *Difference.* The difference between the fundamental and modulating frequencies.

To illustrate, assume that the fundamental frequency is 500 Hz and the modulating frequency is 100 Hz. When these two frequencies are added together, the following sum and difference frequencies are developed:

Fundamental	500
Modulating	100
Sum	600
Difference	400

The sum and difference are harmonics of the fundamental and modulating frequencies and are called *sidebands*. In this case, the output would be the fundamental (500 Hz), the sum (600 Hz), and the difference (400 Hz).

As long as the frequency of the modulating waveform (the center waveform) is quite slow relative to the original—say, 5 Hz—only a tremolo effect results: a slight up and down in volume. Interesting things begin to happen, though, when you start increasing the frequency of the modulating waveform. First, you hear a three-note cluster. At a 100 Hz modulating frequency, you hear a natural major triad composed of a 400 Hz tone, a 500 Hz tone, and a 600 Hz tone. As the modulating frequency goes up, you start to hear two tones moving in opposite directions—one higher in frequency going lower, and one lower going higher. That effect is followed by a single tone accompanied by some interesting harmonic overtones. Finally, as the modulating frequency climbs, three tones are developed. All three tones shift in frequency, but two of them remain in fixed relative positions. You get all these effects from two simple voltage-controlled oscillators.

Sideband frequencies multiply at a very high rate. In this simple example, an output signal was created that had a fundamental of 500 Hz with two sidebands. If you used another set of voltage-controlled oscillators to create the same output, and then mixed those two together, the output would be the 500 Hz fundamental with 8 sideband frequencies!

When sharp-edged waveforms such as sawtooth waves and square waves are used, the effects are compounded well beyond the scope of this book. The reason is that these kinds of waveforms already contain sideband frequencies, whereas clean sine waves do not.

A block diagram of a frequency modulation system is shown in figure 2.22.

Fig. 2.22

Frequency
modulation.

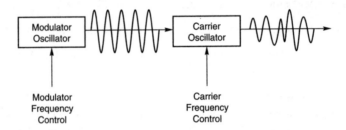

Two oscillators are connected together. The modulator oscillator's output is fed to the input of the carrier oscillator. If the modulator is turned off, the carrier oscillator generates a nice clean sine wave. When the modulator is turned on, however, and its frequency and amplitude varied, it has the effect described in earlier paragraphs and shown in figure 2.19.

The technique used by Sound Blaster is frequency modulation through its FM chip sets. The FM chips are described in greater detail in Chapter 10, "Programming Sound Blaster."

Filters

The next, most essential element of synthesis is a filtering mechanism. Filters selectively reduce the amplitude of some frequencies. To illustrate, the diagram in figure 2.23 shows the frequencies that a person with very good hearing can hear. Our hearing range seems to run from about 15 Hz to about 15,000 Hz. In other words, if your ears are in good shape, you can hear frequencies as low as 15 Hz and as high as 15,000 Hz. Most of us can actually *feel* frequencies below 15 Hz, and some individuals and many animals can hear frequencies well above 15,000 Hz.

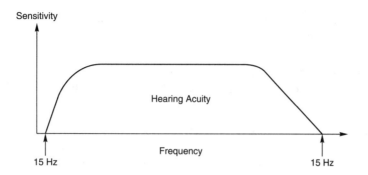

Fig. 2.23

Human frequency
detection.

Actually, the shape of the envelope is different for all of us. You undoubtedly
know someone that cannot hear well in certain circumstances, or perhaps you
have trouble hearing certain frequencies. In those instances, either physical
ear or nerve damage is filtering out certain frequencies. If you had trouble
hearing high-pitched tones, for example, your hearing acuity graph might look
something like that in figure 2.24. In this instance, the physiological hearing
mechanism is acting as a filter, filtering out part of the sounds presented to
your ear drum.

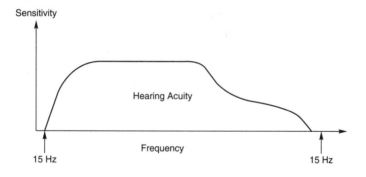

Fig. 2.24

Frequency filtering
through hearing
impairment.

Electronic filters are used to alter sound envelopes and to enhance or dampen
certain frequencies. If your stereo has a graphic equalizer, those sliders that
you move up and down, or back and forth, are actually controlling a set of
frequency filters. The leftmost slider usually controls the lowest range of
frequencies, and the rightmost slider controls the highest range of frequencies. By moving the slider on the right down to its lowest setting and keeping
the other sliders in the middle of their range, you are roughly duplicating the
kind of frequency response shown in figure 2.24.

Electronic filters used in synthesis are usually variable in terms of what frequencies they filter and which frequencies they pass along unfiltered. In most software associated with Sound Blaster, you will see reference to *high-pass* and *low-pass* filtering. High-pass filters do just as the name suggests— they pass higher frequencies unchanged while dampening lower frequencies. Naturally, low-pass filters do just the opposite.

Low-pass filters were originally used by telephone companies. Although humans can hear a much wider band of frequencies, human speech is intelligible at a frequency range of 300 Hz to 3,000 Hz. In other words, although your voice generates harmonics well above 3,000 Hz, it is not necessary for you to hear those harmonics in order to understand human speech.

The telephone companies save a significant amount of money in expensive broad-band amplifiers and can place multiple telephone conversations on a single line by limiting the frequencies transmitted to under 3,000 Hz.

Filters generally use three simple electronic components: the resistor, the coil, and the capacitor. The following discussion provides a very simplistic description of how these three components work. But before starting, you need to understand the difference between voltage and current. *Voltage*, measured in volts, is the electrical potential a circuit has. *Current*, measured in amperes, is the number of electrons available to travel down a wire. For example, if you were capable of sending six million million million electrons down a wire in one second, you would have generated one ampere of current. The static electricity charge that you build up shuffling across a carpeted floor builds a very high potential (several thousand volts) but very little current (microamperes), which mercifully saves your life each time you touch a doorknob. The very high voltage causes the air to be ionized between your finger and the doorknob, and a spark leaps out, but the current is so low that the effect is a minor annoyance. However, the wall outlet in a North American home has a moderately low potential (115 volts), with a very large number of available electrons (usually 15 amperes' worth, and you can do the math to calculate the number of electrons).

A *resistor* acts as a constrictor to an electrical signal, consistently reducing the electrical current flowing through a circuit. As a nonsensical example, if 50 electrons enter one end of a resistor, only 40 may come out the other end. The lost 10 electrons are burnt up in heat.

A *coil* has the unique property of resisting changes in electrical current. In other words, if the current flowing through a coil is constant, the coil has very little impact. If, however, the current passing through the coil gets greater or smaller, then for a short time the coil acts just like a resistor and temporarily reduces the electrical current flowing through it. Once the current is stable, the coil stops resisting and becomes a piece of wire again. If you apply a higher voltage to one end of a coil while measuring what goes on at the other end of the coil, you would see the voltage go up very quickly, while the current comes up very slowly.

The third element is the *capacitor*. All capacitors are fundamentally two metal plates separated by a small gap. The function of the capacitor is to temporarily store electrical energy. One way to think of a capacitor is to view it as a very small battery that can't hold much of a charge. But the important characteristic of a capacitor in a filter is that it takes a certain amount of time to charge a capacitor, and a certain amount of time to discharge it. And when you apply a voltage to one end of a capacitor, current immediately flows out the other end, but the voltage builds up slowly.

(A personal note here. In the preceding paragraphs, great liberties have been taken with physics and the behavior of electronic components. If you want to know how these electronic components really work, a short course or two at your local community college will set you straight. A complete description of electronic theory and the behavior of the resistor, coil, and capacitor is well beyond the scope of this book.)

To summarize, a resistor resists current all the time, a coil resists current only when the current is changing, and a capacitor stores electrical charges. What can you do with these three components? You can make filters!

A low-pass filter passes low frequencies. By connecting two or more of the components in specific ways, you can change the band of frequencies that are passed on down the circuitry. Figure 2.25 illustrates three such circuits.

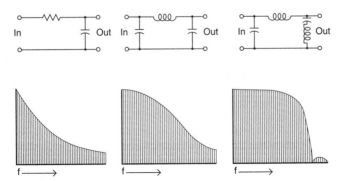

Fig. 2.25

Low-pass filter circuits.

All three circuits shown in figure 2.25 are low-pass filters, and they will filter a range of frequencies as shown. The first circuit uses a resistor (the one with jagged lines) and a capacitor to create a filter that lets very low frequencies through (those on the left of the graph below the circuit), but steadily reduces the amplitude of the higher frequencies. The capacitor's behavior is to, in effect, short all higher frequencies to ground, not letting them pass.

The center circuit uses a coil and two capacitors to create the ski-jump kind of filtering effect where more of the lower frequencies are passed, but then the filter gradually blocks higher frequencies. Remember that the coil reacts to changes in current, and the current changes at a higher rate at higher frequencies. Therefore, the coil is more resistant to higher frequencies and blocks their signals.

The final low-pass filter produces an interesting effect. By using both a coil and a capacitor across the output, the filter sharply cuts off high frequencies, except for that "bounce" at the very highest frequencies where a few are let through.

Sound Blaster's built-in low-pass filter works like the first filter on the left in figure 2.25.

High-pass filters do just the opposite of low-pass filters in that they block lower frequencies and pass higher frequencies. Three high-pass filters are shown in figure 2.26.

Fig. 2.26

High-pass filter circuits.

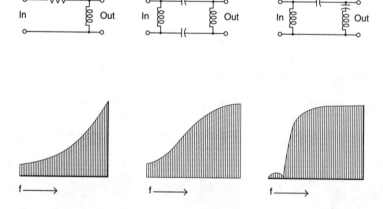

In the case of high-pass filters, the circuitry does just the opposite of its low-pass partner. The filters use the behavior of a coil across the output to effectively short all low frequencies to ground. At low frequencies, a coil acts like a plain piece of wire. At high frequencies (faster current changes), the coil becomes more resistant, and the higher frequencies are allowed to pass without being conducted to ground. Note that the circuitry uses the same components as the low-pass filter but configured in a different manner.

The Sound Blaster high-pass filter works very much like the first filter on the left in figure 2.26.

The final filter used in sound circuitry is the *band-pass* filter. Although Sound Blaster does not contain a band-pass filter, a brief description seems appropriate because audio filters are under discussion. The band-pass filter is typically an adjustable filter that will pass a band of frequencies. Figure 2.27 illustrates a band-pass filter circuit and the resulting filtering.

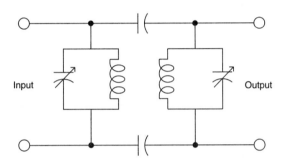

Fig. 2.27

Band-pass filter circuit.

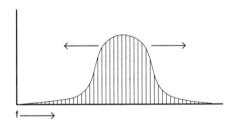

Notice in figure 2.27 that the two capacitors have arrows through them. The arrow indicates that the capacitors are adjustable and that the filter can be tuned up and down the frequency spectrum to pass a specific band of frequencies. The other effect the tunable capacitors have is to allow the width of the band to be adjusted to pass a very narrow range of frequencies or a very wide range of frequencies.

As stated before, Sound Blaster does not contain a band-pass filter, but most other audio equipment does.

Sound Blaster Synthesis

Sound Blaster synthesizes sound by using integrated circuits to generate waveforms instead of using individual oscillators, mixers, and filters. Sound Blaster's integrated circuits include the following:

- A digital signal processor (DSP)

- A frequency modulation (FM) synthesizer

- A mixer (only with Sound Blaster Pro, Sound Blaster 16, and Sound Blaster 16 ASP)

The DSP circuit has two tasks: it handles both the MIDI (Musical Instrument Digital Interface) and the voice operations. In the case of voice (or line-in) operations, whenever you have a microphone plugged into Sound Blaster, the DSP is used to sample the sound in order to translate that organic, analog sound into 1s and 0s the computer can manipulate. When acting as a MIDI controller, the DSP circuit sends commands to and receives commands from a MIDI instrument or instruments connected to Sound Blaster's MIDI port. How Sound Blaster works with MIDI instruments is described in Chapter 6.

The mixer chip is used to mix sounds from various sources, letting you control the volume of each source. For example, sources can be a CD, the microphone, and the line input on Sound Blaster. With the mixer, you can control the various volume levels of each of these inputs.

The FM synthesizer circuits are the sound generators for Sound Blaster. If you have recorded a voice message on Sound Blaster, it was sampled and stored and will be played back by the DSP chip. But if you use the SBTALKER to cause Sound Blaster to speak or you use the FM Organ to play music, Sound Blaster uses its FM synthesizer chips.

The FM synthesizer circuits are divided into elements called *operator cells*, and each operator cell consists of two parts. Recall the earlier discussion about envelope shapes. Sound Blaster's circuitry, illustrated in figure 2.28, contains a component called an *envelope generator* (or wave shaper). The envelope generator controls the shape—the rate of attack, decay, sustain, and release— of the other part of the operator, a phase generator.

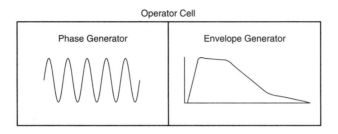

Fig. 2.28

A Sound Blaster
operator cell.

Operators are used in pairs: one operator serves as the modulator oscillator, and the other operator is the carrier oscillator, as shown in figure 2.29.

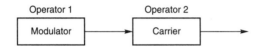

Fig. 2.29

A Sound Blaster
operator pair.

Just as in the synthesizers described earlier in this chapter, the modulator cell is used to modulate the waveform generated by the carrier, which, in turn, produces very complex waveforms.

The operators can be internally connected in two configurations, by way of software commands. For example, you can provide a feedback loop, shown in figure 2.30, which takes a small part of the signal from the output of the carrier operator and feeds the signal back to the input of the modulator operator, providing new and interesting opportunities to create new sounds. Nearly everyone has experienced the capability of a feedback loop to generate new sounds whenever an active microphone is held close to a speaker.

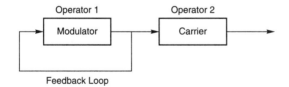

Fig. 2.30

Feedback within
an operator pair.

The operator parameters or variables are controlled through software. In the case of Sound Blaster's repertoire of preprogrammed instrument sounds (piano, harpsichord, bells, drums, and so on), the operators are programmed from the Sound Blaster libraries. The internal libraries indicate the frequency of the waveform generated by the phase modulator portion of the operator, and how the envelope generator should shape the waveform. If you are interested, you can program the operators yourself to experiment with creating new sounds. Programming Sound Blaster is discussed in Chapter 10.

Sound Blaster's FM synthesizer chip has 18 operator cells. These cells can be used in three ways:

- *Nine-channel FM sound.* In this mode, the 18 operator cells are coupled together as modulator and carrier to generate 9 different sounds simultaneously. The sound generated by each operator pair is assigned a channel number—thus, the reference to 9-channel FM sound.

- *Six-channel FM sound plus percussion.* Sound Blaster is automatically capable of producing the sounds of 5 percussion instruments: bass drum, hi hat cymbal, tom-tom, snare drum, and top cymbal. In this mode, 12 operator cells are dedicated to generating 6 channels of FM sound, while the remaining 6 operators produce the 5 percussion sounds.

- *Speech synthesis.* When the output of 3 to 6 operator cells is mixed together, a fair representation of the human voice can be synthesized. Sound Blaster uses tables of preconfigured waveforms to synthesize speech.

In addition to these uses, the FM synthesizer chip has two additional components: a vibrato oscillator and an amplitude modulation oscillator. Recall that *vibrato* is a slight variation of frequency, and amplitude modulation is used to create a tremolo effect.

Summary

This brief overview of sound and synthesis should give you some idea of the bigger picture, at least. Not covered in this chapter are such topics as Fourier synthesis, phase distortion synthesis, linear arithmetic synthesis, or any of the newer techniques that are constantly being developed. The purpose of this chapter was to give you some idea of the complexities of generating sound electronically, as well as some feeling for what a significant step forward Sound Blaster is.

The Sound Blaster family of products is described in the next chapter, including a table that describes the capabilities of each product.

CHAPTER 3

The Sound Blaster Family

The Sound Blaster family of products from Creative Labs, Inc., represents a breakthrough for DOS- and Windows-based PCs. Apple's Macintosh computers have long had built-in sound capability. Sound Blaster has added sound capability to PCs at a reasonable price, opening up a wide world indeed.

The predecessor to the Sound Blaster family was Game Blaster, an add-on card that enables game programmers to add a dimension of excitement to their products by generating sound effects. The first Sound Blaster card, introduced in 1989, was compatible with software written for Game Blaster. In addition, Sound Blaster was compatible with the AdLib sound card. But most important, Sound Blaster could sample audio input from a microphone or other source and store the sounds in digital format.

Since then, the Sound Blaster family has become the defacto standard for PC-based sound cards. Currently, Microsoft is developing its own sound card, and AdLib will certainly stay in competition, as will a number of other companies. So things may change, but you can be fairly certain that new introductions will need to have Sound Blaster compatibility.

This chapter describes the various members of the Sound Blaster family, including two new products added to the lineup in the summer of 1993.

Sound Blaster

All Sound Blaster cards have three basic functions:

- They can sample sound inputs, digitizing the sound and storing it in a sound file for playback or modification.

- They can synthesize the sound of musical instruments and the human voice.

- They can control musical instruments that conform to the Musical Instrument Digital Interface (MIDI) specification.

These functions are explained in greater detail in later chapters of this book. You might want to review Chapters 1 and 2 for an introduction to these ideas. However, a quick summary is in order before you continue.

The task of converting sound into a form that can be stored on a computer is carried out by a digital signal processing (DSP) circuit. The DSP can convert any sound that can be captured by a microphone or that can be fed into Sound Blaster through its Line-In or CD-In connectors (Sound Blaster Pro and 16/16 ASP only). In an oversimplification, the DSP samples the incoming sound signal every few microseconds and stores these samples in a contiguous file. When the time comes to play back the sound, the samples are converted back into audio signals by the DSP. That same DSP is used also to generate special electrical signals that are understood by musical instruments that comply with the Musical Instrument Digital Interface, or MIDI, specification. A number of widely available electronic musical keyboards from companies such as Yamaha, Roland, and Casio are MIDI-compliant. What this means is that your computer and Sound Blaster can control these keyboards—both playing them and recording music played on them. Finally, Sound Blaster itself contains one or more synthesizer integrated circuits. Synthesizers are capable of synthesizing, or imitating, the sound of a wide range of musical instruments, just as the Yamaha, Roland, and Casio keyboards can. All versions of the Sound Blaster family since V1.5 have used synthesizer integrated circuits from the Yamaha company—the OPL-2 and OPL-3 circuits.

The basic Sound Blaster card has gone through a couple of major changes. Version 1.0 of the card included an integrated circuit (IC) set that made the card compatible with the Game Blaster product. Both Sound Blaster V1.5 and Sound Blaster V2.0 contained sockets that accept the ICs for compatibility, but the circuits are not included with the products. This book addresses only Sound Blaster V1.5 and V2.0, Sound Blaster Pro, and Sound Blaster 16/16 ASP.

Figure 3.1 illustrates the V1.5 Sound Blaster card.

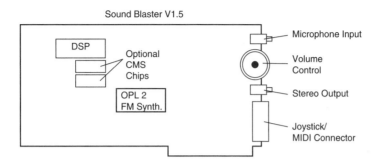

Fig. 3.1

Sound Blaster
V1.5.

Sound Blaster V1.5 has a digital signal processing (DSP) chip for sampling and digitizing audio input through the microphone jack and can sample at rates from 4 kHz to 15 kHz. The FM synthesizer chip is an OPL 2 from Yamaha, capable of generating 11-voice monaural sound. The card also includes two sockets for the CMS 301 chips that allow compatibility with the older Game Blaster. The card supports a joystick/MIDI connector. And like all Sound Blaster cards, the card has a stereo jack that delivers 4 watts of output per channel. The stereo jack can drive a set of stereo headphones directly, a set of powered speakers, or the line-in of a stereo amplifier system.

Sound Blaster V2.0 is a significant enhancement over V1.5. Figure 3.2 illustrates the Sound Blaster card for V2.0.

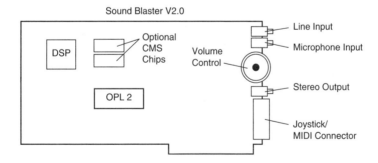

Fig. 3.2

Sound Blaster
V2.0.

Sound Blaster V2.0 has a separate line-in jack, allowing Sound Blaster to be connected to two separate audio sources: a microphone and a line-out audio source. The line-in jack can be connected to a wide variety of electronic products that generate line-out audio signals, including some televisions, stereos, CD players, and VCRs. Only one source can be sampled at a time, however. A new DSP chip samples incoming audio at the same 4 kHz-15 kHz range as in the earlier version, but now supports a higher playback sampling rate of up to 44.1 kHz. What this means is that Sound Blaster V2.0 can play back CD-quality audio that has been sampled and stored by another source, such as Sound Blaster Pro.

Sound Blaster Pro

The Sound Blaster Pro card is yet another step forward. As you can see in figure 3.3, Sound Blaster Pro uses a 16-bit bus slot instead of the 8-bit slot used in previous boards. However, Sound Blaster Pro still uses 8-bit sampling. It also has three new features:

- An additional FM synthesizer chip to produce stereo sounds

- A mixer chip that enables you to mix various sound sources together

- A CD-ROM connector

Two versions of Sound Blaster Pro have been released: V1.0 and V2.0 (see figs. 3.3 and 3.4).

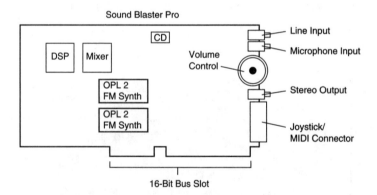

Fig. 3.3

Sound Blaster Pro V1.0.

Sound Blaster Pro V2.0 has a pair of upgraded synthesizer chips, as well as a couple of pins to which you can connect your internal PC speaker line, so that sounds your PC would normally generate are fed to Sound Blaster and out through the speaker system connected to Sound Blaster.

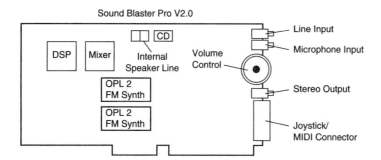

Fig. 3.4

Sound Blaster Pro
V2.0.

The Sound Blaster Pro boards are capable of generating 11 FM stereo voices. A *voice* is an instrument sound. Therefore, Sound Blaster Pro can simultaneously produce the sound of 11 different instruments, in stereo. In addition, the DSP chip can digitize stereo sounds at a sampling rate of up to 22.05 kHz. In monaural, sampling rates can go as high as 44.1 kHz.

The mixer chip lets Sound Blaster receive sound from multiple sources and mix them into a single sampled recording. In other words, you could do a voice-over on top of a CD being played by Sound Blaster, digitizing and storing them both as a single recording.

Sound Blaster 16 ASP

The high-end of the Sound Blaster series is Sound Blaster 16 ASP (ASP stands for Advanced Signal Processor). The greatest improvement is that 16 ASP uses a 16-bit chip to do sampling, bringing its audio frequency response into the range of a standard CD player. In addition, the new processor allows 16-bit compression/decompression to reduce the size of sample files. The improved signal processor capabilities allow this Sound Blaster to move into the arena of speech recognition. The Sound Blaster 16 ASP card is shown in figure 3.5.

The impact of the data compression/decompression capabilities of Sound Blaster 16 ASP should not be underestimated. For example, if you decide to take full advantage of the Sound Blaster 16 ASP's capability to sample stereo audio at the maximum sample rate of 44.1 kHz, what you are demanding of the system is that it store 176,400 bytes of data every second of the recording! No problem, except that you'll chew up vast quantities of your hard disk in very short order. This clearly demonstrates the need for data compression.

Fig. 3.5

Sound Blaster 16
ASP.

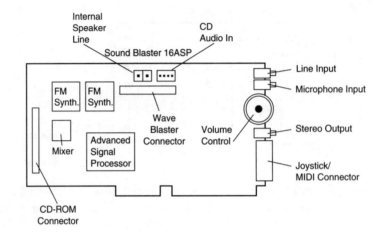

There are two ways to do data compression and decompression: with software or with hardware. The software method is one in which your PC's CPU is called on to compress the incoming data—a task for which the CPU is not ideally suited, although it can be done. The price you pay is in seriously degraded system performance, because the CPU is tied up doing compression and decompression instead of doing the housekeeping chores required by the rest of the system. The second method is to devise a specific integrated circuit to relieve the CPU of that burden. This method is one of the features of Sound Blaster 16 ASP. Creative Labs designed the ASP to handle data compression and decompression for the system. How the process works is shown in figure 3.6.

Fig. 3.6

How the Advanced
Signal Processor
(ASP) handles
data compression.

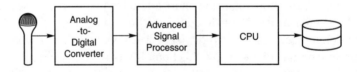

Audio signals are fed from the source (microphone, line-in, or CD) to an analog-to-digital converter that converts the waveforms into 1s and 0s (zeros). The binary information (the 1s and 0s) is then fed to the ASP for compression. In essence, the ASP squeezes all the blank spaces and repeated sounds out of the signal and then passes the digital information on to the CPU for storage on disk. As you can see, if the system did not use the ASP (see the next section on Sound Blaster 16), the CPU would have to take up the task of compressing the data. When it comes time to decompress, the opposite happens. The CPU reads the data off the disk and passes it to the ASP. The ASP decompresses the data before passing it on to the analog-to-digital converter, which is now working in reverse as a digital-to-analog converter. In turn, the digital-to-analog converter routes the newly reconstituted audio signal to Sound Blaster's output connector.

The ASP lends other capabilities to the system as well. It can be used to perform the complex task of processing voice data for speech recognition. The ASP can also be programmed to add special effects such as echo, reverberation, fade-in, and fade-out. Furthermore, the ASP can speed up or slow down playback without altering the original pitch, thus allowing your samples to be compressed or stretched in time. In other words, you can play back your own speech at a faster speed without sounding like one of the chipmunks, or at a slower speed without sounding like you're in a time warp. Finally, the ASP can be used in *speech compaction*, which is the art of shrinking the amount of memory or disk space that sampled speech consumes without making the speech incomprehensible. Sampled speech that formerly took 8,000 bytes of storage per second of speech can be shrunk to approximately 500 bytes of storage per second, which is ideal for transmitting voice files through e-mail or over networks. Previous versions of Sound Blaster could compress voice data, but the ASP chip can compress and decompress very quickly—so quickly, in fact, that it can decompress and play a compressed file without having to do the decompression ahead of time. In versions of audio boards that do not have the ASP chip, the computer itself must carry out the compression and decompression tasks, slowing the processor significantly in some cases.

The 16 ASP also has an improved mixer that can mix 10 channels and do tone control. The new board has a somewhat improved MIDI interface, but of equal importance is a connector that allows a Wave Blaster general MIDI daughterboard to be connected to the 16 ASP. There is more on Wave Blaster later in this chapter.

Sound Blaster 16 ASP has a jumper that lets you bypass the internal 4-watt amplifier and feed unamplified audio output directly into another amplifier through the stereo output connector.

Sound Blaster 16

Sound Blaster 16 is the newest member of the Sound Blaster family. The only fundamental difference between Sound Blaster 16 and Sound Blaster 16 ASP is that the ASP chip is not included. Instead of using the ASP chip to do compression/decompression, Sound Blaster 16 uses software to perform the same task but somewhat more slowly. Sound Blaster 16 can be upgraded to the 16 ASP level.

Wave Blaster

Wave Blaster is an add-on card for both Sound Blaster 16 and Sound Blaster 16 ASP. Wave Blaster does a couple of things for Sound Blaster: it provides general MIDI compliance and greatly enhances the quality of musical sound generated. Wave Blaster contains 4 megabytes of sampled sounds in memory, which are the source for 128 musical instrument presets, 18 percussion presets, and over 40 different effects. In addition, the card provides 32-voice polyphonic playback, which means that, unlike the FM Organ software application that can play only one note at a time, Wave Blaster can play 32 voices simultaneously.

As to MIDI compliance, the Sound Blaster cards comply to a subset of the MIDI standard, but with the Wave Blaster add-on, Sound Blaster 16 and 16 ASP are fully General MIDI compliant.

MIDI Blaster

MIDI Blaster is an external box that is nearly the functional equivalent of Wave Blaster. MIDI Blaster, however, connects to any of the Sound Blaster cards, or any other sound card that provides a MIDI connector. MIDI Blaster provides 20-voice polyphonic playback, with 128 instrument presets, 92 percussion presets, and 46 different effects. MIDI Blaster supports 16 MIDI channels.

Port Blaster

Port Blaster is for anyone who has a laptop computer but wants to be able to make use of sound. Port Blaster is an external box, about the size of a mouse, that connects to the parallel port on your laptop. A lot of the functionality of the Sound Blaster cards has been boiled down into this product, including the OPL 3 stereo synthesizer, 8-bit sampling and playback, and a built-in speaker. Port Blaster is similar in features and function to Sound Blaster 2.0.

CD-ROM Upgrades

Sound Blaster Pro, Sound Blaster 16, and Sound Blaster 16 ASP can be connected to a CD-ROM drive through internal connectors. However, the CD-ROM interface is proprietary to Creative Labs and not generic in any sense. That is not necessarily a negative, and, in fact, even those providers of CD-ROM drives that use the SCSI standard to control the CD-ROM players have proprietary, higher-level controlling software. This proprietary interface lets Creative Labs improve *data transfer performance* (the rate at which data is moved from the CD-ROM player into your computer) as fast as their engineering teams are able. In addition, by feeding audio signals directly from the CD-ROM player into the Sound Blaster card, you can maintain the quality of audio signals. However, it does mean that no "standard" CD-ROM player can be attached to Sound Blaster.

Hardware Summary

Table 3.1 summarizes the capabilities of the various Sound Blaster cards.

Table 3.1 The Capabilities of Sound Blaster Cards

Function	Sound Blaster V2.0	Sound Blaster Pro V2.0	Sound Blaster 16	Sound Blaster 16 ASP
Sample Rates	4-15 kHz	4-44.1 kHz	4-44.1 kHz	4-44.1 kHz
Playback Rates	4-44.1 kHz	4-44.1 kHz	4-44.1 kHz	4-44.1 kHz
Stereo	No	Yes	Yes	Yes
DSP	8 bit	8 bit	8 bit/16 bit	8 bit/16 bit
FM Voices	11	20	20	20
Microphone In	Yes, mono	Yes, mono	Yes, mono	Yes, mono
Mic. Auto Gain	No	Yes	Yes	Yes
Line in	Yes	Yes	Yes	Yes
Speaker Out	Yes	Yes	Yes	Yes
Line Out	No	Yes, internal	Yes, internal	Yes, internal

continues

Table 3.1 Continued

Function	Sound Blaster V2.0	Sound Blaster Pro V2.0	Sound Blaster 16	Sound Blaster 16 ASP
CD Audio In	No	Yes	Yes	Yes
CD-ROM Connector	No	Yes	Yes	Yes
Mixer	No	Yes	Yes	Yes
Tone Control	No	No	Yes	Yes
Voice Recognition	No	No	No	Yes
Sample Compression via Hardware	No	No	No	Yes

Sound Blaster Software

A wide variety of software packages is provided with the Sound Blaster card. The following sections summarize these software applications. A few of them are discussed in greater detail later in this book. (You should be aware that Creative Labs frequently changes the software packaged with the various Sound Blaster products to continue providing the best software available. For this reason, the packages shipped with your Sound Blaster board may differ from those described here.)

In addition to the wealth of software provided with Sound Blaster products, the back of this book contains two disks with additional software that is useful or entertaining (or both). The shareware and sound files provided on those disks are described in Chapter 11.

Drivers

When you install the Sound Blaster software, the installation routine creates a subdirectory to hold all the Sound Blaster drivers. *Drivers* are software programs that take care of all the gritty details of running a Sound Blaster card. Typically, application programs handle the user interface and the bulk of the work but call on a driver program to send messages and data to the Sound Blaster card. For example, the FM Organ program takes care of placing an image of the keyboard on your computer screen, calling up files, and recognizing when you press a key to play a note. But when it comes time to request that Sound Blaster play the note, the FM Organ software sends a message to the driver, which is usually stored in memory, and the driver passes the message along to the appropriate part of Sound Blaster.

All driver files have a DRV extension. The driver file for the FM Organ is called ORGAN.DRV. As you try out various software packages that come with Sound Blaster, you'll occasionally see one complain that it cannot find the appropriate driver, or that the driver is not loaded into memory. Some software requires that the driver simply be in the same directory as the application software. In that case, make sure that you place a copy of the driver with the application. Don't remove the drivers from the driver directory. In other cases, the drivers must be loaded by another program. The file named SBFMDRV.COM, for example, loads the Sound Blaster's FM synthesizer driver into memory for use by other programs. The SBMIDI.EXE file loads the MIDI driver into memory.

FM Organ

Sometimes referred to as the FM Intelligent Organ, this application runs under DOS and allows you to use your PC keyboard to play Sound Blaster's version of an electronic organ. (Actually, it is probably unrealistic to try to play the FM Organ on the PC keyboard. Fortunately, Sound Blaster does have that MIDI port, and if you have a MIDI-compliant keyboard and the MIDI kit, you can use your keyboard to play, rather than use the computer keyboard.) Figure 3.7 shows the FM Organ for Sound Blaster Pro.

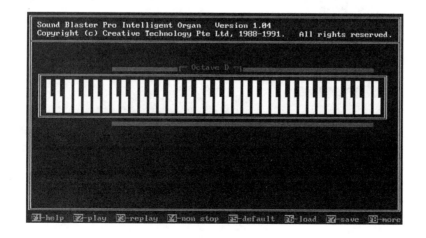

Fig. 3.7

The Sound Blaster Pro version of the FM Intelligent Organ.

The FM Organ (called PRO_ORG when included with Sound Blaster Pro) is a prime example of a monophonic synthesizer application, meaning that the FM Organ can play only one note at a time. Try to play a chord, and the FM Organ will play the key pressed first. (The reason is that the computer cannot sense when you've pressed two keys simultaneously. Stored background rhythms and music don't have this computer keyboard limitation.) The FM Organ can generate 20 different sounds, some of which are quite appealing, and can back you up with 16 different rhythms or accompaniments.

SBTalker

This program uses the Sound Blaster synthesizer chip(s) to synthesize human speech. SBTalker reads text files to you in a fairly mechanical voice. The real entertainment, however, comes from using SBTalker inside another program, called Ask Dr. Sbaitso, in which software makes a feeble but occasionally enjoyable attempt to carry on a conversation (see fig. 3.8). Dr. Sbaitso uses some aged software technology to present a mock interview with you. Those of you that have been in the computer business for a while might remember a program called "Lucy" that made the rounds about 10 years ago. Dr. Sbaitso uses the same methodology—canned responses to key words. The SBTalker program (called READ.EXE) and Dr. Sbaitso do demonstrate the capability of synthesizer chips and programmers to come pretty close to human speech. SBTalker and Dr. Sbaitso must be installed from a separate disk and require an additional 335K of disk space.

Fig. 3.8

A short interview with Dr. Sbaitso.

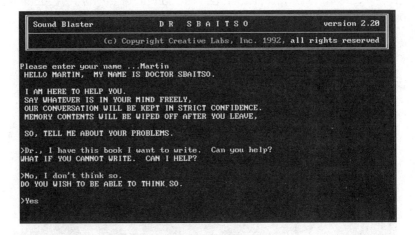

```
 Sound Blaster           D R   S B A I T S O          version 2.20
                 (c) Copyright Creative Labs, Inc. 1992, all rights reserved

Please enter your name ...Martin
HELLO MARTIN,  MY NAME IS DOCTOR SBAITSO.

I AM HERE TO HELP YOU.
SAY WHATEVER IS IN YOUR MIND FREELY,
OUR CONVERSATION WILL BE KEPT IN STRICT CONFIDENCE.
MEMORY CONTENTS WILL BE WIPED OFF AFTER YOU LEAVE,

SO, TELL ME ABOUT YOUR PROBLEMS.

>Dr., I have this book I want to write.  Can you help?
WHAT IF YOU CANNOT WRITE.  CAN I HELP?

>No, I don't think so.
DO YOU WISH TO BE ABLE TO THINK SO.

>Yes
```

Talking Parrot

The Talking Parrot program (not provided with Sound Blaster 16/16 ASP) demonstrates Sound Blaster's sampling and playback capabilities, coupled with a simple animation (see fig. 3.9). When you speak into a microphone connected to Sound Blaster, the card samples your voice and plays it back to you at a little higher rate, while cycling through four frames of parrot artwork. You can use your own animation frames if you like, as long as they have the same file names as the Parrot pictures. Occasionally, the Parrot injects its own comment and has no problem filling quiet spaces with nonsense.

Fig. 3.9

The Talking
Parrot.

Voice Editor II

This DOS-based voice editor (VEDIT2.EXE) is a fairly powerful application you can use to sample, edit, and store VOC files. (VEDIT2.EXE is not provided with Sound Blaster 16/16 ASP.) In figure 3.10, you can see an oscilloscope-like display of a stereo sampling made through the line-in connector. You use the mouse to select specific areas in the sample to edit (cut, paste, and so on) or modify with the Effects menu, which is shown in figure 3.10. In addition, VEDIT2 lets you control your CD-ROM player if you have one attached to your system. The CD-ROM player does not have to be a Sound Blaster CD-ROM. A description of Voice Editor II is included in Chapter 4.

Voice Utilities

A number of utility programs provided with Sound Blaster are quite useful. Among them are utilities that convert sampled files in the Sound Blaster VOC format into WAV files for use with Windows, or vice versa. In addition, there are utilities for recording and playing back VOC files, changing the playback sample rates of VOC files, joining two or more VOC files into a single file, and adding the appropriate file header information to raw sound files to turn them into VOC files. More on file formats and conversion is provided in Chapter 5 and Appendix B.

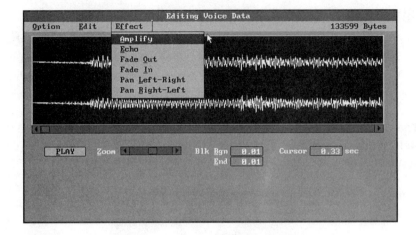

Fig. 3.10

Voice Editor II being used to modify a stereo sound track sampled from the line-in connector.

MMPlay

This program is intended to demonstrate the multimedia capabilities of Sound Blaster coupled with an animation program. In this instance, the program MMPLAY.EXE loads animation files with the FLI extension (FLI is an animation standard developed by Autodesk) and plays back the animations along with sound files. Unfortunately, the demo animation provided with Sound Blaster requires a Super VGA display and will not work on standard VGA display systems. In fact, if you attempt to run MMDEMO.BAT without a Super VGA monitor and card, it tends to hang up the computer.

PC Animate Plus

This is a DOS-based program developed by Presidio Software, Inc. PC Animate Plus is a full-featured animation program provided with Sound Blaster 16/16 ASP, but the program works as well with Sound Blaster and Sound Blaster Pro. A sample animation is shown in figure 3.11. It is a paint program that enables you to draw individual animation frames, cut and paste images across frames, fade in and out, and add sound to your animation. PC Animate Plus is installed from a separate disk and requires an additional 2.7M of disk space.

Voyetra Sequencer Plus

This very powerful MIDI recording and editing program is developed by Voyetra Technologies. The Sequencer Plus Pro package is bundled with the Sound Blaster MIDI kit and with Sound Blaster Pro. This sequencer is described in detail in Chapter 7.

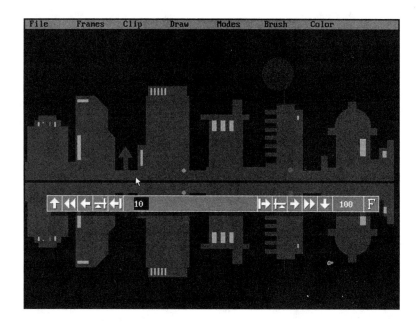

Fig. 3.11

A sample frame
from PC Animate
Plus.

Monologue for Windows

This Windows program can be used to read text and numbers from Windows applications. Monologue uses the same techniques used by SBTalker to read text from one of three sources: the Windows Clipboard, Excel, or a DDE (Dynamic Data Exchange) application that can direct text streams to Monologue. To use Monologue (shown in fig. 3.12), double-click the icon, select which source you want, and then minimize the Monologue window. At that point, you can convert to speech whatever you copy to the Clipboard by pointing to the minimized Monologue icon and clicking the right mouse button. Monologue must be installed from a separate disk and requires an additional 602K of disk space.

Creative WaveStudio

This application is an editor program that lets you edit WAV files. As you know, WAV files are sound files stored in the Windows file format. Creative WaveStudio enables you to merge WAV files, cut and paste elements of the file, add an echo, reverse the sound (play it backwards), and so on. Creative WaveStudio, illustrated in figure 3.13, is described in greater detail in Chapter 9.

Monologue for
Windows used to
read aloud the
Clipboard's
contents or Excel
text.

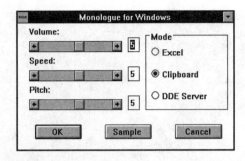

A Creative
WaveStudio
window.

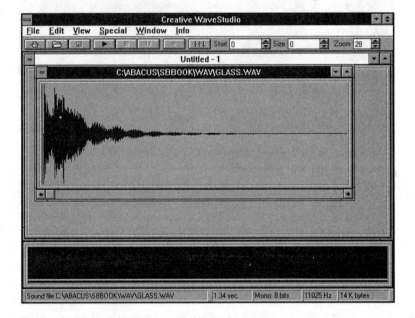

Creative Soundo'LE

The Soundo'LE application can be used to record and play back sound
samples, but more important, it enables you to attach sound files to other
applications by linking or embedding them. Soundo'LE, illustrated in figure
3.14, works in much the same manner as the Object Packager utility provided
with Windows; once you have a WAV file created or edited to your satisfaction,
you can open another Windows application, such as Excel, and then link that
sound file to an Excel spreadsheet.

The sound file is indicated by an icon that shows up in the spreadsheet. Whenever someone clicks the icon, the linked sound file is played back over Sound Blaster. Soundo'LE might be useful in adding audio notes to a word processor document or spreadsheet, or in adding a speech sample to a security system.

Creative Talking Scheduler

This program is fundamentally a computerized scheduling program into which you load appointments. Then, when the time comes to meet an appointment, one of three animated characters (named Simon, Perkins, and Igor) verbally reminds you of the appointment (see fig. 3.15). The Scheduler's power is increased significantly because it can be an OLE (Object Linking and Embedding) client within Windows. In other words, you can link such Windows' objects as text files, graphic images, or other OLE objects to the scheduler so that, when an appointment comes up, you can review relevant documentation.

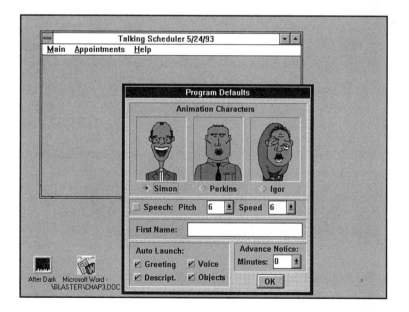

HSC InterActive SE

HSC InterActive SE is a package of three different applications: an icon-based application development system, an icon animator, and a screen capture and manipulate program. A screen shot of HSC InterActive is shown in figure 3.16. HSC InterActive SE must be installed from a separate disk and requires an additional 1.6M of disk space.

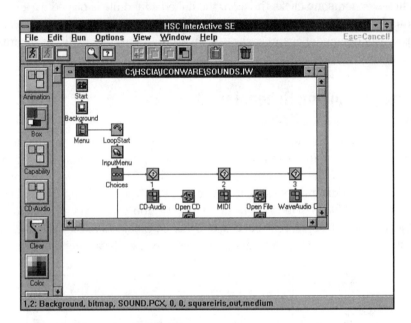

Sound Blaster Installation

If life were perfect, you would simply plug the Sound Blaster card into your PC, turn it on, install the software, and away you'd go. Unfortunately, for most of us, anyway, life is neither perfect nor simple. Personal computers have some characteristics and requirements you should be concerned about.

The CPU inside your computer knows how to take care of itself very well, thank you. It's also pretty good at taking care of the needs of the disk drives, monitor, and keyboard. But when you start adding options beyond those basic three, things get a little complicated.

Each hardware option that you add to your computer—whether it be a CD-ROM controller, sound card, or scanner—requires the CPU to pay attention to it once in a while. The way that Sound Blaster or any other card asks the CPU for attention is by *interrupting* the CPU. The CPU, depending on what kind it is, can handle a fixed number of interrupts, some as high as 10. Sound Blaster begs for attention by issuing an interrupt request, or IRQ, to the CPU. Sound Blaster Pro, for example, can interrupt the CPU on IRQ lines 2, 5, 7, or 10. As the installer of Sound Blaster, you have to worry about what IRQ line number to assign to the card.

Another requirement of each hardware option is that it must work in its own address space. This address space, called the I/O (short for input/output) address or port address, must be unique to each hardware option in your computer. You wouldn't want, for example, the CPU to issue Sound Blaster commands to the I/O address space used by your scanner or FAX/MODEM. Therefore, the second thing you have to worry about is assigning an I/O base address to the Sound Blaster card.

The final requirement is called Direct Memory Access, or DMA. In most cases, when a hardware option wants to move data in and out of your system memory, it passes the data on to the CPU, which takes care of handling memory. But this adds a certain amount of overhead. Hardware that works very fast, like Sound Blaster Pro or Sound Blaster 16 ASP, can't wait for the CPU to move the data around. In this instance, Sound Blaster requires direct access to the memory, bypassing the CPU. Modern PCs have made allowances for this requirement by providing up to three DMA channels: 0, 1, and 3. DMA channel 2 is used for other purposes. Selecting a DMA channel is the third concern you have when installing Sound Blaster Pro, 16, or 16 ASP.

So you have these restraints:

- Every hardware device must work in its own I/O address space.

- Every hardware device should generate its own interrupt request (IRQ).

- Every hardware device should use its own DMA channel or behave itself when sharing.

If the Sound Blaster card is the only hardware option you have in your computer (no modems, serial mouse, scanner, or CD-ROM drive), you don't have many problems. You most likely can leave all the settings at their defaults and install the Sound Blaster card without worrying about a thing. If you're like many of us, however, you have loaded up your computer with a lot of other hardware.

Testing Your System with Snooper

The problem that many of us have when installing new hardware is finding out how all the other hardware in the computer is set up. The best way to do this is to keep a file at your system level that lists the IRQ, I/O address, and DMA channels you've set up for each option. When you install new hardware, you can then update this file. Sadly, not all of us are that organized.

During the installation process, you are required to provide information to the installation program about what I/O address you want your Sound Blaster to use, and which interrupt request line (IRQ) and DMA channel (Pro, 16/16 ASP only) to use. You can accept the default values for these items if you choose, but you do run the risk of having the defaults conflict with other hardware already installed. The only way to prevent those conflicts is to know what is already installed in your system. If you run into a conflict, your only option is to take the case off your computer, remove all the circuit boards, and make note of the existing hardware settings. Then you can select settings for Sound Blaster that do not conflict with other hardware.

Alternatively, you can use software to help in that quest. A utility is included in the software in the back of this book to make life a little easier: Snooper, the system checker.

The Snooper program is terrific at checking out your system hardware. Snooper comes to you courtesy of John Vias, who can be reached at the following address:

> Vias & Associates
> P.O. Box 8234
> Gainesville, FL 32605-8234
> (904) 332-8234

Snooper is a DOS-based program that you run simply by typing **SNOOPER** from the DOS prompt in the Snooper directory. The first screen you see is a summary of your computer's capabilities: the kind of CPU and memory you have, DOS version, and so on. Snooper reads your disk drive to determine how much space you have left. You can tell when Snooper is finished when it fills out the space-used bar in the lower-right corner of the first screen. To have Snooper check out your system, you must press Alt-D. Snooper then begins diagnosing your system to find out how various hardware components are using it.

When Snooper checked out my system, the program found the information shown in figure 3.17.

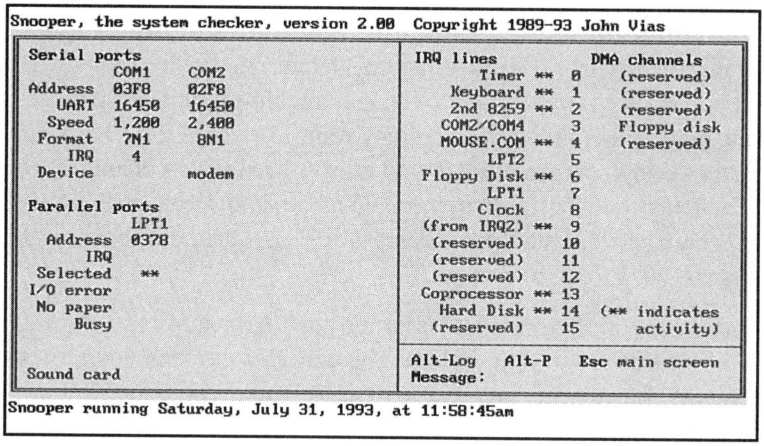

```
Snooper, the system checker, version 2.00  Copyright 1989-93 John Vias

 Serial ports                        IRQ lines             DMA channels
           COM1     COM2                   Timer ** 0        (reserved)
 Address   03F8     02F8                Keyboard ** 1        (reserved)
    UART   16450    16450               2nd 8259 ** 2        (reserved)
   Speed   1,200    2,400              COM2/COM4    3        Floppy disk
  Format   7N1      8N1                MOUSE.COM ** 4        (reserved)
     IRQ   4                                LPT2    5
  Device            modem           Floppy Disk ** 6
                                            LPT1    7
 Parallel ports                            Clock    8
           LPT1                        (from IRQ2) ** 9
 Address   0378                        (reserved)   10
     IRQ                               (reserved)   11
 Selected  **                         (reserved)   12
 I/O error                           Coprocessor ** 13
 No paper                              Hard Disk ** 14    (** indicates
    Busy                               (reserved)   15        activity)

                                     Alt-Log   Alt-P    Esc main screen
 Sound card                          Message:
Snooper running Saturday, July 31, 1993, at 11:58:45am
```

Fig. 3.17

The output of Snooper showing IRQ use.

Keep in mind that what you're trying to find out is whether there are any I/O address, IRQ, or DMA conflicts. Given the wide range of possible I/O addresses, it is pretty unlikely that any address conflicts will occur. However, it's good to check and make sure. In this case, my computer is not using the default Sound Blaster address of 220H, so I can leave that at its default value.

Far more common and troublesome are IRQ conflicts. On the right side of the display is the list of IRQ lines available in my computer, lines 0 through 15. Some of the IRQ lines have predetermined uses. For example, the keyboard always uses IRQ1, the clock uses IRQ 8, and so on. If you take a moment to look at the Snooper output, you can see that my system is using two serial ports, COM1 and COM2. The COM1 port is using IRQ line 4 (my serial mouse), so IRQ 4 is not available. The modem in my computer is using COM2, and although it doesn't show, IRQ 3; so IRQ 3 is not available. However, I do not have a second printer and am not using the second printer port, LPT2. This means that LPT2's IRQ 5 is available. And again, the default IRQ setting for Sound Blaster Pro is IRQ 5, so no change is needed there.

The DMA channels are shown at the far right in figure 3.17. My PC uses DMA channels 0 through 4. Most DMA channels are shared by the hardware in today's PCs and are marked as reserved, which means that they are available. Notice that in my system, though, DMA channel 3 is used by the floppy disk controller. Because of this, DMA channel 3 is not available for use, even though the Sound Blaster Pro documentation says that most floppy disk controllers use channel 2 and that DMA channel 3 is available. This is one of the reasons why running a program like Snooper is valuable before you install any optional hardware like Sound Blaster.

Sound Blaster Pro uses DMA channel 1 by default. According to Snooper, that should be OK. But if you appear to be running into problems such as sound working only some of the time, you may want to change the DMA channel. I found, for example, that setting Sound Blaster Pro to DMA channel 0 worked better and more reliably in my system. What I do know from running Snooper is that I should not set the Sound Blaster Pro DMA channel to channel 3. I can use channels 0, 1, or 2, however.

The bottom line on all this is that it's far too easy to run into conflicts when you install new hardware in your system. The best strategy is to keep track of all assignments. But if you don't know what they are, use Snooper to dig the information out of your system. I recommend that you run Snooper before beginning the Sound Blaster installation. But whatever you do, make note of how you set up the Sound Blaster card because you might have to change it later.

Installing Sound Blaster Software

Sound Blaster software installation is very similar from one product to the next. This discussion describes in some detail how the installation process works and which of your system files are modified. Keep in mind, however, that the manual and README.TXT file that come with your Sound Blaster are the final authority on how Sound Blaster software is installed, and far more current and up-to-date than any book can be. If you discover a conflict between the information provided here and the information provided with your Sound Blaster, please consider the Sound Blaster documentation the final authority. No book can keep pace with potential changes in software.

After you have used Snooper to determine what should be appropriate hardware settings for your Sound Blaster, you can begin software installation. All Sound Blasters use fundamentally the same installation process:

1. You set the base address, interrupt request (IRQ), and DMA jumpers on the circuit board.

2. You run INSTALL from disk #1, which tests the board to make sure that it's working.

3. INSTALL then modifies AUTOEXEC.BAT (and CONFIG.SYS for Sound Blaster 16/16 ASP).

When installation is complete, you reboot your system, and everything should run.

If you have Windows, an extra step is required to load the appropriate driver software and configure Windows. You set up the Windows environment by running the WINSETUP.EXE program in your Sound Blaster directory from Windows, using File Manager or the Control menu.

Running INSTALL

Begin software installation by placing disk #1 in the appropriate drive. Then begin the installation program by typing the drive letter followed by the name of the program. For example, if you place disk #1 in drive B, you enter the following at the prompt:

B:INSTALL

The installation program starts, presenting an opening screen similar to that shown in figure 3.18.

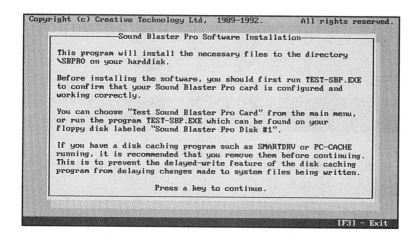

```
                 ┌─Sound Blaster Pro Software Installation─┐
                 │                                          │
                 │  This program will install the necessary files to the directory
                 │  \SBPRO on your harddisk.
                 │
                 │  Before installing the software, you should first run TEST-SBP.EXE
                 │  to confirm that your Sound Blaster Pro card is configured and
                 │  working correctly.
                 │
                 │  You can choose "Test Sound Blaster Pro Card" from the main menu,
                 │  or run the program TEST-SBP.EXE which can be found on your
                 │  floppy disk labeled "Sound Blaster Pro Disk #1".
                 │
                 │  If you have a disk caching program such as SMARTDRU or PC-CACHE
                 │  running, it is recommended that you remove them before continuing.
                 │  This is to prevent the delayed-write feature of the disk caching
                 │  program from delaying changes made to system files being written.
                 │
                 │              Press a key to continue.
                 │
                 └──────────────────────────────────────────┘

                                                          [F3] - Exit
```

Fig. 3.18

The opening installation screen, similar for all Sound Blaster cards.

One difference between the Sound Blaster 16/16 ASP installation program and the other installation programs is that the 16/16 ASP does not give you the option of running the test program described in figure 3.18. If you are installing Sound Blaster or Sound Blaster Pro, you should run the test to make sure that the hardware was installed correctly and is working.

The installation program actually calls up another program to run the tests:

System	Test Program Name
Sound Blaster	TEST-SBC.EXE
Sound Blaster Pro	TEST-SBP.EXE
Sound Blaster 16/16 ASP	TESTSB16.EXE

You can run the test program from DOS independently whenever you like.

When the test program starts, an opening screen appears, as shown in figure 3.19. This happens to be the opening screen for Sound Blaster Pro, but all three screens are similar.

Fig. 3.19

The opening screen for the test program.

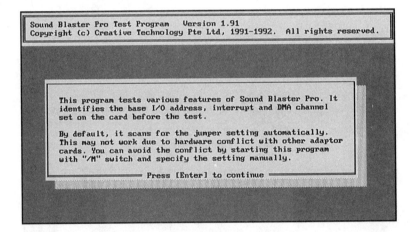

```
Sound Blaster Pro Test Program    Version 1.91
Copyright (c) Creative Technology Pte Ltd, 1991-1992.  All rights reserved.




        This program tests various features of Sound Blaster Pro. It
        identifies the base I/O address, interrupt and DMA channel
        set on the card before the test.

        By default, it scans for the jumper setting automatically.
        This may not work due to hardware conflict with other adaptor
        cards. You can avoid the conflict by starting this program
        with "/M" switch and specify the setting manually.
                        ══ Press [Enter] to continue ══
```

As the screen states, the program automatically checks your Sound Blaster card for jumper settings.

The Test Program

The test program checks each part of the hardware installation: the I/O address, the interrupt line, and the DMA channel. The test program first checks whether Sound Blaster responds to the default settings. If not, the program then checks all the alternative settings.

The first thing tested is the I/O address that Sound Blaster is using. Usually, the default address of 220H is just fine. Again, using Snooper should tell you whether any other add-on cards are using that address; if so, you can change Sound Blaster.

The next test checks whether the interrupt line is working, as shown in figure 3.20.

Again, if you have used Snooper, you should know whether you can safely use the default interrupt line (5) or whether you need to change it.

The final hardware test is to see what DMA channel Sound Blaster is set for, as shown in figure 3.21.

DMA channel conflicts are very difficult to detect. Even though other hardware in your computer might be using the DMA channel, they probably don't use it all the time. The test routine may check the DMA channel and see that it is working. However, a little later, DMA channel conflicts may crop up because the other hardware decided to use the channel. In some cases, you won't know that a DMA channel conflict exists until a problem occurs. This is unfortunate but true.

16/16 ASP NOTE

The opening screen warns you to disable any programs such as SMARTDRV.EXE that may be running before you begin installation. You can do this by opening the AUTOEXEC.BAT file with your favorite editor and inserting the letters REM and a space at the beginning of the line containing SMARTDRV.EXE. For example, your AUTOEXEC.BAT file may contain the following line:

```
LH /L:0;1,42384 /S C:\DOS\SMARTDRV.EXE
```

This line loads the program SMARTDRV.EXE into high memory. To disable SMARTDRV.EXE during Sound Blaster 16/16 ASP installation, modify this line to read

```
REM LH /L:0;1,42384 /S C:\DOS\SMARTDRV.EXE
```

By adding the letters REM and a space in front of the line, you are telling DOS to ignore this line during boot-up. After you make this change in your AUTOEXEC.BAT file, save the file and reboot your computer.

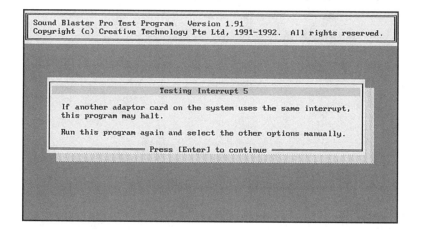

Fig. 3.20

The test program checking whether Sound Blaster is using the appropriate interrupt line.

Fig. 3.21

The test program checking whether Sound Blaster is able to use the DMA channel you selected.

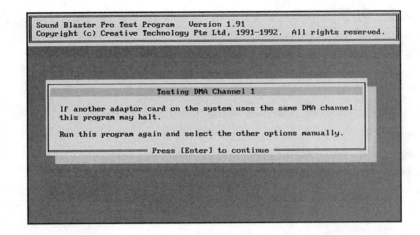

16/16 ASP NOTE

Sound Blaster 16 and 16 ASP use two DMA channels: one channel for the low 8 bits of the address bus, and one for the high 8 bits.

When the test program is satisfied that the Sound Blaster card is configured correctly and is responding, it runs a musical test. The test menu shown in figure 3.22 lets you play a short piece of music—and plays a sampled sound to make sure that Sound Blaster is working correctly.

Fig. 3.22

The test menu that lets you hear Sound Blaster for the first time.

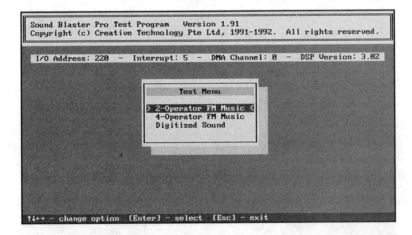

When the sound tests are completed, the installation program moves on to the next step: modifying your AUTOEXEC.BAT file, and in the case of Sound Blaster 16/16 ASP, modifying your CONFIG.SYS file.

Modifying the DOS System Files

The next step in installation is to add some lines to the AUTOEXEC.BAT file so that all the appropriate software is started when you turn on your computer. Sound Blaster and Sound Blaster Pro add the following two lines to the AUTOEXEC.BAT file:

SET BLASTER=A220 I5 D0 T4

SET SOUND=C:\SBPRO

The first line is used by Sound Blaster application software to find out where the card is and to access it properly. In this case, Sound Blaster is at address 220 and uses interrupt line number 5 and DMA channel 0:

Parameter	Description
A220	I/O address 220H
I5	Interrupt line 5
D0	DMA channel 0
T4	Type of Sound Blaster card

The second line added to AUTOEXEC.BAT tells other applications where the Sound Blaster software is located. Of course, if you were installing Sound Blaster V2.0, the second line would read

SET SOUND=C:\SB

Because Sound Blaster Pro has a mixer that can set various volume levels, it adds a third line to AUTOEXEC.BAT:

C:\SBPRO\SBP-SET /M:12 /VOC:12 /CD:12 /FM:12

This line sets the volume levels for each of these sound sources:

/M:12	Master Volume
/VOC:12	Voice Output
/CD:12	CD Input
/FM:12	FM Chip Input

If you would like to change the initial settings for the Sound Blaster Pro mixer chip, simply change the values in this line. A lower number reduces volume. You can set each value as high as 15.

Sound Blaster 16 and 16 ASP add the following four lines to the AUTOEXEC.BAT file:

    SET BLASTER=A220 I5 D0 H6 P300 T6

    SET SOUND=C:\SB16

    C:\SB16\SBCONFIG.EXE /S

    C:\SB16\SB16SET /M:220 /VOC:220 /CD:220 /MIDI:220 /TREBLE:0

The first of these lines sets the Sound Blaster 16/16 ASP environment:

Parameter	Description
A220	I/O address 220H
I5	Interrupt line 5
D0	DMA channel 0
H6	High DMA channel 6
P300	MIDI port I/O address 300H
T6	Type of Sound Blaster card

As indicated before, Sound Blaster 16 and 16 ASP use two DMA channels. Sound Blaster 16 and 16 ASP also provide the option of changing the MIDI port address from 330H to 300H. Finally, the 16 ASP is a type 6 card.

Sound Blaster 16 and 16 ASP have software-programmable interrupt and DMA channel jumpers. That is, instead of having to physically set the jumpers, you can use the SBCONFIG.EXE program to set them. In fact, each time you boot your computer, your AUTOEXEC.BAT file runs the SBCONFIG program to configure Sound Blaster. The third line added to AUTOEXEC.BAT runs the Sound Blaster 16/16 ASP configuration program. The /S parameter tells the configuration program to configure the Sound Blaster 16/16 ASP interrupt line and DMA channels according to the environment line (SET BLASTER=) just described.

The fourth line added to the 16/16 ASP AUTOEXEC.BAT file runs the Sound Blaster mixer program to set the mixer chip to initial values:

Parameter	Description
/M:220	Master Volume
/VOC:220	Voice Output
/CD:220	CD Input
/MIDI:220	MIDI Volume
/TREBLE:0	Treble/Bass

The maximum setting for each parameter is 255.

One other change is made to your DOS environment when you install Sound Blaster 16 ASP, and that is to point to the new Advanced Signal Processor device in the system. At installation, the following line is added to CONFIG.SYS:

    DEVICE=C:\SB16\DRV\ASP.SYS /P:220

This line tells DOS the path name of the controlling software and the I/O address of the Sound Blaster 16 ASP card. This line is not added when you install Sound Blaster 16.

Windows Installation

After you have the DOS installation completed, you can move on to the Windows installation, which makes the appropriate modification to your Windows WIN.INI file, creates a Sound Blaster program group, and adds the Windows program icons to the group.

You run the Windows installation program from Windows. One way to do this is to click the **F**ile menu item in Program Manager, choose **R**un, and enter the appropriate path name and program name (see fig. 3.23).

When you start the Windows installation program, a small dialog box appears, as shown in figure 3.24, and installation begins.

Click OK, and the installation gets under way. Very quickly, the following lines are added to two groups in the SYSTEM.INI file:

    [drivers]
    MIDI=sbp2fm.drv
    Aux=sbpaux.drv
    Wave=sbpsnd.drv
    MIDI1=sbpsnd.drv

```
[sndblst.drv]
Port=220
Int=5
DmaChannel=0
```

If this were a Sound Blaster or Sound Blaster 16/16 ASP installation, the file names and settings would be slightly different. These lines should not be altered. If you happen to change the hardware settings on your Sound Blaster board, rerun the installation program to ensure that all variables are set correctly.

Fig. 3.23

Running the Windows installation program.

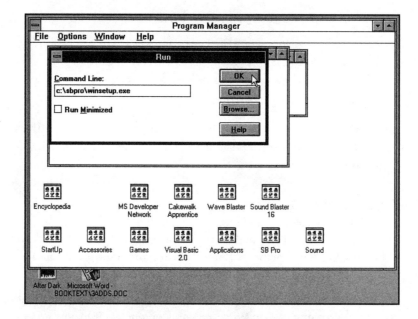

Sound Blaster Inputs and Outputs

The Sound Blaster cards have a variety of input and output connectors. The following text describes each one briefly and tells whether you need to be concerned about any aspects of connecting other equipment to Sound Blaster.

Microphones

Nearly any standard mono microphone can be plugged into the microphone jack; but if you are interested in recording high-quality audio at high sample rates, you should invest in a moderately high-quality microphone—in the

$25-$75 range. Avoid the microphones sold for portable cassette tape recorders. The quality just isn't up to acceptable levels in most cases. Sound Blaster 16/16 ASP includes a microphone with the package.

Fig. 3.24

The dialog box that starts the installation process.

The input impedance of the microphone jack is 600 ohms, with a sensitivity range of 10-100 mV for Sound Blaster Pro, and 10-200 mV for Sound Blaster 16 ASP. The Sound Blaster Pro and 16/16 ASP versions have automatic gain control, which means that the microphone amplifier is automatically turned up as sound volume goes down, and vice versa. In any case, Sound Blaster versions with the mixer chip let you directly control the volume of the microphone.

Speakers

The speaker output for all Sound Blaster cards is connected to an on-board amplifier that generates 4 watts of power per channel, with a load impedance of 4 or 8 ohms per channel. A standard mini stereo-jack-to-RCA-connector converter cable is provided with some Sound Blasters, but if you don't have one, you can use standard cables found at any audio store.

Sound Blaster 16/16 ASP has a jumper you can use to bypass the on-board amplifiers, if you like, and feed unamplified audio as a line-out signal through the speaker jack (see fig. 3.25). This feature is primarily used by serious audiophiles who know that any small amplifier will add a certain amount of noise and distortion, and who want unadulterated output from the synthesizer and DSP chips. If you are connecting the speaker jack to an amplifier, you should move the jumpers on the OPSL and OPSR pins to bypass the on-board audio amplifier.

Fig. 3.25

Jumpers allow the speaker jack to be used as a line-out jack (Sound Blaster 16/16 ASP only).

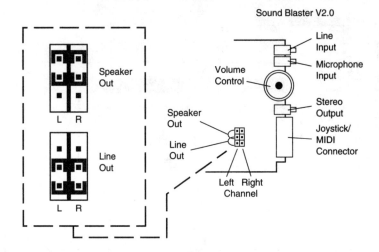

Line-In

The line-in connector accepts audio signals at line levels, meaning that they are at very low amplitude and not controlled by the source's volume knob. You can connect any audio source that has a line-out jack to the Sound Blaster line-in connector.

Line-Out

You can use the Sound Blaster 16/16 ASP speaker output jack as a line-out connector by setting the jumpers to the "line out" position shown in figure 3.25.

Joystick/MIDI Port

The 15-pin D-connector on the back of the Sound Blaster cards is a dual-function connector in that it supports both a standard game joystick and a MIDI adaptor cable for connecting Sound Blaster to MIDI instruments.

On-Board Connectors

You can use a number of connectors on-board the Sound Blaster cards. The following paragraphs describe these connectors.

CD-ROM Audio In

The CD-ROM Audio In connector is available if you want to feed audio signals from your own CD-ROM player into Sound Blaster. There are four pins:

Pin	Signal
1	Ground
2	CD Left Channel
3	Ground
5	CD Right Channel

The signal levels expected at these pins are line-in levels. Do not feed amplified audio signals into the CD-ROM Audio In connector.

CD-ROM Controller

Sound Blaster Pro and Sound Blaster 16/16 ASP have a CD-ROM controller connector at the rear of the card. This connector is a proprietary interface and uses a standard developed internally at Creative Labs. Only CD-ROM players sold by Creative Labs can be attached to this connector.

PC Speaker

Sound Blaster Pro and Sound Blaster 16/16 ASP have a two-pin connector that you may be able to connect to your PC speaker output on your motherboard. That would enable the PC motherboard to use Sound Blaster as a speaker, rather than use the small speaker provided with your computer.

Most PC speaker connectors have one pin on the motherboard connected to +5 Vdc, while the other pin carries the data out. Make sure that you connect the +5 Vdc line to pin 1 of JP1, as suggested here:

Pin 1   To +5 Vdc on motherboard

Pin 2   To data-out pin on motherboard

Be careful! If you make a mistake and misconnect these wires, you may damage the motherboard or Sound Blaster. If you do, it's most likely that your warranty will not be honored.

CHAPTER 4

Finding and Editing Sounds

Now that you have a sound machine in your computer, where do you get the sounds? The answer is, "Almost anywhere you want." However—and there is always a *however*—what you do with those sounds is not entirely up to you. You can buy sound clips on disk or CD, or you can take the more exciting route and make your own.

Sampling sound is just another way of recording sound, and people have been recording sound for as long as it has been possible to do so. In 1878, Thomas Edison patented the phonograph, which sampled sound and stored it on a thin sheet of tinfoil wrapped around a cylinder. Valdemar Poulsen of Denmark patented the first magnetic recorder in 1898, with which sound was electronically recorded on a steel wire. And the forebearer of all tape recorders—the Magnetophon—was introduced in 1936 by AEG Telefunken, using plastic tape created by BASF. So for over 100 years, people have been sampling sound and storing it for later playback.

The greatest difference between sampling as done with Edison's phonograph and sampling with Sound Blaster is that Sound Blaster converts the sound into digital ones (1s) and zeros (0s), as explained in Chapter 2. Mr. Edison's phonograph turned sound into squiggles imprinted on the tinfoil, and later on plastic disks known to a few historians as *records*.

Today, nearly all popular music takes advantage of sampling. There have, in fact, been lawsuits over unauthorized digital sampling, where one artist has "borrowed" a particular musical riff from another artist and used it in a recording. The technology used in the music industry is the same as that available to you with Sound Blaster—with enhancements, of course.

This chapter covers a variety of information but concentrates on using Sound Blaster and the DOS-based Voice Editor II software, which is provided with Sound Blaster and Sound Blaster Pro to record and edit your own samples. Voice Editor II is not provided with Sound Blaster 16 and 16 ASP. Users of those products can refer to Chapter 9 and the Creative WaveStudio product for information on editing sound files in the Windows environment.

Sampling and the Law—Who Really Owns "Beam Me Up, Scotty"?

Almost every sound track from a movie, stage play, record, CD, radio show, or television show is copyrighted. And the law protects these sounds in exactly the same way that it protects printed matter. If you go to your local library and pull a book or magazine from the shelf and take it to the copy machine, you will likely see a warning about copying information posted somewhere near the copier. The same is true with the video tapes you rent. The next time you rent a video, don't fast-forward past the warning; instead, read it. It might say something like this:

> Licensed only for noncommercial private exhibition in homes. Any public performance, other use, or copying is strictly prohibited. All rights under copyright reserved.

This copyright statement says that *all* the information on the video tape, including the sound, is owned by someone else and that you cannot copy or reproduce the information. Only the copyright owner can do the following:

- Reproduce or authorize reproduction of the copyrighted material

- Make derivative works or changes to the material

- Distribute, license, or sell the material

These exclusive rights last for 50 years past the life of the author.

Do you have the right to sample the sound track from *Star Trek: The Next Generation* or from any of the *Star Trek* movies? No, you do not. That sound track belongs to Paramount Communications, which owns all the images and sounds you can see or hear in the television show or the movies.

Second question: Is Paramount Communications going to come pounding on your door if you sample McCoy's verbal abuse of Spock just to use when you exit Windows? Probably not. Some companies may not mind if you take a sample or two for your own use. But keep in mind that these sounds must be for your use, on your computer. They cannot be scattered across the world either as a sound file or as part of a program you may write—particularly if you're going to make any money from the effort.

If you want to compile a disk full of samples from movies, television, and records, go ahead. But keep this disk for your own use. If you decide to get rich distributing this disk commercially or as shareware, you'd better line up a terrific copyright infringement attorney. You'll need one.

The best bet is to consider carefully *before* you sample someone else's work. Think how you'd feel if you spent $40 million on a sound track, only to have parts of it stolen for someone else's profit. Sample away, but use good sense!

Sampling with Sound Blaster

Plugging a microphone into the back of your computer is the quickest way to get started in the sampling business.

First, a little bit about microphones. Various kinds of microphones are available, with prices ranging from under ten dollars to hundreds of dollars. In general, microphones come in two flavors: directional and omnidirectional. *Directional* microphones have to be pointed in the general direction of the sound source. *Omnidirectional* microphones pick up sound from nearly all directions. Which is better? It depends on what you're trying to do. If you're recording in a place that has a lot of noise coming from one direction—say, that printer fan in the corner—a directional microphone would be better. However, if you want to record all the sounds of a place, or if you don't know which direction the sound will come from, an omnidirectional microphone is probably better. If you want to do only general-purpose recording while sitting at your computer, either type is probably fine.

The second consideration is how to avoid those nasty "pops" when you speak into the microphone. People seem to fall into three categories when using a microphone: those who have "microphonophobia" and hold it as far away as possible; those who think that intimacy is the best policy and hold the microphone lovingly to their faces; and those who know that microphones are best held about 6 inches from the mouth, slightly below a horizontal line drawn from the mouth outward. Holding a microphone too far away guarantees that all the noises around will be sampled, along with the far-off, dim sound of the person you're trying to record. Holding a microphone too close ensures that speech will be muffled and accompanied by nose noises. As to the horizontal line, you must try to keep the microphone out of the way of that high-velocity air that escapes your mouth whenever you use the letter P in a sentence.

Remember also that your microphone doesn't need to be connected to your Sound Blaster card all the time. With a high-quality portable recorder, you can go out in the field and record sounds from other places, bring them back to your desk, and sample them at your leisure.

One of the tools you will need in order to do sampling with the Sound Blaster is a sound editor. Sound editor software enables you to sample sounds, modify them if you choose, and then store them in disk files for later replay. Both Sound Blaster and Sound Blaster Pro include a software product called Voice Editor II (the program's file name is VEDIT2). Sound Blaster 16 and 16 ASP do not include Voice Editor II but do have the Windows WAV file editor, Creative WaveStudio, which performs the same tasks. Creative WaveStudio is described in Chapter 9.

Using Voice Editor II to Record Sounds

To start recording sounds, you may want to use Voice Editor II (VEDIT2), the DOS-based sound editor that is installed with Sound Blaster and Sound Blaster Pro. Make sure that your microphone is connected to the appropriate jack in the Sound Blaster card, and then switch to the directory containing VEDIT2. (The default installation places VEDIT2 in this path: C:\SBPRO\VOCUTIL\VEDIT2.EXE.)

When you start VEDIT2, you first see the program load two drivers, as shown in figure 4.1.

The CT-VOICE.DRV driver resides in memory and controls Sound Blaster's voice input and sampling capabilities. The other driver, CTVDSK.DRV, loads and stores voice files in memory. Voice files have the VOC extension.

After VEDIT2 is running, the initial menu screen appears and offers the menu items shown in figure 4.2.

```
Creative Voice Editor    Ver 2.15
Copyright (c) Creative Technology Pte Ltd, 1991. All rights reserved.

CT-VOICE.DRV version : 2.12
CTVDSK.DRV version : 2.12
```

Fig. 4.1

The Voice Editor
startup screen,
showing two
drivers being
loaded.

```
 File   Record   Play   Pack   Edit   CDisc   Volume
```

Fig. 4.2

The VEDIT2 menu
bar.

You can select the menu items by using the mouse or by holding down the Alt
key while pressing the underlined letter of the menu item. There are seven
main menu items:

- **F**ile. Load existing voice files and save new voice files or portions
  (blocks) of voice files.

- **R**ecord. Set sound source, sampling rates, and filtering, and whether
  voice data is to be saved to memory or disk.

- **P**lay. Play back voice data from memory or disk, or play back selected
  blocks of voice data from a voice data file containing multiple blocks.
  (Blocks are described later in this chapter.)

- **Pa**ck. Compress voice data in memory or in disk files.

- **E**dit. Modify voice data.

- **C**Disc. Control a CD player connected to your computer.

- **V**olume. Set the volume levels for sound sources as well as the master
  volume.

The following discussion does not cover each menu item in detail. Instead, you
should use this discussion as an introduction to Voice Editor—and as a
launching-off point for your own experimentation with VEDIT2.

Begin by choosing the **R**ecord menu item. As shown in figure 4.3, you have several options. Choose the first option: **S**etting.

Fig. 4.3

The Voice Editor
Record menu.

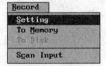

You use the **S**etting dialog box (shown in Fig. 4.4) to select the sound source, the filtering, the sample rate, and where the sound is to be stored.

Fig. 4.4

The **S**etting dialog
box.

For this session, you want to record using the microphone, so choose **Micro**-phone if it isn't already chosen.

The sampling rate you select determines the quality of the recording, as well as how much memory and/or disk space the recording will consume. The higher the sample rate, the higher the quality and the more memory used. A sampling rate of 8 kHz is just adequate for sampling voice, while a sampling rate of 44.1 kHz is about as good as it gets—CD quality. If you choose **U**ser Defined, you can set your own sampling rate.

Notice that the bottom of the dialog box displays the maximum recording time. When you change the sampling rate, the maximum recording time changes. At lower sampling rates, recording time is high. At higher sampling rates, recording time is reduced. The reason for this difference is that much more data is being saved at higher sample rates. In this example, you're recording to memory; consequently, the recording time is based on the amount of conventional memory available in your computer. At a sampling rate of 11,000 samples per second, with each sample consuming 1 byte in mono or 2 bytes in stereo (SB Pro only), a recording chews up 11,000 bytes of memory every second. If you change the sample rate to 44,100 samples/second, then memory is consumed at 44,100 bytes per second in mono and at 88,200 bytes per second in stereo. The rate of consumption is even higher when you are using Sound Blaster 16 or 16 ASP because each sample uses 2 bytes of space instead of the 1 byte used for each sample by Sound Blaster and Sound Blaster Pro.

The To **D**isk option lets you record to your disk drive instead of to conventional memory, thereby increasing the amount of time you can record to the amount of free disk space you have in bytes.

The filtering setting depends on the rate at which you want Sound Blaster to sample your voice. Choose Lo **F**ilter if you sample at the 8 kHz or 11 kHz rate, **H**i Filter for rates from 12 kHz through 35 kHz, and **N**o Filter for rates greater than 36 kHz. The reason for these filter settings will be obvious when you record at the lower sample rates and play back the results. At the lower sample rates, quality of recording is poor, suitable for speech only. The Lo **F**ilter setting filters out a lot of spurious electronic noise.

Choose **8** kHz for the sampling rate and choose **N**o Filter. If you have Sound Blaster Pro, you have the option of recording in stereo by clicking the **S**tereo button. However, the microphone input to Sound Blaster and Sound Blaster Pro is monaural, so you needn't waste memory or disk space recording in stereo. If you were sampling from the line-in plug, or from a Creative Labs CD player, you might want to record in stereo.

After you have selected the appropriate options, click **O**K at the bottom of the dialog box.

Next, start recording. Choose the **R**ecord menu and then choose To **M**emory. The Voice dialog box appears, and you're recording (see fig. 4.5). Clearly and distinctly speak into the microphone. When you're finished, click the **S**top button. (By the way, if your microphone has an On/Off switch, make sure that it's in the On position before recording.)

Fig. 4.5

The Voice dialog box, which tells you that Voice Editor is sampling sound and storing it in memory.

When you stop recording, an information box appears, like the one shown in figure 4.6.

Voice file block
information.

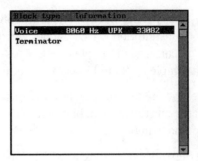

The information box describes the recording in terms of the following block
types:

Header	A block that defines the voice file type.
Voice	Voice data, in either mono or stereo.
Silence	A block of silence within a voice file. Silence can be added or removed.
ASCII Text	A block of ASCII text. ASCII text can be included in a voice file, providing comments on the voice block to follow, for example.
Marker	A block used by other software applications to trigger an action. For example, a computerized slide show could use a marker block inside a voice file to trigger the next slide.
Repeat	A block that tells the software playing the sound file to repeat the next voice block a selected number of times.
End Repeat	A block that tells the playing software to stop repeating a block.
Terminator	A block that marks the end of a sound file. All sound files end in a terminator block.

The voice file you just recorded contains only two blocks: Voice and Terminator. If you load a voice file created by someone else, you may see several blocks
of the types just listed, but in this instance, a simple voice recording will use
only two block types.

The box also indicates the sampling rate (8060 Hz in figure 4.6; your display
may be different if you used a different sampling rate), whether the sample is

packed (UPK means unpacked), and the number of bytes of memory used during the sampling. Suppose that you sample "This is a test. One, two, three, four, five, six, seven, eight, nine, ten" at a sample rate of 8 kHz. This recording would consume 33,082 bytes of memory.

Why all this stuff? Because the editor lets you modify a sound file by adding repeats, silences, and markers, and by deleting voice blocks. Suppose that you build a sound file containing several bird sounds and your voice announcing each bird. You might want to add one or two seconds of silence before each voice block containing bird sounds. You can use VEDIT2 to accomplish this effect by loading several different block types in sequence. In other words, the editor performs as a *sequencer*, letting you play sounds and silences in order.

One other thing that you need to know a little about is data compression. As discussed earlier in this chapter, recording voice data at high sample rates uses a lot of memory and disk space. Voice Editor lets you compress voice data so that it takes up less space. The UPK indicator in the block description box indicates that the voice sample you just recorded is not compressed. To compress the voice data in memory or to compress a voice file, choose **P**ack from the menu bar and then choose either **M**emory to compress the voice data currently in memory, or **D**isk to compress a voice file. You get the option of compressing the data up to a maximum of 4 to 1 (a 1,000-byte sample is compressed into 250 bytes). The 4-to-1 compression ratio will result in some degradation of playback, whereas the 2-to-1 compression ratio will result in very little degradation.

Should you want to add a text string to your voice file identifying it as yours, or add a marker block, select **I**nsert from the **E**dit menu. From that submenu, you can insert or append any of the following four block types: Silence, Marker, ASCII, and Repeat.

Using Voice Editor (VEDIT2) to Edit Sounds

You can modify the sound you just recorded by choosing **E**dit from the main menu and then choosing **M**odify. You then see a graphical representation of the sound you recorded—as if you had attached the microphone to the input of an oscilloscope—an electronic instrument that displays changes in voltage over time. As figure 4.7 will show, the jagged lines indicate the recorded volume and frequency of a voice. Your screen will look different, depending on what you said, the natural frequency range of your voice, how loudly you spoke, and where you held the microphone. (Because Sound Blaster's microphone input is mono, you made a single-channel recording. Had you been editing a stereo recording, you would see two lines instead of one.)

When you select **Mo**dify, a new menu bar is displayed, along with the waveform. The **O**ption menu item has the following functions:

- **S**plit block. This option splits a voice recording into two different sound blocks. Each block is listed in the voice block box. To split a recording, move the cursor to the point at which you want to insert the split, and then chose this menu item. The recording will be split at the point at which you place the cursor, and the block on the right will no longer be displayed.

- **E**dit Sampling Rate. This option enables you to change the playback sample rate of the recording.

- **Ex**it. This option lets you exit the Modify screen and get back to the main screen.

The **E**dit menu enables you to cut and paste parts of the waveform data. You can edit out any click sounds, for example, or you can reorganize the order in which words are spoken. You take action on a part of the waveform by highlighting the sounds you want to change, either with the mouse or the keyboard. When using the mouse, position the pointer at the beginning of the sound you want to select, and then hold down the left mouse button and drag the highlight to the right. To do the same thing without a mouse, use the Tab, Shift-Tab, comma, and period keys to move the waveform cursor (a vertical bar in the waveform display) left and right. When you have the waveform cursor at the beginning position, press Ctrl-B. Now use the Tab or period key to move the highlight to the right. When you have the sound highlighted, press Ctrl-E.

Here are the options on the **E**dit menu:

- **S**ave. This option saves to a file the highlighted portion of the voice data.

- **C**ut. Use this option to delete the highlighted portion of voice data. You can paste the deleted data into another location by using the Paste option.

- **P**aste. Use this option to paste voice date that has been previously cut.

- **F**ill. This option overwrites the selected data with silence. When you select this option, you are asked to enter a Fill value. The default is 128, which you probably will want to use.

- **I**nsert. This option enables you to insert a block of silence, pushing the selected voice data to the right on the display and outward in time. As with **F**ill, you are given the option of entering a silence value, but you may as well use the default value of 128.

The **Eff**ect menu provides options that let you modify the voice data by adding certain sound effects:

- **A**mplify. This option enables you to increase the volume of the highlighted voice data by a percentage. To change the default percentage, move the cursor to the value box and enter a new value. After you enter the new value, press Enter and either click OK or press the O key.

- **E**cho. You can add an echo effect to the highlighted sound data by choosing this option. You are prompted for two values. The percentage of echo effect is actually the magnitude of the echo (how loud you want the echo to be). The other value is the delay in milliseconds. To create a moderately loud echo at a reasonable time, try the values of 50 percent and 10, respectively.

- Fade **O**ut. This option fades the highlighted sound data down to silence.

- Fade **I**n. This option causes a fade-in effect by reducing the beginning of the sound data to silence, and then bringing it up to its original volume.

- Pan **L**eft-Right. If you have Sound Blaster Pro, you can shift the sound playback from the left speaker to the right speaker by using this option.

- Pan **R**ight-Left. This option shifts the sound from the right speaker to the left speaker.

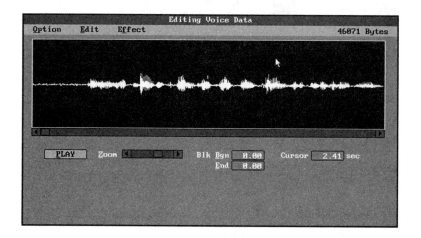

Fig. 4.7

The editing screen within Voice Editor II.

Using figure 4.7 as a reference point, take a look at your voice data. The leftmost part of the display indicates when recording started. You see a slight hesitation before speaking begins, and then you see the first word—*this*.

Because the recording is longer than can be shown on the screen at once, a horizontal scroll bar beneath the display lets you scroll back and forth from the beginning to the end of the recording. If you want to squeeze the display into a single dialog box—or stretch it out to see all the detail—use the **Z**oom control located to the left of center, below the display.

Notice the mouse arrow within the display. Just below the display is a box labeled Cursor, followed by a number given in seconds. In this instance, the arrow is pointing to a spot 2.41 seconds into the recording. If you move your mouse back and forth within the display, the time changes.

To play the recording, simply click the **PLAY** button.

Next, you can edit the sound in several interesting ways. Figure 4.8 shows the front of the waveform expanded a little with the use of **Z**oom control. You start by removing that blank space at the beginning of the recording. To do this, move the arrow to near the beginning of the recording. Then, holding down the left mouse button, drag the arrow to the right, until it's positioned as shown in figure 4.8. Release the mouse button.

Fig. 4.8

Using the mouse to highlight a block of sound.

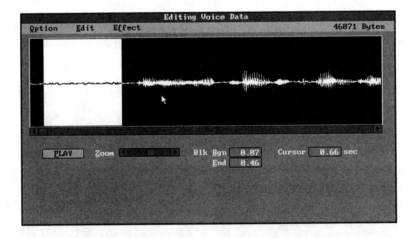

You've now highlighted a block of sound for Voice Editor to cut, copy, or otherwise modify. Now that the block is highlighted, you can play that block by clicking the **PLAY** button. Or you can choose **E**dit from the menu bar and then choose **C**ut to remove the unwanted silence.

To cut out the silence, choose **E**dit and then **C**ut. After you've cut the silence out of the recording, position the arrow anywhere on the display and click once. The highlight lines disappear.

Next, you can modify all or part of the recording, as shown in figure 4.9. Choose **Effect** from the menu bar, and the special effects options appear. As described earlier, these options let you amplify the recording, add an echo, fade in or out, and pan left or right.

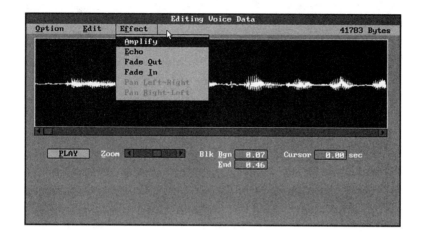

Fig. 4.9

The Effect menu.

To modify a single portion of the recording, choose the sound by holding down the left mouse button and dragging the pointer in the direction you want to move. Choose **Effect** from the menu bar and then choose the special effect you want. To modify the entire recording, move the cursor arrow to the far-left side of the display and click once; any changes you make will then be made to the entire recording.

The Fade **O**ut and Fade **I**n options bring the sound within a highlighted area up and down gradually. The Pan options work only with stereo recordings; these options modify the sound file so that the recording seems to shift from the left speaker to the right speaker while being played back.

Another way to modify sound files is to cut and paste. Figure 4.10 shows a word (*test*) highlighted in the recording. See if you can isolate a single word in your recording by highlighting a section of the display; then click **P**LAY to play this section.

After you select a block, choose **E**dit from the menu bar. From here, you can cut or move the block. You can also insert silence or replace a selected chunk of sound with nothing.

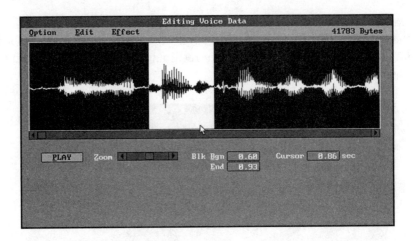

Fig. 4.10

The waveform representing the word *test* is highlighted, and can now be cut out or otherwise modified.

Finally, choose **O**ption from the menu bar and then choose **E**dit Sampling Rate. The Edit Sampling Rate dialog box appears (see fig. 4.11). This option lets you modify the playback rate—from very slow to very fast. If you recorded the original sample at 8 kHz, you can slow the playback by moving the slider bar to the left, down toward 4 kHz. By moving the slider to the right, you can play back the recording so quickly that you'll have a hard time understanding the words. The playback rate is changed for the entire recording.

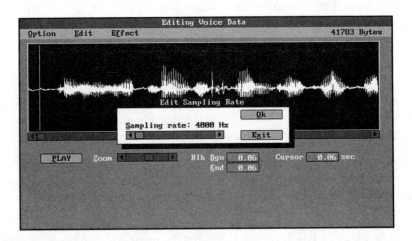

Fig. 4.11

The **E**dit Sampling Rate menu item lets you change the playback rate of the recording.

When you have a recording that satisfies you, you will need to exit the Modify screen and return to the main screen. From the **O**ption menu, choose E**x**it. Now choose **F**ile and then **S**ave. The editor prompts you for a file name and path in which to store the file, which has a VOC extension. To load another file into the editor, select **F**ile and then **L**oad. You are then prompted to select a file name to be loaded.

Experiment with all these options. You'll be delighted at how you can change a simple recording into something new and interesting. Try to sample as many different sounds as you can, and then modify them by stretching or compressing the time, adding an echo, cutting and pasting blocks, or even playing sounds backwards. The sky is the limit!

Sound Blaster Record and Play Utilities

Sound Blaster is provided with a set of utilities to record and play voice data files. Sound Blaster and Sound Blaster Pro have two utilities named VREC and VPLAY, used to record and play VOC files, respectively. Sound Blaster 16/16 ASP, in addition to providing VREC and VPLAY, offers two similar utilities, WREC and WPLAY, that record and play Windows WAV files. To use any of the record utilities, you must have a monaural microphone connected to the Sound Blaster MIC input.

These utilities are DOS command-line utilities. You enter the command, followed by the file names and parameters necessary to complete the task. Because Microsoft Windows uses Sound Blaster, you cannot run these utilities from Windows.

VREC

The sound-recording utility is VREC.EXE. If you own Sound Blaster V2.0, you will find VREC in the VOXKIT subdirectory. The Pro and 16/16 ASP versions have VREC in the VOCUTIL subdirectory.

The VREC command is substantially the same with all three versions of Sound Blaster. However, differences do exist, having to do with increased capabilities of one version over another.

Sound Blaster V2.0

The Sound Blaster version of VREC is a rather straightforward recording utility. You can record without using any of the options, or you can set recording parameters and limits. When you enter VREC without any options or parameters, the following help screen appears:

```
Creative Disk Voice Record   Version 2.21
Copyright (c) Creative Labs, Inc., 1991. All rights reserved.
Copyright (c) Creative Technology Pte Ltd, 1991. All rights reserved.

Usage: VREC filename [/B:kk] [/S:hh] [/T:ss] [/Q] [/X="command line"]

        /B:kk   set buffer size. Range of kk = 1 - 32
        /S:hh   set sampling rate. Range of hh = 4000 - 15000
        /T:ss   set time limit for recording. Range of ss = 1 - 65535
        /Q      set to quiet mode
        /X="command line"   execute the command line directly where command
        line is a set of executable statement.
```

At a minimum, you must provide VREC with a file name in which to store the voice data. You do not need to add the file name extension (VREC does it for you), but if you choose to add an extension, it should be VOC.

The following parameters are used with VREC:

filename	This is the name of the file in which you want data stored.
/B:*kk*	This option is the recording buffer size. VREC uses a memory buffer in which to store voice data while recording. By default, VREC uses 16K of memory as a buffer. You can change the buffer size in 1K increments. The buffer can be set to a minimum of 1K or a maximum of 32K by replacing *kk* with a value of 1 to 32.
/S:*hh*	You set the recording sampling rate with this option. Sound Blaster V2.0 can record at sampling rates ranging from 4,000 to 15,000 samples per second. The default value is 8,000. When entering the sample rate, leave out any commas. For example, replace *hh* with 15000.
/T:*ss*	This option sets a recording time limit in 1-second increments. You can limit recording time to as little as 1 second or as high as 65,535 seconds, depending on available disk space. Remember that at a sample rate of 8,000 samples per second, you are storing slightly more than 8,000 bytes of information every second of recording. If you want to record for the maximum of 65,535 seconds, you will need

524,280,000 bytes of disk space at a sample rate of 8,000 (65,535 x 8,000 = 524,280,000). This option does not work when you are using the /X option (see the last entry in this list). For example, you can replace *ss* with 30 to limit recording time to 30 seconds.

/Q   This option turns off all messages during recording except error messages. While recording, VREC usually displays your command options. Use /Q to suppress the display of these messages.

/X="*command line*"   You can insert a DOS command on the same line with VREC, and when recording is completed, that DOS command will be executed. The command must be in quotation marks.

Suppose that you want to record a sample of background conversation at a party and store it in a file named PARTY.VOC. You can use the default sample rate of 8,000 samples per second, which is suitable for most conversation, and the default buffer size will probably be sufficient. However, you want to limit the recording time to 10 seconds, and at the end of the recording session, play back the sounds you recorded. Here is the command you use:

VREC PARTY /T:10 /X="VPLAY.EXE PARTY.VOC"

As soon as you press Enter, recording begins. At the end of 10 seconds, recording stops, and the recorded sounds are played back. You can use any legitimate DOS command. For example, if you want to display the current directory after recording, you enter this command:

VREC PARTY /T:10 /X="DIR"

While recording, VREC displays the following message:

```
During the recording, you can use
        [Esc]           key, to stop the voice immediately
        [S]             key, to go to DOS
```

This message means that you can stop recording at any time by pressing the Esc key. If you're making a long recording and want to use the computer for other things while recording, you can press the S key, which returns you to DOS. Recording continues in the background, and you can return to VREC by typing **EXIT** at the DOS prompt.

Sound Blaster Pro

VREC for Sound Blaster Pro has all the features of VREC for Sound Blaster V2.0. New options are available with the Pro, however, and some existing options have changed. VREC has the following format:

VREC *filename* [/B:*kk*] [/A:*ii*] [/F:*hh*] [/S:*hh*] [/M:*mm*] [/L:*nn*] [/T:*ss*] [/Q] [/X="*command line*"]

Here are both the new and the changed options available with Sound Blaster Pro:

/B:*kk*	Sound Blaster Pro uses a double-buffering technique that consumes twice as much memory space for data buffering. When you set the buffer size to 32, the program uses 64K of memory for buffering. The range for *kk* is from 2 to 32.
/A:*ii*	You can record from one of three sources: the microphone input, the internal CD input, or the Line-In. Replace *ii* with MIC, CD, or LINE.
/F:*hh*	This option turns on the filtering capabilities of Sound Blaster Pro. Replace *hh* with LOW to perform low-pass filtering or with HIGH to perform high-pass filtering.
/S:*hh*	The sampling rate range is higher with the Pro, and you can record in stereo from the CD or Line-In inputs. If you are recording in mono, *hh* can range from 4,000 to 44,100. If you are recording in stereo, the range can be from 4,000 to 22,050. When entering the sample rate, leave out any commas.
/M:*mm*	This option sets the recording mode to either monaural or stereo. Replace *mm* with MONO or STEREO.
/L:*nn*	You can adjust the volume of the Line-In from 0 (volume all the way down) to 15 (all the way up).

The /T, /Q, and /X options work exactly as they do with Sound Blaster V2.0.

Suppose that you want to record a 15-second stereo sound bite from an external CD player connected to the Sound Blaster's Line-In connector. You want to use the maximum sampling rate to achieve the highest quality, and you want to use high-pass filtering to keep those sharp edges on the higher frequencies. Here is the command you use:

VREC SNDBITE.VOC /A:LINE /F:HIGH /S:22050 /M:STEREO /T:15

Note again that whenever numbers are entered, you must not include the comma you might ordinarily use to separate the numbers into thousands.

Sound Blaster 16/16 ASP

The newest Sound Blasters have expanded stereo sampling rates and can sample in either 8- or 16-bit mode. The new mixer chip adds significant functionality to VREC as well. VREC has the following format:

VREC *filename* [/B:*kk*] [/A:*ii*] [F:*hh*] [/C:/*xx*] [/R:*xx*] [/S:*hh*] [/M:*mm*] [L:*nn*] [/T:*ss*] [/Q] [/X="*command line*"]

Here are the options that differ from those used with Sound Blaster Pro or are new to VREC:

/A:*xx* [+*xx*]	This option selects the recording source, which can be the microphone (MIC), internal CD (CD), Line-In (LINE), or Sound Blaster's FM synthesizer (FM). You can add sources together to record input from more than one source at a time. Simply place a plus sign (+) between each source name, as in MIC+LINE+FM.
/R:*xx*	This option sets the sample size in bits. For 8-bit sampling, replace *xx* with 8. For 16-bit sampling, use 16.
/C:*xx*	Used for Sound Blaster 16 ASP only, this sets the data compression type. *xx* can be CTADPCM, ALAW, or MULAW. If this option is not used, no compression is applied to the file.
/S:*xx*	You set the sample rate with this option. The rate can range from 5,000 to 44,100 in either stereo or mono.

All other options are identical in function to those used with Sound Blaster and Sound Blaster Pro. For examples of how to use VREC on Sound Blaster 16/16 ASP, refer to the earlier descriptions of Sound Blaster and Sound Blaster Pro.

WREC

The WREC utility, available with Sound Blaster 16/16 ASP, is a variant of the VREC utility. WREC records sounds in Windows WAVE format and assigns the file names the WAV extension. Here is the format for WREC:

WREC *filename* [/B:*kk*] [/A:*ii*] [F:*hh*] [/R:*xx*] [/S:*hh*] [C:/*xx*] [/M:*mm*]
[L:*nn*] [/T:*ss*] [/Q] [/X=*"command line"*]

The WREC command works the same way as VREC for the 16/16 ASP, with the following exception:

/S:*xx*   Windows WAV files can be recorded with only one of these sampling rates: 11,000, 22,050, or 44,100.

In all other ways, WREC is identical to the Sound Blaster 16/16 ASP VREC utility.

VPLAY

The playback utility is VPLAY, or WPLAY when playing back WAV files. This command works exactly the same as with Sound Blaster V2.0, Pro, and 16/16 ASP. You use one of the following formats:

VPLAY *filename* [/B:*kk*] [/T:*ss*] [/Q] [/X=*"command line"*]

WPLAY *filename* [/B:*kk*] [/T:*ss*] [/Q] [/X=*"command line"*]

At a minimum, you can enter VPLAY followed by the name of the file you want to hear. Or you can use the following options:

/B:*kk*   This is the playback buffer size. VPLAY uses a memory buffer to store voice data from the disk while playing back. You can change the buffer size in 1K increments. The buffer can be set to a minimum of 1K or a maximum of 32K for Sound Blaster V2.0, or a range of 2 to 32 for the Pro and 16/16 ASP.

/T:*ss*   This option sets the playback time. You can limit the playback time by replacing *ss* with a number equal to the number of seconds you want to hear sound.

/Q   This option turns off all messages during playback except error messages. While playing a file, VPLAY usually displays what your command options are. Use /Q to suppress the display of these messages.

/X=*"command line"*   You can insert a DOS command on the same line as VPLAY, and when playback is completed, the DOS command will be executed. The command must be in quotation marks.

Suppose that you want to play back the first five seconds of a file named NOISE.VOC and then execute the DOS command CLS to clear the screen. The complete command looks like this:

VPLAY NOISE.VOC /T:5 /X="CLS"

During playback, a message screen appears, allowing you to control playback as it happens. The following commands can be used during playback:

Esc   Pressing the Esc key stops playback immediately and returns you to DOS.

Space   Pressing the space bar pauses playback. You resume playback by pressing the space key again.

Enter   VOC files can contain elements that repeat a number of times in what is called a loop. To force VPLAY to immediately break out of the currently playing loop and stop playing, you press the Enter key. When you press Enter, VPLAY exits to DOS.

Tab   The Tab key forces VPLAY to break out of the currently playing loop and move on to the next part of the file, if there is a next part. If the loop is the last thing in a file, pressing the Tab key causes VPLAY to exit to DOS.

S   Pressing the S key during playback causes VPLAY to continue playing the voice file, but shifts you to the DOS prompt during playback so that you can perform other tasks. In other words, pressing S causes the voice file to be played in the background.

As a reminder, WPLAY works in exactly the same way as VPLAY, except that you must give the name of a file with the WAV extension. Otherwise, playing a voice file is as simple as can be. If you forget what the options are, you can enter **VPLAY** or **WPLAY** with no file name or other parameters, and a help list is displayed.

Sound Blaster Mixers

Sound Blaster Pro and 16/16 ASP have mixer chips that allow recording and playback sources to be mixed together. Both DOS and Windows versions of the mixer utility software are available, allowing you control over the mixer chip. The following discussion covers both varieties of mixer software.

Sound Blaster Pro Mixer for DOS

There are two Sound Blaster Pro mixer utilities. SBP-SET is a standard DOS command-line application that can accept parameters and options. The other is a terminate-and-stay-resident (TSR) program called SBP-MIX.EXE. Both are located in the SBPRO directory.

The TSR version, SBP-MIX, is a graphical program; when you press the Alt-1 hot key combination, a window is displayed on-screen, and you can control the various sound sources with slider bars. SBP-SET, however, must be used with command-line parameters. In either case, control of the mixer chip is very similar.

SBP-SET

With the SBP-SET command, you use the following syntax:

SBP-SET [/Q] [/R] [/M:*l,r*] [/VOC:*l,r*] [/FM:*l,r*] [CD:*nn*] [/X:*nn*] [/ADCF:*xx*] [/ADCS:*xx*] [/LINE:*l,r*] [ANFI:ON,OFF] [DNFI:ON,OFF]

The volume settings for each source are whole numbers ranging from 0 to 15. In most cases, you must enter a value for both the left and right channels, separated by a comma.

Here are the available parameters:

/Q	Activate Quiet mode. Usually, when you enter an SBP-SET command, the program responds by telling you what is being changed. This parameter forces SBP-SET to perform the command without printing any response on-screen. When the command is completed, the DOS prompt is displayed.
/R	Reset the mixer chip.
/M:*l,r*	Set the master volume.

/VOC:*l,r*	Set the volume for sampled voice data playback.
/FM:*l,r*	Set the volume for the FM synthesizer.
/CD:*nn*	Set CD volume. CD input is monaural, and only one value is required.
/X:*nn*	Set microphone volume. Microphone input is monaural, and only one value is required.
/ADCF:*xx*	Set input filter to low pass (LOW) or high pass (HIGH).
/ADCS:*xx*	Select the recording source. Possible sources are the microphone (MIC), internal CD connector (CD), and Line-In connector (LINE).
/LINE:*l,r*	Set Line-In volume.
/ANFI:ON,OFF	Turn input filter ON or OFF.
/DNFI:ON,OFF	Turn output filter ON or OFF.

Suppose that you want to set master volume to the middle of its range, set microphone volume near the highest level, record from the microphone, and apply a low-pass filter to the input. Here is the command you use:

    SBP-SET /M:8,8 /X:6 /ADCS:MIC /ADCF:LOW /ANFI:ON

SBP-MIX

When you enter the SBP-MIX program, it is loaded into memory and stays there as a TSR program until you remove it. You access SBP-MIX by holding down the Alt key and pressing 1. To change the hot key, type

    SBP-MIX /k*key*

at the DOS prompt, where *key* is the new key combination you want to use. For example, to set the hot key combination as Alt-7, enter

    SBP-MIX /k<Alt-7>

Then you can activate SBP-MIX by pressing Alt-7.

To remove SBP-MIX from memory, enter

    SBP-MIX /u

As noted, SBP-MIX is a graphical program that allows you to adjust volumes with slider-bar images on-screen. When first activated, SBP-MIX opens a full-screen window containing a dialog box. Using the arrow keys, you can choose from the dialog box the item you want to change. After you have made your selection, press Enter. A new box appears with the appropriate number of sliders. You select the slider you want to move by pointing to it with the mouse; or by pressing the left- or right-arrow key, which moves a selection box. When you have the appropriate slider selected, move it up or down with the up- or down-arrow key, or hold down the left mouse button and slide the mouse up and down. You can adjust the following controls:

Card reset	This control resets the mixer chip on the Sound Blaster card.
MASTER volume	This control sets the master volume and is divided into three sliders: left, right, and both.
VOC volume	This is the volume setting for VOC data files. You control the channel volume for left, right, and both.
LINE volume	This controls the input volume from the Line-In connector. This, too, is a stereo control.
CD volume	CD volume is in mono and has a single slider to control volume.
MIC volume	This is a mono control with a single slider to set the input volume level from the microphone.
FM volume	This is a stereo control that selects the input volume from the Sound Blaster FM synthesizer chips.
FM channel	This control is used to steer output from the FM synthesizer to both speakers, just the left speaker, or just the right speaker. Or you can mute the output entirely.
ADC channel	Sound Blaster Pro contains an analog-to-digital converter (ADC) that performs digital sampling, which is the act of converting sound into numbers stored in a disk file. This control lets you select the sound source to be sampled. You choose the microphone, CD, or Line-In as your source. You can also set low-pass or high-pass filtering.

ADC test on/off	You can test whether the ADC is working by turning on the test feature. As the source sends sound to the ADC, notes are graphically shown in a line across the bottom of the screen while sound is being sampled.
Hidden mode	Hidden mode is particularly useful during multi-media presentations if you want to make a mixer change without bringing up the mixer control screen. By turning on Hidden mode, you control the mixer during the presentation by using key-board commands. These commands are described next.
Exit	This option leaves SBP-MIX.

SBP-MIX Hidden mode allows you to change mixer controls from the key-board, without bringing up the SBP-MIX screen. The following commands are available only when Hidden mode is ON:

Master Volume	Ctrl-Alt-M
Voice	Ctrl-Alt-V
Line-In	Ctrl-Alt-L
CD	Ctrl-Alt-C
FM Output	Ctrl-Alt-F
Microphone	Ctrl-Alt-I
Increase Volume	Ctrl-Alt-U
Decrease Volume	Ctrl-Alt-D
Quiet Mode (Mute)	Ctrl-Alt-Q

To illustrate how Hidden mode works, run through the following exercise:

1. Start SBP-MIX by changing to the SBPRO directory, typing **SBP-MIX**, and pressing Enter.

2. When the SBP-MIX screen appears, choose Hidden mode with either the arrow keys or the mouse. Then press Enter.

3. Highlight ON and press Enter. Now click OK (if you're using a mouse) or press the Esc key to go back to the main menu.

4. Choose Exit to return to DOS.

At this point, SBP-MIX is resident in memory, and you can call up the program by pressing Alt-1. Hidden mode is now enabled, giving you keyboard control over mixer settings. Next, you can play a little MIDI music:

1. Type **SBMIDI** and press Enter. This loads the Sound Blaster Pro MIDI player into memory.

2. Change to the subdirectory PLAYMIDI.

3. Type **PLAYMIDI JAZZ.MID** and press Enter. You should start to hear music coming from your speakers or headphones.

4. Select the mixer master volume by entering Ctrl-Alt-M.

5. Decrease the playback volume by entering Ctrl-Alt-D. Hold down the keys until the volume decreases to silence.

6. Now increase playback volume by entering Ctrl-Alt-U. As you hold down the keys, you will hear the volume steadily rising.

7. To mute playback, momentarily hold down Ctrl-Alt-Q. The sound will stop. Hold down Ctrl-Alt-Q again to resume sound output.

To change the volume of any source, you must select the source first; you can then use Ctrl-Alt-U or Ctrl-Alt-D to control volume. Once a source is selected, it stays selected until you change the source or exit the program.

Sound Blaster Pro Mixer for Windows

Control of the Sound Blaster Pro mixer while in Windows is rather easy, because Sound Blaster provides a very graphical and easy-to-understand mixer control panel, shown in figure 4.12. The Windows mixer control panel gives you complete control over most mixer functions.

Fig. 4.12

The Sound Blaster Pro mixer control panel.

As you can see in the figure, the control panel is laid out much like a physical mixer control panel. Each volume control has two sliders (except the microphone) that you can either move independently or lock together by checking the Lock L/R Vol box.

Here are the mixer controls (from left to right):

Mas	Master output volume
MIDI	MIDI music playback volume
CD	CD input volume
Mic	Microphone input volume
Lin	Line-In input volume
Voc	Playback volume for VOC file

In the upper-right corner of the control panel, you can set the input source for the Sound Blaster Pro's analog-to-digital converter (ADC), which is the device that samples sound and stores it in memory or on disk. You can also select a filter to filter incoming sound that is being sampled. And at the lower-right corner of the panel, you can test any of the inputs to make sure that everything is working correctly. If, for example, you had selected the microphone as the ADC source and clicked **S**tart Test, any sounds that the microphone picked up would be displayed in the little vertical window next to the source buttons. To save your mixer settings, click **S**ave and then exit the mixer.

Sound Blaster 16/16 ASP Mixer for DOS

Two Sound Blaster 16/16 ASP mixer utilities are available. SB16SET is a standard DOS command-line application that can accept parameters and options. The other is a TSR program called SBP16MIX.EXE. Both are located in the SB16 directory.

The TSR version is a graphical program. When you press the Alt-1 hot key combination, a window is displayed on-screen, and you can control the various sound sources with slider bars. You can enter the SB16SET program with or without command-line parameters; when you enter SB16SET without parameters, it becomes a graphical interface program. In any case, control of the mixer chip is very similar.

SB16SET

When you type **SB16SET** and press Enter, the mixer control panel shown in figure 4.13 is displayed.

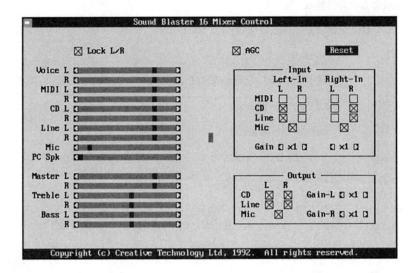

You can use SB16SET with the mouse or with the arrow keys, Tab key, and Enter key. When using a mouse, point to a slider and, while holding down the left button, move the mouse back and forth. To change the setting of a check box, point to the check box and click the left mouse button. If you do not use a mouse, you can position the highlight with the up- and down-arrow keys and the Tab key. To change the state of a check box, press the space bar. Use the left- and right-arrow keys to move a selected slider back and forth.

Down the left side of the screen are the slider controls to set various source and output volume levels, as well as bass and treble levels. At the right, check boxes enable you to select left- and right-channel input sources, set the gain, and select which input source is sent to the output.

At the top of the screen, the Lock L/R check box is used to lock both left and right mixer knobs together, keeping volume settings the same in both channels. You use the AGC check box to select Automatic Gain Control for microphone input. The AGC feature allows the mixer to automatically adjust microphone amplification for various sound levels. In other words, quiet sounds will be amplified and very loud sounds will be reduced in volume.

The Reset button resets all mixer settings to their default values.

The Input box on the right side of the screen controls what signals are fed to the Sound Blaster output. Left-channel input (Left-In) can be the left channel, right channel, or both channels of a MIDI song, CD output, Line-In, or single microphone input. The same is true of the right-channel input (Right-In). The gain controls multiply the input volumes by 1, 2, 4, or 8 times the original setting.

The Output box works in exactly the same way as the Input box. You can select whether CD input is fed to the left or right output channels, for example. And the Gain buttons multiply output volumes by 1, 2, 4, or 8 times. When you finish setting the mixer controls, click the box in the upper-left corner of the screen or press the Esc key to exit SB16SET.

The other method of using SB16SET is to enter SB16SET as a DOS command, followed by one or more optional parameters. When you enter the SB16SET as a DOS command with parameters, the control screen just described is not displayed.

The SB16SET command uses the following syntax:

SB16SET [/H] [/Q] [/R] [/M:l,r] [/VOC:l,r] [/MIDI:l,r] [/FM:l,r] [/CD:l,r]
    [/LINE:l,r] [/TREBLE:l,r] [/BASS:l,r] [/SPK:nn] [/MIC:nn]
    [/AGC:ON|OFF] [/IPGAIN:l,r] [/OPGAIN:l,r] [/OPSW:] [/IPRSW:]
    [/IPLSW:]

The volume settings for each source are whole numbers ranging from 0 to 255. In most cases, you must enter a value for both the left and right channels, separated by a comma. Here are the available parameters:

/H	Display help.
/Q	Activate Quiet mode. Usually, when you enter an SB16SET command, the program responds by telling you what is being changed. This parameter forces SB16SET to perform the command without printing any response on-screen. When the command is completed, the DOS prompt is displayed.
/R	Reset all mixer settings to their default levels.
/M:l,r	Set master output volume to a value within the range of 0 (silence) to 255. You must provide a setting for both channels.

/VOC:*l,r*	Set voice (VOC or WAV file) output volume to a value within the range of 0 (silence) to 255. You must provide a setting for both channels.
/MIDI:*l,r*	Set MIDI song output volume to a value within the range of 0 (silence) to 255. You must provide a setting for both channels.
/FM:*l,r*	Set FM synthesizer input volume to a value within the range of 0 (silence) to 255. You must provide a setting for both channels.
/CD:*l,r*	Set CD input volume to a value within the range of 0 (silence) to 255. You must provide a setting for both channels.
/LINE:*l,r*	Set Line-In input volume to a value within the range of 0 (silence) to 255. You must provide a setting for both channels.
/TREBLE:*l,r*	Set treble control to a value within the range of 0 to 255. You must provide a setting for both channels.
/BASS:*l,r*	Set bass control to a value within the range of 0 to 255. You must provide a setting for both channels.
/SPK:*nn*	If you are using Sound Blaster as your PC speaker, set PC speaker output volume to a value within the range of 0 (silence) to 255.
/MIC:*nn*	Set microphone input volume to a value within the range of 0 (silence) to 255.
/AGC:ON|OFF	Turn Automatic Gain Control (AGC) ON or OFF.
/IPGAIN:*l,r*	Select an input mixer gain value of 1, 2, 4, or 8. You must provide a setting for both channels.
/OPGAIN:*l,r*	Select an output mixer gain value of 1, 2, 4, or 8. You must provide a setting for both channels.
/OPSW:	Select output sources. The following inputs can be fed to the output: MIC, CDL, CDR, LINEL, and LINER. To select a source, follow the source name with a plus (+) to include the source or a minus (–) not to include a source.

/IPRSW:	Select right-channel input sources. The following are valid mixer inputs: MIC, CDL, CDR, LINEL, LINER, MIDIL, and MIDIR. To select a source, follow the source name with a plus (+) to include the source or a minus (–) to not include a source.
/IPLSW:	Select left-channel input sources. The following are valid mixer inputs: MIC, CDL, CDR, LINEL, LINER, MIDIL, and MIDIR. To select a source, follow the source name with a plus (+) to include the source or a minus (–) not to include a source.

Suppose that you want to set master volume to the middle of the range, turn AGC off, feed microphone input to the output with a gain of 4, and select MIDI input as the left- and right-channel mixer input (turning off CD, Line, and Microphone left and right inputs). Here is the command you use:

```
SB16SET/M:130,130/AGC:OFF/OPSW:MIC+ CDL- CDR- LINEL- LINER-
    /OPGAIN:4,4 /IPLSW:MIDIL+ MIDIR- CDL- LINEL- MIC-
    /IPRSW:MIDIR+ MIDIL- CDR- LINER- MIC-
```

As you can see, setting the mixer by using a DOS command is seemingly more complex—but useful if you are controlling sound from a batch file, for example.

SB16MIX

When you first enter the SB16MIX program, it is loaded into memory and stays there as a TSR until you remove it. You access SB16MIX by holding down the Alt key and pressing 1. To change the hot key, type

```
SB16MIX /kkey
```

at the DOS prompt, where *key* is the new key combination you want to use. For example, to set the hot key combination as Alt-7, you enter

```
SB16MIX /kAlt-7
```

Then you can activate SB16MIX by pressing Alt-7.

To remove SB16MIX from memory, enter

```
SB16MIX /u
```

As stated previously, SB16MIX is a graphical program that allows you to adjust volumes with slider-bar images on-screen. When activated, SB16MIX displays three cascading (overlapping) windows. Use the Page Up and Page Down keys to move between the windows. Use the Tab key to move between selections within the window, or point to a selection by using the mouse. To move a selection, point to it and, while holding down the left mouse button, drag the selection to the new location. Or make your selection with the Tab key and then use the arrow keys to change values.

The top window is the Volume window, which allows you to select volume levels within a range of 0 (silence) to 31. Those sources with stereo capability have two sliders, one for each channel. To lock the slider bars together, select Lock ON at the bottom of the window. To mute playback, select Mute ON. Here are the controls you can adjust:

MASTER	Master volume
VOICE	Volume settings for VOC data files
LINE	Input volume from the Line-In connector
CD	CD volume control
FM	Stereo control that selects the input volume from the Sound Blaster FM synthesizer chips
MIC	Mono control with a single slider to set the input volume level from the microphone

If you are using Sound Blaster as your PC speaker, you can set the speaker volume to one of three levels in the lower-right corner of the window.

The second window controls tone and gain. You can set bass and treble tone control for each channel. The gain controls select record and output gain levels. If Lock is set to ON, gain changes affect both channels. If you set Lock to OFF, you can control individual channel gain.

The third window controls input and output sources. When you select a source, an icon in the shape of a pair of 1/32 notes appears next to the source name.

SB16MIX enables you to change mixer controls from the keyboard, without bringing up the SB16MIX screen. The following commands are available whenever SB16MIX is loaded into memory:

Master Volume	Ctrl-Alt-M
Voice	Ctrl-Alt-V
Line-In	Ctrl-Alt-L
CD	Ctrl-Alt-C
FM Output	Ctrl-Alt-F

Microphone	Ctrl-Alt-I
Increase Volume	Ctrl-Alt-U
Decrease Volume	Ctrl-Alt-D
Quiet Mode (Mute)	Ctrl-Alt-Q

To illustrate how these functions work, run through the following exercise. Start SB16MIX by changing to the SB16 directory and typing SB16MIX; then press by Enter.

At this point, SB16MIX is resident in memory, and you can can call it up by pressing Alt-1. Next, play a little MIDI music:

1. Type **SBMIDI** and press Enter. This loads the Sound Blaster 16/16 ASP MIDI player into memory.

2. Change to the subdirectory PLAYMIDI.

3. Type **PLAYMIDI JAZZ.MID** and press Enter. You should start to hear music coming from your speakers or headphones.

4. Select the mixer master volume by entering Ctrl-Alt-M.

5. Decrease the playback volume by entering Ctrl-Alt-D. Hold down the keys until volume decreases to silence.

6. Now increase playback volume by entering Ctrl-Alt-U. As you hold down the keys, you will hear the volume steadily rising.

7. To mute playback, momentarily hold down Ctrl-Alt-Q. The sound will stop. Hold down Ctrl-Alt-Q again to resume sound output.

To change the volume of any source, you must select the source first; then you can use Ctrl-Alt-U or Ctrl-Alt-D to control volume. After you select a source, it stays selected until you change the source or exit the program.

Sound Blaster 16/16 ASP Mixer for Windows

The Windows Mixer application provides access to all mixer controls. When you double-click the Mixer icon, the dialog box shown in figure 4.14 is displayed. All mixer functions are accessed from the mixer control panel.

The volume controls for the various sound sources are provided as sliders. You can point to a slider knob and, while holding down the left mouse button, drag the knob up and down the control panel. If you prefer, you can lock the left- and right-channel knobs together by selecting **O**ptions from the menu bar and

Fig. 4.14

The Sound Blaster 16/16 ASP mixer control panel.

clicking **L**ock L/R Vol. The left- and right-channel volume controls are locked when a check mark appears next to the menu item.

The master volume and tone settings are quickly available from this dialog box, as are the left and right gain selectors. You can set gain multiplication to be 1, 2, 4, or 8 times the volume settings. You can select input signals to be routed directly to the output by clicking the appropriate button in the lower-right corner of the window.

To set recording sources, choose **S**ettings from the menu bar and click **R**ecording. Figure 4.15 shows the recording control panel that appears.

Fig. 4.15

Recording mixer controls accessed with the **S**ettings menu item.

Within this box, you select what sources will be fed to the left- and right-channel inputs, as well as what kind of gain multiplication factor you want to apply. When the AGC (Automatic Gain Control) box is selected, the mixer automatically adjusts source volume levels.

Line-In Sources

Nearly every piece of moderately sophisticated entertainment electronics has a line-out jack somewhere. CD Players, televisions, VCRs—all have an audio output capability.

We're not talking about speaker outputs here. Most speaker outputs are connected to amplifier systems that generate enough power to fry the line-in circuitry on the Sound Blaster card.

Typically, low-power audio signals are transferred via one of two kinds of connectors: the ministereo headset jack like those used by the microphone and line-in jacks on the Sound Blaster card; and the tried-and-true RCA plug, usually coming in the dynamic colors of red and white. If you see a label marked *audio out*, *Line Out*, or something similar, you're probably safe in connecting that signal to Sound Blaster's line-in jack. Your Sound Blaster card undoubtedly came with one converter cable to convert RCA plugs to the ministereo plug. Extra cables are readily available at most audio equipment retailers.

When connecting audio sources to Sound Blaster's line-in connector, make sure that any volume controls which appear to control the output of the audio source are turned down initially. In other words, if you're going to pull sound samples from a videotape playing in your VCR, and your VCR has volume controls on the front panel, begin with these controls turned down. If you have connected a line-out plug to Sound Blaster's line-in jack, you needn't worry about volume levels. They are already set to appropriate levels.

You can use Voice Editor to check the volumes of incoming signals, as shown in figure 4.16. The editor's Scan Input function lets you look at the sound levels coming in through whatever source you've selected.

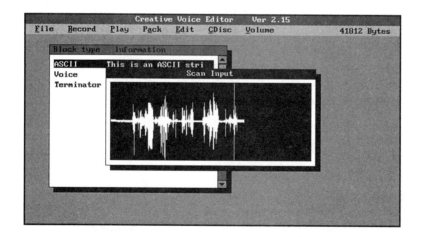

Fig. 4.16

Voice Editor's Scan Input function, used to make sure that appropriate sound levels are coming into Sound Blaster.

To use the Scan Input function, first start Voice Editor by changing to the appropriate directory and typing **VEDIT2** at the DOS command line. When the editor starts, choose the **R**ecord option, go to Setup, and choose the appropriate input, such as microphone or line-in. Then choose **Sc**an Input from the **R**ecord menu.

Scan Input turns your computer into an oscilloscope—it shows you the sound waveform as it is coming into Sound Blaster. At this point, you can adjust the output of the VCR or other audio source to correct audio levels. A correct audio level is not much different from that shown in figure 4.16. If you have connected to a line-out audio source, the sound levels are already at appropriate levels. If you have connected to a source that gives you control over the audio levels, adjust the loudness so that the loudest parts look nearly like those shown in the figure. Do not turn up the audio source to the point where the vertical lines are banging into the top and bottom of the display window. That kind of volume causes serious clipping and distortion. In addition, in music particularly, the quiet parts are supposed to be *quiet*. Don't adjust the volume to get maximum input on a quiet segment of music if the music is going to get very loud later. The loud part will be distorted.

You adjust the incoming volume for Sound Blaster Pro and 16/16 ASP with the **V**olume menu item from VEDIT2's main screen. The earlier Sound Blaster does not have a mixer chip, and therefore volumes for each sound source cannot be individually adjusted. Three signal sources can have their volumes individually adjusted: **V**oice, **C**Disc, and **L**ine In. When you select a particular option, a slider bar is used to set a volume level for that source. The **V**oice option is used to set the volume for the microphone input. **C**Disc adjusts volume of the signal coming in over the internal CD audio plugs, and **L**ine In adjusts the level of the signal coming in through the line-in jack. The **M**aster volume control is used to control the final recording level.

Although VEDIT2 lets you record in stereo, you cannot edit just one track of a stereo recording. All editing changes affect both tracks.

CD Players

You have a couple of options when sampling from CD players. If you're lucky enough to have a newer CD-ROM player with both data and audio capabilities, you're already set. Simply connect either the line-out or ministereo jack to

Sound Blaster's line-in jack. The Voice Editor program has a CD-ROM controller feature, called **C**Disc on the main menu, that gives some control over CD-ROM players connected to your computer. Frankly, Voice Editor is not a reliable CD-ROM controller. My system has a Magnavox CDD 461 CD-ROM. When playing audio discs, Voice Editor can play only tracks 1, 2, and 13 of one of my CDs. The other CD-ROM programs, particularly in Windows, have no such problems. Choosing **C**Disc from the main screen brings up a single option: **C**D Player. Choosing **C**D Player brings up a dialog box that resembles the control panel of your CD player, enabling you to select a particular track, start playing, pause, fast-forward to the next track, and so on.

If you want to sample from audio-only CDs, the process is exactly the same as if you were sampling from a stereo or VCR. The CD player probably has a line-out jack somewhere that you can connect to. If you're using a portable CD player, plug the cable from Sound Blaster's line-in jack into the CD player's headphone jack.

CHAPTER 5

Saving Sounds

Sounds are saved as sound files. Because of the wide variety of sound file formats—there seem to be as many file formats as there are companies that make software and hardware to work with sound—and because certain sound files consume enormous amounts of disk space, this chapter discusses how sound files are created.

The chapter begins with a discussion of saving digitized sound and then covers several utilities that convert files from one format to another. The discussion includes utilities that convert files for other computer platforms—such as Mac, Amiga, and Sun—to PC-compatible formats.

Saving Sound: Sampled Sound versus Sequencer Instructions

Begin by considering the difference between saving an actual digitized or sampled sound and saving a file to a synthesizer. When you sample a sound and store it on hard disk, you are actually storing a digital *representation* of the sound. When the sound is played back, the digital data is fed to a digital-to-analog converter (DAC) and converted back into audio signals. The higher the sample rate, the more data must be stored and converted. That's why a voice sample of you saying, "This is a test. One, two, three, four, five, six, seven, eight, nine, ten," takes around 40 kilobytes of memory at a sample rate of 11 kHz.

Most synthesizers come with a canned set of musical or percussion sounds already. Suppose that you just want to play these sounds in a specific order and within a specified time interval. Now, the sound file no longer needs to contain the actual sounds. Instead, it contains *instructions* to the synthesizer that say, in effect, "Play this sound at this time." The software that helps you build those instructions and play the sounds is called a *sequencer*. The file, called a *sequencer file*, is much smaller than the actual sound files.

File Formats

Table 5.1 lists most of the sound file and sequencer file formats you are likely to encounter. (Keep in mind that this list is not definitive; new formats are being developed regularly.)

Table 5.1 Sound File Extensions

File Extension	Description
AU	Audio files that run on Sun workstations.
BNK	Sound Bank files, usually containing sound patches.
CMF	The original Sound Blaster file format, no longer supported by Creative Labs. CMF files rely on the availability of the C/MS chip set used in the original Game Blaster and Sound Blaster V1.0 cards.
IFF	Amiga IFF sound files.
MID	MIDI-compatible sequencer files.
MOD	Digital recordings made on a Commodore Amiga computer.
NOT	Files created by the Musician shareware program.
NST	Song files created by the TrakBlaster, ScreamTracker, and Tetra programs running on the Amiga computer. The NST files are extensions of the MOD file; the difference is that MOD files can sequence 15 instruments, whereas NST files can sequence 31 instruments.
ORG	Files saved by Sound Blaster's Intelligent Organ.
PRN	Piano roll notation.
ROL	AdLib sound card files. The AdLib sound player is called JUKEBOX, and compatible files are sometimes referred to as JUKEBOX files. ROL files do not contain definitions for instrument sounds and must be accompanied by BNK files that contain instrument data. In the past, Bank files consisted of multiple instrument files that ended with the INS extension, but those files are no longer supported by AdLib.

File Extension	Description
ND	Sound files for use with GRASP animation software.
NG	Sequencer files created by Voyetra's SP Pro.
SOU	Files from any of several sound programs, including Apple Macintosh sound files.
VOC	Voice files, saved by Sound Blaster voice utilities. VOC files contain sampled sounds, which are digitized versions of sound. Samples taken with a fast sample rate require large amounts of disk space unless compressed. The VOC file format is described in Appendix B.
WAV	Windows sound files. Can be linked or embedded in Windows applications. WAV files are sampled only at rates of 11 kHz, 22 kHz, or 44 kHz.
WRK	Sound files created by the CAKEWALK program.

This list is not exhaustive, but it does cover the basics.

File Converters

As you browse through bulletin boards and over CompuServe, Prodigy, and the other national services, you find sound files in all their various flavors. The disks that come with this book contain a collection of shareware. One subdirectory contains a number of converter programs that run under DOS and convert one sound file type to another. The rest of this chapter briefly describes those programs.

> **NOTE**
>
> The file converters described in the following pages are used to convert the contents of a song or sound file. The converters do not reformat a disk so that the files can be played on another machine. In other words, you will not find a utility here that will let your PC read Macintosh disks. These utilities will, however, let you convert an Amiga sound file that you've downloaded from a bulletin board onto your PC.

Using Creative Labs Converter Utilities

The three utilities described here are provided with Sound Blaster. JOINTVOC combines multiple voice files into a single file, VOC2WAV converts WAV files to VOC files, and WAV2VOC converts VOC files to WAV files.

Joining Two VOC Files

The JOINTVOC utility enables you to merge two or more VOC files into a single file. You can also accomplish the following tasks:

- Insert silence between the joined sound files.

- Insert markers between the joined sound files. Markers can be used by other software programs to cause an action.

- Repeat a sound file within the new file.

To run JOINTVOC, enter this command at the DOS prompt:

JOINTVOC /T*targetfile*.VOC [*file1*.VOC]... [/S*xx*] [/M*xx*] [/R*xx*] [/RE]

Here are the definitions of the parameters:

/T*targetfile*.VOC	The name of the file you are creating that will contain the contents of the other files.
file1.VOC	The name of the first file to be merged.
/S*xx*	A silence period between the joined files; the period, defined by *xx*, is set in units of 0.1 seconds.
/M*xx*	A two-byte marker defined by *xx*. Markers cannot be heard, but they can be detected by other software applications.
/R*xx*	The parameter to repeat the next file *xx* times.
/RE	The parameter to stop repeating.

Suppose that you want to merge BILL.VOC with BOB.VOC to create a new file named BILLBOB.VOC. The new file will have a silence period of one second between the two files. Use this command:

JOINTVOC /TBILLBOB.VOC BILL.VOC /S10 BOB.VOC

To put BILL.VOC first in the new file, to follow it with a one-second silence and a marker, and to repeat BOB.VOC three times, use this command:

JOINTVOC /TBILLBOB.VOC BILL.VOC /S10 /M33 /R3 BOB.VOC /RE

Now you have a file named BILLBOB.VOC that contains one copy of BILL.VOC and three copies of BOB.VOC, separated by a one-second silence and a silent marker containing the number 33. Fun, huh? This marker can be any number and is used by other software to trigger an action. For example, a multimedia presentation could use markers embedded in the sound file to trigger the next slide or next video clip. Markers are simply indicators to perform a function and are not heard.

If you are the owner of Sound Blaster Pro, you can use VEDIT2 to look at the merged files and see the block types, as shown in figure 5.1 and described in Chapter 4, "Finding and Editing Sounds."

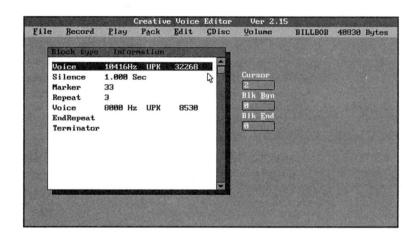

Fig. 5.1

Using VEDIT2 to show the block types when two files are joined.

VOC-to-WAV Conversion

The VOC2WAV utility converts Sound Blaster VOC files to Microsoft Windows WAV files. The command takes the following form:

VOC2WAV *source*.VOC *target*.WAV [/C:*xx*] [/R:*xx*] [/S:*xx*] [L:*xx*]

Here are the command parameters:

source.VOC	The name of the source VOC file.
target.WAV	The name of the WAV file you want to create.
/C:*xx*	The parameter to convert the source file to mono or stereo; $xx = 1$ for mono, and $xx = 2$ for stereo. If the original VOC file is in mono, the mono track repeats on both stereo channels.
/R:*xx*	The sampling rate for the target WAV file. Set xx to 11, 22, or 44.

/S:*xx*   The parameter to convert the silence block contained in a joined VOC file to a WAV file data block. Set *xx* = ON to convert the silence; set *xx* = OFF not to convert the silence.

/L:*xx*   The parameter to replicate the repeat information in a joined VOC file. Set *xx* = ON to have the sound block repeated an equivalent number of times in the WAV file. Set *xx* = OFF not to repeat the sound block.

To convert a VOC file to a WAV file without any changes, enter the following:

  VOC2WAV *filename*.VOC

Suppose that you have a mono sound file named WOLF.VOC and want to convert it to a stereo WAV file named WOLVES.WAV. You enter

  VOC2WAV WOLF.VOC WOLVES.WAV /C:2

This creates a stereo file named WOLVES.WAV, where the original mono recording is repeated on both tracks.

WAV-to-VOC Conversion

The WAV2VOC utility converts WAV files to VOC files. You use the following command syntax:

  WAV2VOC *source*.WAV *target*.VOC [/O] [/8] [/M]

Here are the command parameters:

source.WAV   The WAV file to be converted to a VOC file.

target.VOC   The name of the VOC file you want to create.

/O   The parameter to generate the older VOC file format for early Sound Blaster machines. The default is the current format.

/8   The parameter to convert 16-bit WAV files to 8-bit VOC files.

/M   The parameter to convert stereo WAV files to mono VOC files. The default is to create a stereo VOC file.

For example, to convert a WAV file named GLASS.WAV to a VOC file with the same name, enter

WAV2VOC GLASS.WAV GLASS.VOC

If you want to convert a 16-bit stereo WAV file to the older 8-bit mono VOC format, enter

WAV2VOC GLASS.WAV GLASS.VOC /8 /O /M

Converting Amiga Sound Files

The Amiga computer has long had the capability of sampling sounds and storing them as data files. The following converters enable you to convert the Amiga IFF voice data file to VOC format, as well as the Amiga MOD music sequencer files to a standard MIDI format usable by Sound Blaster.

IFF-to-VOC Conversion

Kevin S. Bachus has written IFF2VOC to convert Amiga IFF files to Sound Blaster VOC files. When IFF2VOC is installed, you can enter the following command from the DOS command-line prompt to run the program:

IFF2VOC *filename*

The *filename* is the name of the IFF file to be converted to a VOC file.

Because the converter program expects the file extension to be IFF, you do not need to enter an extension. IFF2VOC creates a new file with the same name but a different extension. For example, the command

> **NOTE**
>
> Appendix D provides instructions for installing the programs provided with this book.

IFF2VOC BACH

looks for the file named BACH.IFF and creates a new file named BACH.VOC.

MOD-to-MID Conversion

Many sound files are available that have been created on Amiga computers. Alexander Stock created a program called MOD2MIDI, which converts Amiga MOD files into MID files. You can play this program on Sound Blaster using a MIDI sequencer program (see Chapters 6, 7, and 8).

The MOD2MIDI utility has many capabilities and enables you to make several MIDI channel and voice assignments—concepts described in detail in

Chapter 6. It is beyond the scope of this chapter, however, to delve into any of the capabilities of this utility, except for the most obvious: converting MOD files to MIDI files. After you read Chapter 6, the options available with this utility will be obvious.

The quickest way to make a conversion is to accept MOD2MIDI's instrument assignments by pressing the Esc key at each of its option windows until it asks whether you want to continue. Press Y, and MOD2MIDI converts the file.

Converting Macintosh Sound Files

Like the Amiga, the Apple Macintosh has long had sound capability. Many of the sampled sound files that are available on CompuServe and other bulletin board systems are Macintosh files. In most digitized sound files, the actual sound data is in a relatively standard format typically called raw data. In front of the raw data, manufacturers add a file header that contains information about the data and how it is best played. Sound files created on a Macintosh are structured this way. You can extract the raw sound data from Macintosh SND files—without the header information—and then add the appropriate Sound Blaster file header information. In this way, you can convert sampled sound files from the Macintosh format to Sound Blaster format.

> **NOTE**
>
> Not all files with the SIT extension are equal. In other words, not all archive files with the SIT extension can be unarchived with extractors like unStufIt, described in the following section.

Because disk space and transmission time over commercial computer networks are fairly expensive, Macintosh files containing sound data are usually compressed into archive files to save space. You often run across Macintosh files that have been compressed with StuffIt, a popular archiver program. StuffIt files end with the extension SIT; Macintosh sound files within the archive typically have the extension SND. After you extract the sound file from the archive, you can use the VOC-HDR.EXE utility provided with Sound Blaster to convert the SND file into a VOC file.

unStufIt

You begin by extracting the sound data from the archive. Thanks to CABER Software, a DOS utility called unStufIt is available that extracts files archived with the Macintosh StuffIt program. StuffIt archives usually have an SIT extension. unStufIt lists all the files contained in the archive and extracts any or all of them for you.

To use unStufIt, enter the following command at the DOS prompt:

UNSTUFIT /D X *filename*.SIT *filename*.SND

Replace *filename*.SIT with the name of the archived file that contains the sound data, and *filename*.SND with the name of the file you want unStufIt to create.

Suppose, for example, that you have an archived file called BACH.SIT that contains the first eight notes of Bach's Toccata and Fugue in D Minor. Use the following procedure to extract and convert the SND file:

C>UNSTUFIT /D X BACH.SIT BACH.SND

This command de-archives the sound file data and stores it in another file called BACH.SND.

> **NOTE**
>
> Macintosh files contain two parts: the resource fork and the data fork. The data fork is the only part of the file you need to be concerned with—hence, the /D switch used on the unStufIt command line. The X parameter means "extract" and must be included in the command line.

SND-to-VOC Conversion

At this point, use the VOC-HDR command, provided with your Sound Blaster card, to add a VOC header to the sound data. This section describes the process to convert BACH.SND to BACH.VOC.

First, you must enter the VOC-HDR command at the DOS prompt:

VOC-HDR BACH.SND BACH.VOC

With this command, you are asking VOC-HDR to add a header to the file BACH.SND and save the new file as BACH.VOC. After you enter the command, VOC-HDR dumps the following information on the screen:

```
Creative Voice Header Fixer Version 2.00
Copyright (c) Creative Labs, Inc., 1989-1991. All rights reserved.
Copyright (c) Creative Technology Pte Ltd, 1989-1991. All rights
reserved.
Create bach.voc with data in bach.snd
File without header
 (1) 8 bit
 (2) 4 bit
 (3) 2.5 bit
 (4) 2 bit
 (5) Stereo
File format ( 1 - 5):1
```

At this point, you are prompted to enter the file type. The file can be a normal, uncompressed 8-bit sound file; or the file can be a compressed sound file, created with one of Creative Labs' standard compression techniques (4 bit, 2.5 bit, or 2 bit). If the sound file is a stereo recording, you would enter 5. In this case, the file is not compressed and is a monaural recording, so a value of 1 was entered.

Next, you are prompted to enter the sampling rate for the file. If you do not know it, you may have to experiment with different sampling rates to find the rate that sounds correct during playback. In the following case, the sampling rate was 22,050, so that value was entered without the command:

```
Enter sampling rate for this file:
4000 - 44100 Hz (Mono) 11000 - 22050 Hz (Stereo) :22050
```

When you have all the required information entered, the program asks you whether everything is correct. If you think you have everything right, press Y and then press Enter:

```
Is everything correct ? ( Y or N ) : y
Start copying...
Completed
C:>
```

At this point, you have a file named BACH.VOC in the working directory. If the sound file plays too slowly or too quickly, run VOC-HDR again and change the sample rate.

Converting Sun Workstation Sound Files

Kevin S. Bachus built a utility called SUN2VOC to convert Sun's AU sound files to VOC files that are compatible with Sound Blaster. Running the program is quite simple. You enter the utility name followed by the name of the Sun audio file to be converted:

> SUN2VOC *filename*.AU

The utility does the conversion and creates a file with the same name but with the VOC extension.

Sound Converter

The Sound Converter utility converts many types of sound files into WAV or RAW files. You use the following command syntax:

> SNDCONV *fromfile tofile* [*sample rate*]

The *fromfile* parameter can be a sound file with any of the following extensions:

> WAV   VOC   SND   RAW

The *tofile* parameter can be either a WAV file, suitable for use with Microsoft Windows, or a RAW file, to which you can attach a voice header to create a VOC file, using the VOC-HDR utility described earlier.

Musical Instrument Digital Interface

6

By 1980, electronic synthesizers of all varieties were hitting the streets, as was the first wave of personal computers. It became more and more difficult for musicians to interconnect electronic instruments from different manufacturers—so difficult, in fact, that anyone interested in being in the electronic music field nearly had to have a degree in electronics technology to make a sound!

As occasionally happens in this world, enlightened people got together and came up with a solution. The summer of 1983 saw the first release of the Musical Instrument Digital Interface (MIDI) specification. The MIDI specification was a document agreed to by nearly all the manufacturers of electronic instruments, and became the default standard (though it is not a true standard) for the electronic music industry.

The MIDI specification addresses two issues:

- The hardware interface between two or more instruments

- The software commands passed between two or more instruments

Unlike the audio interface that connects your cassette player to your amplifier, no sound—real or digitized—passes between two MIDI instruments. The MIDI interface is used only to pass instructions, called *messages*, to the MIDI instrument. The receiving MIDI instrument is responsible for accepting the message and configuring its own synthesizer in such a way as to create the appropriate sound at the appropriate time. This "message passing" is how computers became a natural partner in the electronic music industry. Fundamentally, all a computer does is pass messages back and forth. Sound Blaster uses its MIDI connector to issue and receive MIDI commands to and from MIDI-compatible instruments.

The MIDI specification has survived remarkably well over the years, primarily because it is strict in certain areas and very loose in others, giving musical instrument manufacturers and performers a great deal of flexibility. MIDI is used today by both professional and amateur musicians, with a huge number of enthusiasts willing to share information and techniques. The Sound Blaster's MIDI capabilities will be used extensively in the future for multimedia presentations, as well as in the home music studio.

This chapter is dedicated to explaining MIDI, starting with the hardware.

The MIDI Hardware Interface

Connecting two dissimilar pieces of electronic equipment can be tricky unless some pretty clear agreements are made ahead of time. Both power and signal voltages must be present at the correct levels and polarities. Some degree of isolation is a necessity because you don't want instrument A to melt down instrument B with a faulty signal or an accidentally switched wire. Finally, both instruments have to be synchronized to work together. The MIDI hardware interface specification solves all these problems in a neat and understandable way.

MIDI is, as its name implies, a digital interface. A stream of ones and zeros, in the form of high voltages and low voltages, is passed between instruments. Figure 6.1 shows an illustration of how voltage levels correspond to digital information. A digital 1 is represented when the signal voltage is high—near +5 Vdc (volts direct current). A digital 0 is represented when the voltage is near 0 Vdc.

Fig. 6.1

Voltage levels corresponding to digital information.

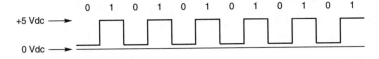

The Sound Blaster MIDI interface (or any other MIDI-compliant interface) transmits digital information by way of a single output line. Digital information is received by a separate line. To achieve isolation between the sending and receiving units, the MIDI specification requires that optical isolators be used by the receiving circuit. A simplistic version of the interface between two MIDI instruments is shown in figure 6.2.

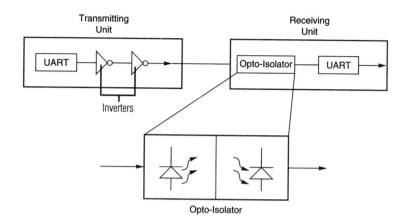

Fig. 6.2

The MIDI interface uses optical isolation to protect one instrument from another.

Both units contain a device called a Universal Asynchronous Receiver/Transmitter, commonly referred to as a UART. The UART is an integrated circuit used to turn parallel data from your computer into serial data that can be sent over a single wire. The transmitting MIDI unit's UART sends the stream of 1s and 0s through a couple of inverters and onto the cable leading to the receiving unit.

The receiving unit contains a device called an opto-isolator, which contains one light-emitting diode (LED) and one photo diode. When the signal from the sending unit gets to the input of the opto-isolator, it turns the light-emitting diode on and off. The light from the LED shines on the photo diode inside the isolator. The photo diode is sensitive to light and turns itself on and off in response to the LED. This on-and-off signal is fed to the receiving unit's UART. In this rather clever way, the 1s and 0s are transmitted from the sending unit's UART to the receiving unit's UART without having any actual physical contact between the two UARTS. Furthermore, the side of the opto-isolator containing the LED is powered by the sending MIDI unit, while the side containing the photo-diode is powered by the receiving unit. Thus, the two MIDI units achieve complete electrical isolation from one another.

Of course, most MIDI units are both receivers and transmitters, and contain both sets of electronics.

Another circumstance requires a bit more electronic circuitry, and that is when you want to control more than one instrument at a time. For instance, you may have your Sound Blaster MIDI port connected to a Yamaha keyboard, but would also like to control a drum machine. In that instance, what you need is a MIDI THRU port, as shown in figure 6.3.

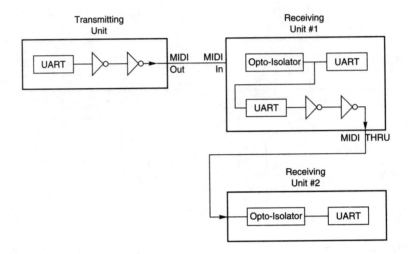

Fig. 6.3

MIDI Out, MIDI In, and MIDI THRU.

Within the receiving MIDI instrument, just after the signal is passed from the opto-isolator but before it gets to the UART, the signal branches and goes to another MIDI transmitter unit called MIDI THRU. Any commands issued by the transmitting unit are passed along to the second unit, which can have yet another MIDI THRU port and pass commands along to yet another unit. The MIDI THRU function is shown in figure 6.4.

Fig. 6.4

Multiple MIDI instruments being chained together with the MIDI THRU port.

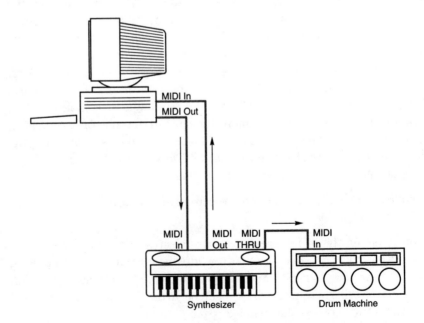

Several MIDI units can be connected in this manner, but signal timing gets to be a serious problem because of delays in the circuitry. The last unit on a long MIDI chain has very little time to intercept commands and stay in synchronization with the first unit.

For more detailed information on MIDI interface hardware, see Appendix C. There you can find a schematic of the circuitry required by the standard, as well as information on building your own Sound Blaster MIDI interface cable.

The MIDI Instruction Word

If you wanted to send digital information—a series of ones and zeros—to a MIDI instrument, you would send a series of square waves, with each low voltage representing 0 and each high voltage representing 1.

The question "How do I distinguish one zero from another zero?" possibly comes to mind. Good question. The MIDI specification handles this problem in two ways. First, the specification says that the digital information will be passed from one instrument or controller to another at a fixed rate of speed. That rate is 31,250 *bits* per second. A bit is either a 1 or a 0.

A transfer rate of 31,250 bits per second means that each bit takes approximately 0.000032 seconds (32 microseconds) of time. In other words, if you were watching the voltage on the signal line and it stayed near zero for 32 microseconds, you would know that a 0 bit was passed over the line. If, however, the voltage on the signal line was near +5 Vdc for those 32 microseconds, you would know that a 1 bit was passed over the line.

OK, now you can recognize a one or a zero. But the instrument or controller sending the signal to another instrument has to notify the receiving instrument that it is sending some digital information. In other words, the two boxes on either end of the MIDI cable must be synchronized. The MIDI specification handles synchronization by specifying how many bits make up an instruction, and then putting a start bit at the beginning of the instruction and a stop bit at the end of the instruction. The MIDI specification says that each instruction is eight bits long. So, if you add it all up, as shown in figure 6.5, you can see that each MIDI instruction consists of one start bit, the eight instruction bits (called a byte), and one stop bit. The start and stop bits are ones (1s).

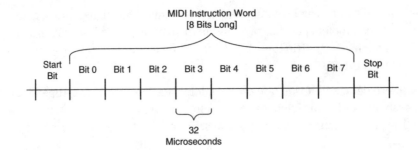

A MIDI message can be as short as a single 8-bit instruction (byte) or many bytes long, but in any case, the message is divided into two parts: a *status byte* followed by one or more *data bytes*. In some instances, only a status byte is issued. In most instances, a status byte is followed by one or more data bytes. The status byte always has a 1 in the most significant position (1xxxxxxx), and a data byte always has a zero in the most significant position (0xxxxxxx).

When a MIDI system is first started, for example, the controlling instrument (your Sound Blaster card) usually issues a System Reset command to get all the instruments synchronized. The System Reset is a status byte by itself, with no following data bytes, as shown here:

Message	Status Byte	Data Byte	Description
System Reset	11111111	None	System Reset

NOTE

Every status and data byte has start and stop bits. In this book, however, the start and stop bits are not shown.

If you were to look at Sound Blaster's MIDI Out line with an oscilloscope when a System Reset message is being sent, you might see something like the waveform shown in figure 6.6.

As shown in figure 6.6, the MIDI Out line goes to its 1 state (a high voltage in this description) at the beginning of the start bit, and stays high for each 32-microsecond chunk of time until the end of the stop bit. Therefore, any MIDI instrument connected to Sound Blaster when it issues the System Reset message will know that when the MIDI Out line goes to a 1 state and stays there for 320 microseconds, it should reset itself. Where did the 320 microseconds come from? Add it up. There are 8 data bits plus 1 start bit and 1 stop bit, totaling 10 bits all together. Each bit lasts for 32 microseconds.

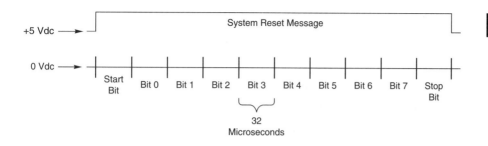

Fig. 6.6

Sound Blaster's
MIDI Out line
issuing a System
Reset message.

Now look at a more interesting message than System Reset. Figure 6.7 illustrates the MIDI System Start message, which is represented with the bit pattern in the instruction shown here:

Message	Status Byte	Data Byte	Description
System Start	11111010	None	System Reset

The fifth and seventh bits in the byte are set to zero, and that zero state is shown in the waveform issued by Sound Blaster.

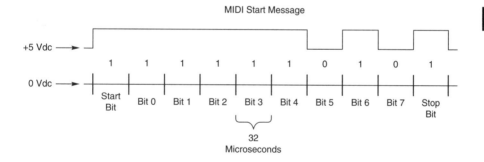

Fig. 6.7

The MIDI System
Start message.

You can begin to see how messages are passed between Sound Blaster and the MIDI instrument. In both of the preceding examples, no data follows the status byte, which is not the usual case. After all, Sound Blaster does more than reset and start MIDI instruments. There are many different types of MIDI messages.

MIDI Message Types

Refer again to figure 6.4. The Sound Blaster MIDI port is connected to a synthesizer and, by way of the synthesizer's MIDI THRU port, to a drum machine. How does Sound Blaster issue one message to the synthesizer and another message to the drum machine? By assigning channel numbers to each of them. A number of specific MIDI messages, called channel voice messages, are used to send data to specific channel numbers. The last 4 bits of a MIDI channel voice message status byte are used to indicate which of up to 16 channels are to act on a specific message. An instrument can have one or more channels assigned to it. In addition, it has become a MIDI practice to use channel 16 as the drum channel.

As you might guess, there are messages you will want to direct to a specific instrument on a specific channel, and messages you will want to direct to all instruments, such as the System Reset message discussed earlier in this chapter.

Therefore, MIDI messages are divided into two specific categories: *channel* messages and *system* messages.

System Messages

The MIDI specification states that there are three kinds of system messages: real-time, common, and exclusive. These are described here:

Real-time   These system messages are for all units attached to the MIDI system, and they are used to synchronize all the units. These messages can be sent at any time and are critical to keeping everything playing together. The real-time messages are described in table 6.1. Real-time system messages contain no data bytes.

Common   These system messages are intended for all units attached to the MIDI system. The common messages, listed in table 6.2, are used in part to make sure that all instruments are playing the same song and starting at the same point in the song.

Exclusive   These system messages are used by specific MIDI instrument manufacturers to send messages that only their machines will understand. The exclusive message format is shown in table 6.3.

Table 6.1 Real-Time System Messages

Status Byte	Data Byte	Description
11111000	None	*Timing Clock*. Used to synchronize the system to play at the same tempo. This message is sent 24 times for every quarter note.
11111001	—	Undefined.
11111010	None	*Start*. Tells all instruments to start playing from the beginning of the song. When you are using the Voyetra SP Pro MIDI sequencer, for example, pressing the space bar to begin playing results in this message being sent to all units.
11111011	None	*Continue*. Tells all instruments to begin playing again at the time of the next clock. This message is used with the following Stop message.
11111100	None	*Stop*. Instructs all MIDI units to stop playing.
11111101	—	Undefined.
11111110	None	*Active Sensing*. An optional message mostly used as a marker to indicate that the system is still active. If used, this message is sent every 300 milliseconds to let other units on the MIDI system know that it is still active.
11111111	None	*System Reset*. Initializes all the units on the system to their power-on states.

Table 6.2 Common System Messages

· Status Byte	Data Byte	Description
11110001	—	Undefined.
11110010	0LLLLLLL 0HHHHHHH	*Song Position Pointer.* This message is three bytes long, with two data bytes following the status byte. The first data byte provides the least significant digit, and the second data byte provides the most significant digit. The number represented by the data bytes indicates the number of MIDI beats since the start of the song. A MIDI beat is counted every 6 MIDI clocks. When a song is started from the beginning, the MIDI beat is typically set to zero. If you want to begin a song elsewhere, you can enter the starting beat number with this message.
11110011	0SSSSSSS	*Song Select.* Tells the system which song to play. To play song 7, for example, the data byte would be set to 0000111.
11110100	—	Undefined.
11110101		Undefined.
11110110	None	*Tune Request.* Used only on MIDI systems that have an analog synthesizer connected. Tune Request asks all analog synthesizers to tune their oscillators.
11110111	None	*EOX.* The End of System Exclusive message, used to terminate a message issued to a specific manufacturer's hardware.

Table 6.3 Exclusive System Messages

Status Byte	Data Byte	Description
11110000	0NNNNNNN	*Begin Exclusive Message.* Indicates the beginning of an exclusive message. Each manufacturer is assigned an identification number that is used in the data byte following the status byte.
	0XXXXXXX	Any number of bytes may be issued following the Begin Exclusive Message as long as they all start with a zero.
	0XXXXXXX	After the last exclusive byte is sent, the EOX message must be sent (see table 6.2 listing the common system messages).

The system messages give the MIDI sequencer overall control of a MIDI system. Specific messages for the generation of sound are given as channel messages.

Channel Messages

Channel messages are issued to specific instruments on specific channels. Again, a channel message consists of a message status byte followed by one or more data bytes. And again, the channel number is specified by the last four bits of the channel message.

There are two types of channel messages:

Mode	Mode messages define the instrument's response to the other kind of channel message: the voice type.
Voice	Voice messages are used to control the instrument's voices— that is, the piano, harpsichord, funky clavichord, and so on.

A MIDI instrument can be assigned more than one channel number and can therefore receive messages on more than one channel. However, usually one of the channels assigned to the instrument is called the *basic* channel, and the other channels are called the *voice* channels. In fact, multiple basic and voice channels can be assigned. For example, if your synthesizer is capable of generating eight voices, you might want to configure it as two four-voice synthesizers, each with its own basic channel and four voice channels. In this way, you have turned your synthesizer into two synthesizers.

Why is it important to have a basic channel? Because mode channel messages are issued over the basic channel, while voice channel messages are issued over the voice channels. (The basic channel carries voice messages in addition to mode channel messages.)

As an example, my Casio MT-640 keyboard recognizes MIDI channels 1 through 4, with channel 1 as the basic channel. Each channel is polyphonic in that more than one note can be played simultaneously, as in table 6.4.

Table 6.4 Casio MT-640 Channel Capabilities

Channel	Notes
1	6
2	4
3	2
4	4

Furthermore, each channel can be assigned one of Casio's preset voices, from either the keyboard or Sound Blaster. For example, I could set up the Voyetra SP Pro MIDI sequencer (covered in Chapter 7) to issue percussion sounds on channel 4. Channel 1 could be set for piano, channel 2 for jazz organ, and channel 3 for jazz guitar.

In the case of the Casio, in addition to receiving voice messages over channel 1, I can use the same channel to receive mode messages.

Mode Messages

Mode messages are issued only over the basic channel. A MIDI instrument can be configured in four modes. The different modes have to do with what kinds of voice messages the instrument pays attention to.

There are two parts to the mode message: omni, and poly or monophonic response. When set to Omni-On, the MIDI instrument will respond to all incoming voice messages, regardless of what channel they come in on (so long as the instrument is capable of receiving that channel). When set to Omni-Off, the instrument will respond to voice messages on only its basic channel, except in the case of mode 4.

The other part of the mode message has to do with whether the MIDI instrument responds by playing a single note (monophonic) or multiple notes simultaneously (polyphonic). Table 6.5 summarizes the four modes.

Table 6.5 MIDI Channel Mode Messages

Mode	Definition	Description
1	Omni-On Poly	Responds to incoming voice messages on each possible channel, playing polyphonically.
2	Omni-On Mono	Responds to incoming voice messages on each possible channel, playing monophonically.
3	Omni-Off Poly	Responds to incoming voice messages only on the basic channel, playing polyphonically.
4	Omni-Off Mono	Responds to incoming voice messages only on the indicated channels, playing monophonically.

As with all other MIDI messages, mode messages are sent as binary 1s and 0s. Table 6.6 lists the mode messages. When a mode is changed, all notes are turned off.

Table 6.6 Channel Mode Messages

Status Byte	Data Byte	Description
1011*nnnn*	0ccccccc	Mode messages, where *nnnn* = basic channel number
	0vvvvvvv	

When: *Meaning:*

ccccccc = 122	Local Control
vvvvvvv = 0	Local Control Off
vvvvvvv = 127	Local Control On

Local Control is optionally used to alter the signal paths in the MIDI instrument. With Local Control Off, keyboard data goes to MIDI Out, and the synthesizer is controlled by MIDI In.

ccccccc = 123	All Notes Off
vvvvvvv = 0	

This message simply turns all voices off.

ccccccc = 124	Omni Mode Off
vvvvvvv = 0	

This message switches to Omni-Off mode.

ccccccc = 125	Omni Mode On
vvvvvvv = 0	

This message switches to Omni-On mode.

ccccccc = 126	Mono Mode On
vvvvvvv = M	(where M is the number of channels)
vvvvvvv = 0	(number of channels equals the number of voices in the receiver)

This message turns Mono mode on and uses three data bytes. The third data byte, when set to a number from 1 to 16, specifies the number of channels that are to receive voice messages. When the third

Status Byte	Data Byte	Description
		data byte is set to zero, the receiving MIDI instrument assigns all its voices, one per channel, from the assigned basic channel, up to a maximum of 16.
		ccccccc = 127 Poly Mode On vvvvvvv = 0
		This message turns Mono mode off.

The mode messages give you some control over how various instruments will respond to voice messages, which are discussed next. At power-up, all MIDI instruments should default to mode 1.

Voice Messages

Voice messages are really what causes sound to be played. The voice messages give you control over what note will be played, when it will be played, how long it will sound, and how it will sound. Table 6.7 lists the MIDI voice messages. The last four bits of the status byte (*nnnn*) are used to select which channel the message will be sent to.

Table 6.7 Voice Messages

Status Byte	Data Bytes	Description
1000*nnnn*	0kkkkkkk	*Note Off.*
	0vvvvvvv	This message turns off the note indicated by the 0kkkkkkk data byte. kkkkkkk can range in value from 0 to 127. A value of 60 equals middle C on the keyboard.
		The 0vvvvvvv data byte is used by synthesizers with keystroke velocity sensors. The value can be set from 0 to 127. If no velocity sensors exist, the value should be set to 64.

continues

Table 6.7 Continued

Status Byte	Data Bytes	Description
1001*nnnn*	0kkkkkkk	*Note On.*
	0vvvvvvv	This message turns on the note indicated by the 0kkkkkkk data byte. kkkkkkk can range in value from 0 to 127. A value of 60 equals middle C on the keyboard.
		The 0vvvvvvv data byte is used by synthesizers with keystroke velocity sensors. The value can be set from 1 to 127. If 0vvvvvvv is set to 0 (zero), the note is turned off. Any Note On message should be followed by a Note Off message at some later time.
1010*nnnn*	0kkkkkkk	*Polyphonic Key Pressure (polyphonic aftertouch).*
	0vvvvvvv	This message controls the aftertouch for a specific note. The note is selected by the first data byte, and the pressure value is selected by the second data byte.
1011*nnnn*	0ccccccc	*Control Change.*
	0vvvvvvv	This message lets the MIDI sequencer manipulate and select the internal instrument controllers and switches found inside most MIDI instruments. The various controllers are assigned a specific control number (the first data byte, 0ccccccc), and values (0vvvvvvv) can be sent to each controller. The control numbers have distinct groupings but are not specifically defined by the MIDI specification. Note the following groupings (where MSB = most significant bit and LSB = least significant bit):

Status Byte	Data Bytes	Description
		ccccccc: *Description:*
		0 Continuous Controller 0 MSB
		1 Continuous Controller 1 MSB (Modulation Wheel)
		2 Continuous Controller 2 MSB
		3 Continuous Controller 3 MSB
		4-31 Continuous Controllers 4-31 MSB
		32 Continuous Controller 0 LSB
		33 Continuous Controller 1 LSB (Modulation Wheel)
		34 Continuous Controller 2 LSB
		35 Continuous Controller 3 LSB
		36-63 Continuous Controllers 4-31 LSB
		64-95 Switches (On/Off)
		96-121 Undefined
1100*nnnn*	0*ppppppp*	*Program Change.* This message lets you select which preset or program to play. The value of 0*ppppppp* can range from 0 to 127.
1101*nnnn*	0*vvvvvvv*	*Channel Pressure (monophonic aftertouch).* This message is used to control aftertouch, which can be sensed on some synthesizer keyboards by pressure sensors. The pressure value is set within the data byte and can range from 0 to 127.
1110*nnnn*	0*vvvvvvv*	*Pitch Wheel Change.*
	0*vvvvvvv*	The two data bytes are used to select a pitch wheel value used for pitch bending. The first data byte sets the least significant number, and the second sets the most significant number.

With this set of voice messages, you can select a specific program voice, define the note the voice is to play, define how quickly the note is struck and how hard, and determine how quickly the note is released. You can control how much a note's tone is bent with a pitch wheel. And you can manipulate the various other electronic controllers found in today's synthesizers, such as a modulation wheel, a foot peddle, or breath control.

By far, the easiest way to take advantage of MIDI is to do so through a sequencer, which relieves you of the burden of sending MIDI messages.

Sound Blaster as a MIDI Instrument

Thus far in this chapter, you've read about MIDI instruments as external devices. In fact, a MIDI instrument is any synthesizer with a MIDI port. Sound Blaster itself is capable of acting as a MIDI instrument. When you use the Voyetra SP Pro MIDI sequencer, you will find that you can send MIDI commands to one of two places: an external MIDI instrument or the synthesis components built into your Sound Blaster board.

General MIDI and Microsoft

There is a difference between the general MIDI specification and the way Microsoft has implemented MIDI compliance in its software products.

A general MIDI instrument supports 32-note polyphony over 16 channels. Assuming that most PC-based MIDI controllers and instruments would be stretched to perform that well, Microsoft elected to redefine the specification a bit.

As shown in table 6.8, Microsoft's version of MIDI divides MIDI instrument groups into two: Basic MIDI and Extended MIDI.

Table 6.8 Microsoft's Two MIDI Specifications

	Basic MIDI	Extended MIDI
Channels	13-15 16 for percussion	1-16 10 for percussion
Voices	3	9
Polyphony	6 melodic notes 5 percussion	16 melodic notes 8 percussion

Under Microsoft's guidelines, Basic MIDI devices are to listen on channels 13 through 15 for melodic notes and to use channel 16 for percussion. Extended MIDI devices use all 16 channels and listen on channel 10 for percussion. The Sound Blaster and Sound Blaster Pro cards fit Microsoft's definition of Basic MIDI devices.

MIDI Sequencers

A MIDI sequencer is a software program that runs on a MIDI controller. In this instance, the MIDI controller under discussion is your Sound Blaster board; however, there are any number of MIDI synthesizers that can act as controllers.

In brief, the sequencer is designed to allow you to issue messages to a MIDI instrument or receive messages from a MIDI instrument. In addition, the sequencer should enable you to enter notes without a keyboard, change the length and timing of the note, let you change the program or preset that will play the note, and let you record multiple tracks of notes, much like a multitrack tape recorder.

How you issue messages is greatly simplified by the sequencer, although still not extremely easy. You need to be aware of how MIDI works and how your sequencer works with MIDI instruments.

Channels

Sound Blaster issues messages to MIDI instruments by using up to 16 different channels. It can be a little confusing to think of different channels, when at the beginning of this chapter, you discovered that MIDI is a serial communications protocol, with only one line out and one line in. How can you have multiple channels with only one signal line? Again, you can have multiple channels by assigning a channel number to every MIDI instrument and then putting that channel number at the beginning of every message sent down the wire. In that way, the MIDI instrument knows to pay attention to only those messages that are addressed to it.

Each instrument connected to the MIDI network has at least one basic channel over which mode messages are issued. For example, the Casio MT-640 used during the development of this book recognizes four channels. Some MIDI instruments can have more than one basic channel assigned.

Programs, Patches, and Presets

The term *program* seems freely interchangeable with the words *preset* and *voice,* and with the word *patch.* In any case, programs are sounds the synthesizer is preset to generate. In other words, the Casio MT-640 has 20 presets, voices, programs, or patches—letting you select a jazz organ sound instead of a pipe organ. The Casio has another 20 rhythm presets to generate waltz, samba, and reggae rhythms (to name a few).

Some MIDI instruments allow you to download one or more new voices. A series of new voices is typically stored in a file called a *sound bank,* which can be downloaded from your computer or other MIDI controller into certain synthesizers.

The standard patches are listed in table 6.9.

Table 6.9 MIDI Instrument Patch Assignments

Note	Sound	Note	Sound
0	Piano	15	Dulcimer
1	Bright Acoustic Piano	16	Hammond Organ
2	Electric Grand Piano	17	Percussive Organ
3	Honky-Tonk Piano	18	Rock Organ
4	Rhodes Piano	19	Church Organ
5	Chorused Piano	20	Reed Organ
6	Harpsichord	21	Accordion
7	Clavinet	22	Harmonica
8	Celesta	23	Tango Accordion
9	Glockenspiel	24	Acoustic Nylon Guitar
10	Music Box	25	Acoustic Steel Guitar
11	Vibraphone	26	Electric Jazz Guitar
12	Marimba	27	Electric Clean Guitar
13	Xylophone	28	Electric Muted Guitar
14	Tubular Bells	29	Overdriven Guitar

Note	Sound	Note	Sound
30	Distortion Guitar	55	Orchestral Hit
31	Guitar Harmonics	56	Trumpet
32	Acoustic Bass	57	Trombone
33	Electric Bass Fingered	58	Tuba
34	Electric Bass Picked	59	Muted Trumpet
35	Fretless Bass	60	French Horn
36	Slap Bass 1	61	Brass Section
37	Slap Bass 2	62	Synth Brass 1
38	Synth Bass 1	63	Synth Brass 2
39	Synth Bass 2	64	Soprano Sax
40	Violin	65	Alto Sax
41	Viola	66	Tenor Sax
42	Cello	67	Baritone Sax
43	Contrabass	68	Oboe
44	Tremolo Strings	69	English Horn
45	Pizzicato Strings	70	Bassoon
46	Orchestral Harp	71	Clarinet
47	Timpani	72	Piccolo
48	String Ensemble 1	73	Flute
49	String Ensemble 2	74	Recorder
50	Synth Strings 1	75	Pan Flute
51	Synth Strings 2	76	Bottle Blow
52	Choir Aahs	77	Shakuhachi
53	Voice Oohs	78	Whistle
54	Synth Voice	79	Ocarina

continues

Table 6.9 Continued

Note	Sound	Note	Sound
80	Synth Lead 1 Square Wave	101	Synth SFX 6 Goblins
81	Synth Lead 2 Sawtooth Wave	102	Synth SFX 7 Echo Drops
82	Synth Lead 3 Caliope	103	Synth SFX 8 Star Theme
83	Synth Lead 4 Chiff	104	Sitar
84	Synth Lead 5 Charang	105	Banjo
85	Synth Lead 6 Solo Synth Voice	106	Shamisen
86	Synth Lead 7 Bright Saw Wave	107	Koto
87	Synth Lead 8 Bass and Lead	108	Kalimba
88	Synth Pad 1 Fantasia (New Age)	109	Bagpipe
89	Synth Pad 2 Warm	110	Fiddle
90	Synth Pad 3 Poly Synth	111	Shanai
91	Synth Pad 4 Space Voice (choir)	112	Tinkle Bells
92	Synth Pad 5 Bowed Glass	113	Agogo
93	Synth Pad 6 Metal	114	Steel Drums
94	Synth Pad 7 Halo	115	Woodblock
95	Synth Pad 8 Sweep	116	Taiko Drum
96	Synth SFX 1 Ice Rain	117	Melodic Drum
97	Synth SFX 2 Sound Track	118	Synth Drum
98	Synth SFX 3 Crystal	119	Reverse Cymbal
99	Synth SFX 4 Atmosphere	120	Guitar Fret Noise
100	Synth SFX 5 Brightness	121	Breath Noise

Note	Sound	Note	Sound
122	Seashore	125	Helicopter
123	Bird Tweet	126	Applause
124	Telephone Ring	127	Gunshot

Not all instruments that claim MIDI compliance use this standard patch table. For example, the Casio MT-640 uses the patch table shown in table 6.10.

Table 6.10 Casio MT-640 Patch Table

Note	Sound	Note	Sound
0	Piano	10	Electric Piano
1	Harpsichord	11	Funky Clavichord
2	Vibraphone	12	Jazz Guitar
3	Jazz Organ	13	Organ
4	Pipe Organ	14	Accordion
5	Brass Ens	15	Strings
6	Flute	16	Chorus
7	Bells	17	Synth-ens
8	Wood Bass /Piano	18	Electric Bass /Slap Bass
9	Percussion 1	19	Percussion 2

Now it should be extremely clear why MIDI sequencers, including the Microsoft Windows Sound functions, allow you to create "patch maps." To play a MIDI song on my Casio that calls for a harpsichord, I must tell the sequencer to *map* note 6 to note 1 to play the song correctly. In other words, when it comes time to play a harpsichord note, instead of issuing a MIDI message telling the Casio to play note 6 per the MIDI specification, the sequencer sends a message saying play note 1.

There is another set of sounds used in MIDI music these days, having completely to do with percussion. MIDI channel 16 is usually reserved for percussion sounds, and MIDI-compliant percussion instruments create the sounds shown in table 6.11.

The Ultimate Sound Blaster Book — page 146

146 The Ultimate Sound Blaster Book

Table 6.11 MIDI Percussion Sounds

Note	Drum Sound	Note	Drum Sound
35	Bass Drum	59	Ride Cymbal
36	Bass Drum	60	High Bongo
37	Side Kick	61	Low Bongo
38	Snare Drum	62	Muted High Bongo
39	Hand Clap	63	Open High Conga
40	Electric Snare	64	Low Conga
41	Tom 1	65	High Timbale
42	Closed High Hat	66	Low Timbale
43	Tom 2	67	High Agogo
44	Pedal High Hat	68	Low Agogo
45	Tom 3	69	Cabasa
46	Open Hi Hat	70	Maracas
47	Tom 4	71	Short Whistle
48	Tom 5	72	Long Whistle
49	Crash Cymbal	73	Short Guiro
50	Tom 6	74	Long Guiro
51	Ride Cymbal	75	Claves
52	Chinese Cymbal	76	High Wood Block
53	Ride Bell	77	Low Wood Block
54	Tambourine	78	Mute Cuica
55	Splash Cymbal	79	Open Cuica
56	Cowbell	80	Mute Triangle
57	Crash Cymbal	81	Open Triangle
58	Vibraslap		

If you had a drum machine connected to your MIDI system and you used channel 16 as the percussion channel, sending MIDI messages that tell the machine to play the notes listed in table 6.11 would result in having those sounds played.

Tracks

Most MIDI sequencers enable you to record multiple tracks just as though you were recording multiple sound tracks on a tape recorder. If you make a mistake on one track, you can record over your mistake without changing any of the other tracks. Sequencers allow you to edit the notes on each track, changing note length as well as the start and stop of a note.

Quantization—Note Alignment

Some of us (and I am at the top of the list) are very interested in making music, but we're lousy keyboard players. Because MIDI sequencers keep track of what note is played, when it starts, and when it stops, a good sequencer can help those of us with marginal skills by applying quantization to our music. *Quantization* simply means that the synthesizer does its best to line up the beginning and ending of the note you played with the beginning and ending of the bar in which it was played. In other words, if you were trying to play a quarter note at the beginning of a bar but you pressed the key a little bit late, the sequencer can make its best guess of when you meant the note to start, and shift it to begin a little sooner.

One of the unfortunate side effects of quantization is that it tends to make music very stiff and rigid, removing a lot of the human element that really good musicians add to playing by starting a note just when they want to—which may *not* be at the exact beginning of a bar. If the sequencer you use has a quantization feature, use it sparingly. Music has some relationship with mathematics, but generally should not sound quite so mathematically precise.

CHAPTER 7

The Voyetra SP Pro MIDI Sequencer

The Sound Blaster MIDI Kit provides a DOS-based MIDI sequencer package with every MIDI cable. Until recently, the sequencer packaged in the MIDI Kit was the Voyetra SP Pro MIDI sequencer. Most recently, however, Creative Labs has begun shipping the Cakewalk sequencer from Twelve Tone Systems, Inc., instead of the SP Pro sequencer. However, because the majority of MIDI Kits that are in user hands today include the SP Pro software rather than the Cakewalk product, this chapter is devoted to the SP Pro sequencer. The Cakewalk sequencer is quite similar in function, though, and includes a few improvements over the Voyetra product. If you understand how the SP Pro sequencer works, you certainly won't have any trouble making the transition to the Cakewalk package. If you have neither sequencer but are running Windows, jump immediately to Chapter 11 and take a look at WinJammer, one of the most sophisticated Windows-based MIDI sequencers available. And best of all, WinJammer is included with this book.

SP Pro is a good example of a flexible, mostly user-friendly, DOS-based MIDI sequencer. Included with the shareware packages in the back of this book is the WinJammer program from Dan McKee, which contains many of the same functions as the SP Pro program, but in a Windows environment.

MIDI sequencers are programs that enable you to build a sequence of instructions for MIDI instruments. In the case of SP Pro, you can send instructions to the Sound Blaster synthesizer (which can serve as a MIDI instrument), to an external MIDI instrument connected to Sound Blaster's MIDI connector, or to both.

This chapter walks you through the making of a simple MIDI recording with the SP Pro. Once you've become familiar with SP Pro, you can transfer that basic knowledge to nearly any MIDI sequencer.

I have always been a firm believer that the quickest way to learn how any computer software works is by playing with it. And I use "playing" in the literal sense. Have some fun! If what you're trying to do doesn't work right the first time, so what? Poke around in dark corners. Experiment. See what happens when you change things. You will learn faster and enjoy it too.

The Basic Song-Building Process

Typically, the process of building a song with a MIDI sequencer includes these basic steps:

1. Connect whatever MIDI equipment you are going to use as a note source. In other words, if you have a MIDI keyboard, connect the keyboard to Sound Blaster with the MIDI cables. If you do not have a MIDI keyboard, you can use SP Pro's internal synthesizer, which simulates a keyboard on your computer.

2. Select a tempo that works for your particular song, and then turn on the metronome so that you can hear the beat.

3. Record the first track of the song. The first track can be the percussion, the melody line, or the background—it's entirely up to you. It can be as simple as a bass drum beating once every click of the metronome or, if you're an agile keyboardist, a syncopated background rhythm that will amaze your friends.

4. Record the 2nd, 3rd, or 17th track.

5. Go back and edit the whole song or edit individual tracks until you're happy with the way the song sounds. You can delete tracks, change the key of different tracks, and even change the instrument that plays on each track.

6. Save the song on disk. Actually, you will want to save the song several times throughout its development, or even save different versions of the song.

The easy thing about MIDI recording is that the MIDI source you are using, whether it is an external MIDI keyboard or SP Pro's internal synthesizer, is capable of being an entire orchestra. To lay down a single bass drum track, for example, all you need to do is start the SP Pro recording and then press any key on the keyboard once for every click of the metronome. But, you say, that sounds like a piano! Yes, it does. However, because MIDI instruments are programmable, any instrument in the entire MIDI repertoire is available to you. You can change the programming so that the key you pressed sounds like a bass drum—or a glockenspiel, if you prefer.

When you're ready to lay down the second track, you have a choice of 128 different instruments to play, all from your MIDI keyboard.

SP Pro's Main Screen

The Main screen of SP Pro, shown in figure 7.1, is divided into three basic areas: the status area, the work area, and the menu area (containing the main menu). In addition, you can access pop-up menus from the menu names that appear in all uppercase letters.

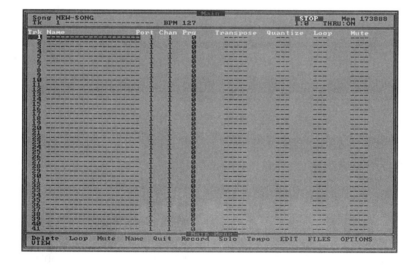

Fig. 7.1

SP Pro's Main screen.

The Status Area

The *status area* is at the top of the screen and provides the following information (see fig. 7.2):

Song	Displays current song file name. If you haven't started a song yet, this displays NEW-SONG until you record some music and name the song.
Tk	Indicates track currently selected in the work area.
BPM	Shows tempo in beats per minute.
STOP	Indicates whether you are playing or recording a track.
Mem	Shows conventional memory available to store sequencer instructions.
1:0	Indicates which bar and beat of the bar is currently being played or recorded (for example, the third beat of the fifth bar is shown as 5:3).
THRU	Tells whether you have turned on the MIDI THRU capability of your MIDI instrument (whether it is Sound Blaster or an external MIDI keyboard or drum).

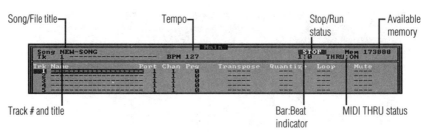

Fig. 7.2

The status area of the Main screen.

The Work Area

Most of the work you will do with a MIDI file goes on in the *work area* (see fig. 7.3). This is where the tracks are laid down, to borrow a phrase from the recording industry. In this window is listed each sound track, to a maximum of 64, in your recording and the name of the track (you can name it anything you like). You select tracks by moving the highlight around with the mouse or the arrow keys on the keyboard.

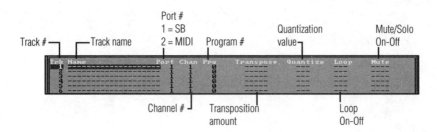

Fig. 7.3

The SP Pro work area where you build a recording.

Each track line provides the following information after the track number and track name:

- *Port.* SP Pro is capable of sending MIDI instructions to either Sound Blaster or the MIDI unit connected to Sound Blaster's MIDI connector. When the port number is set to 2, the song will be played on Sound Blaster, *and*, if MIDI THRU is turned on, the song will be played on the MIDI unit connected to Sound Blaster's MIDI connector. When the port number is set to 1, MIDI instructions are directed only to the unit connected to Sound Blaster's MIDI connector. Sound Blaster itself will ignore the MIDI commands.

- *Chan (channel number).* Recall from Chapter 6 that there are 16 possible MIDI channels, each capable of playing one or more notes.

- *Prg (program number).* This is the number that determines the instrument sound to be generated by the track. There are 128 melodic sounds possible and 47 different percussion sounds.

- *Transpose.* You use this column to transpose a track to a scale different from the one in which it was originally recorded.

- *Quantize.* In this column, you select a quantization value to line up the notes you entered with the beginning and ending of the beat.

- *Loop.* When you record a track, you can turn looping on so that the track is played over and over again until the end of the song. Looping is most useful in percussion tracks (no point in hitting the bass drum over and over again for a hundred bars). You can record a single bar of beats and then loop that bar repeatedly until the end of the song.

- *Mute.* This column lets you either mute (silence) an individual track or solo a track by muting all the other tracks.

These nine columns give you fundamental control over your recording environment.

The Menu Area

The *menu area* is at the bottom of the screen and is used to perform specific functions on the selected track (see fig. 7.4). Some of the options (in all uppercase) in the main menu shown in this figure open additional windows.

You choose items from the menu area by typing the first letter of each menu item. Or, if you're using a mouse, you can click the left and right mouse buttons simultaneously. A mouse window then opens, which you can move through with the mouse (see fig. 7.5). You choose a menu item by placing the mouse pointer on it and then double-clicking with the left mouse button. To exit the mouse window without making a selection, press the Esc key or choose the (Close menu) item in the mouse window.

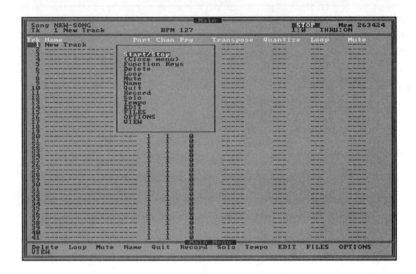

The following options are available in the main menu:

Delete   Deletes the selected track.

Loop   Loops the selected track. When you loop a track, the loop column for that track shows the word loop.

Mute   Mutes or silences the selected track. To silence all tracks except the selected track, choose the Solo option.

Name   Names a track after you've recorded it. If you try to assign a name to a blank track, SP Pro complains.

Quit   Exits SP Pro. When you choose Quit, the software asks whether you're sure you want to quit. Press Q again.

Record	Prepares SP Pro to record a track. If you have highlighted a track that has already been recorded, SP Pro asks whether you want to record over the existing music. When you choose Record, the word REC appears in front of the Stop/Run indicator in the status area. To start recording, press the space bar.
Solo	Mutes all tracks except the selected track.
Tempo	Sets the metronome tempo when recording, or the playback tempo when playing back a recorded piece.
EDIT	Opens the Edit screen, which is discussed in more detail later. The Edit screen allows you to manipulate individual notes in a song by moving them in time, length, and pitch.
FILES	Opens the Files screen, allowing you to save new or edited files, or load existing music files for editing. The Files menu at the bottom of this screen is described later in this chapter.
OPTIONS	Opens the Options window, enabling you to turn on the metronome, set MIDI THRU, and set various other options, described later in this chapter.
VIEW	Opens the View screen, showing which channels are playing in which measures. The View menu options at the bottom of the View screen are described later in this chapter.

To introduce you to some of the functions in the Main screen, the next few paragraphs step you through loading a simple MIDI song, correcting a flaw, and playing around a little.

Bad Mary—A Tutorial

Included on the disks in the back of this book is a file named BADMARY.MID, with apologies to all the Marys that may read this book (you will soon see the reason for the title). BADMARY.MID is a MIDI file that was created simply to show you a few of the primary features of SP Pro.

Loading BADMARY.MID

Start SP Pro by changing to the directory that contains the program, which is usually C:\VOYETRA. The directory should contain a file named SP.BAT, which is the DOS batch file to load the Voyetra drivers and start SP Pro. Type **SP** and press Enter.

When you enter the command SP, the software loads a couple of drivers into memory and then checks to see where your Sound Blaster card is installed. Finally, the Main screen appears (refer to fig. 7.1).

Next, you need to load the file. When you press the F key, the SP Pro Files screen is displayed, as shown in figure 7.6. The Files screen defaults to song files with the SNG extension.

SNG # extension

Fig. 7.6

The SP Pro Files screen showing song (SNG) files.

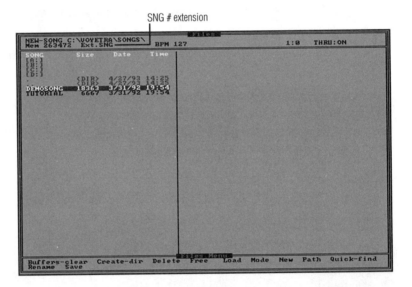

The current directory contains two songs in Voyetra's SNG sequencer format, as you can see. But you're looking for a MIDI file, so you need to change the file type that SP Pro will search for. Press M to choose the Mode menu item at the bottom of the Files screen. That brings up the MIDI Files screen, as shown in figure 7.7. There are actually three different file modes: SNG files, MIDI files, and ROL files generated for AdLib sound cards. You cannot save files in the ROL format, but SP Pro will load the ROL files, and you can save them in either MIDI or SNG format.

MID extension

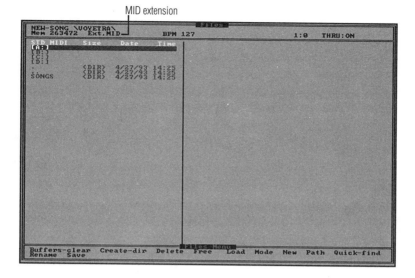

Fig. 7.7

The SP Pro MIDI
Files screen.

Now you have to find the file BADMARY.MID and load it. For this example, the
file is assumed to be on a floppy disk in drive B. To access drive B, move the
selector bar (the highlight) to the line containing [B:] and press Enter. If the
file is located on another floppy drive in your system or has been installed in
a directory on your hard drive, select the appropriate drive, followed by the
appropriate subdirectory.

After you've found BADMARY.MID, highlight the file, as shown in figure 7.8,
and press L to load the file into SP Pro.

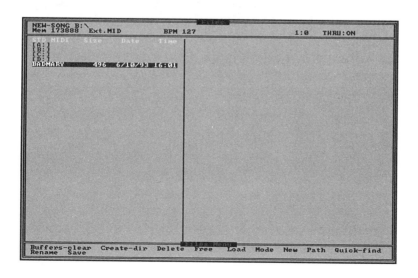

Fig. 7.8

The BADMARY file
highlighted,
showing the
amount of
available memory,
file extension,
name, size, and
date and time of
creation.

When SP Pro begins loading the file, you are asked whether you want to continue, because the file you have selected will be merged with any songs you have already loaded into SP Pro. Press Enter.

As loading continues, the menu area at the bottom of the Files screen changes (see fig. 7.9). You have the option of accepting the tempo, or time signature (timesig), of the file you're loading by choosing Meters. Or, if you're merging this file with a song you already have in memory, you can ignore the time signature of the song being loaded and instead use the tempo of the song in memory. In this example, no other song exists in memory, so use the time signature provided with the file. Choose Meters and press Enter.

Fig. 7.9

Accepting the time signature (timesig) of the song file.

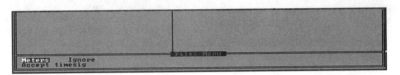

Now the file should be loaded, and your screen should look something like that in figure 7.10.

You can see quite a lot of information on this screen. The song title is at the top of the screen, along with the indicator showing what track is currently selected. The song is not playing—hence, the STOP indicator in the upper-right corner. And the tempo for this particular masterpiece is set to 95 beats per minute.

Fig. 7.10

The BADMARY.MID file loaded and ready to be played.

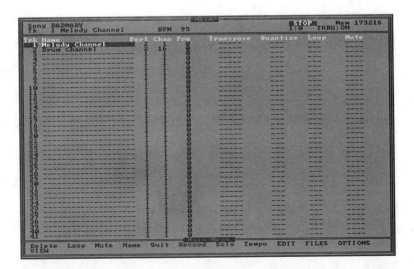

Two other tracks are being used: one is labeled Melody Channel, and the other is labeled Drum Channel. Both tracks are set to play on the Sound Blaster synthesizer (port 2). Track 1 will play on channel 1, and track 2 will play on channel 16, the general MIDI percussion channel. If this song were structured to be Windows Multimedia compliant, you would use channel 16 for percussion in basic MIDI, or channel 10 for extended MIDI.

Each of the tracks will play the zero (0) program from the MIDI default program assignments. In this case, track 1 will play an acoustic grand piano (sort of), and track 2 will play an acoustic bass drum.

OK, OK, a MIDI song loaded. What's next? Play it! Press the space bar to start playing, and again to stop playing.

Now having heard BADMARY.MID, you understand the reason for the name. Mary and her little lamb have a bad note staring rather obviously out of the bushes, which you will fix in a little while.

But first, take some time to find out what your Sound Blaster card is capable of doing. After all, it can play 128 different instruments, and some of them sound rather outrageous. To make changes in the Main screen, move the highlight to the area you want to change, and enter a new number or value for each of the following:

- *Prg*. Here you can pick a new instrument. To begin with, highlight the program number for track 1 and then enter a new number, ranging from 0 to 127. When you've entered the new number, press Enter followed by a space to see how the instrument you've selected sounds.

- *Transpose*. To transpose the melody line to a new key, move the highlight to the Transpose column for track 1 and press the plus (+) or minus (–) key on your keyboard to shift the melody line up or down by a half step.

- *Loop*. Set both tracks to loop by moving the highlight to any item on the track and pressing L. Then, when you play the song, it will endlessly repeat until you either press the space bar again or turn off looping by pressing L for each track.

- *Mute/Solo*. You can solo either track by moving to the track and pressing S. Or you can mute the selected track by pressing M. In either case, pressing the appropriate key again will turn off muting or soloing.

You may want to close the book at this point and spend the next few minutes experimenting. When you're done poking around, a bad note awaits repair.

Fixing Bad Mary's Bad Note

If you are an adventurous person, you've probably spent more time trying out new sounds than you thought you would. But now it's time to find the bad note in the song.

First, it would be helpful to get an idea of the scope of the song. The easiest way to do that is to use the VIEW option from the main menu. When you press V, the View screen comes up, as shown in figure 7.11. In this screen, you can cut and paste songs by measure and begin recording new tracks in the middle of a song. The View menu options in the View screen are described later in this chapter.

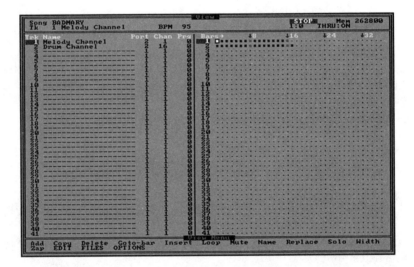

Fig. 7.11

The View screen.

The View screen differs from the Main screen in that the right side of the screen is replaced with a grid showing the bars in which each track is playing. A dot means that nothing was recorded for that bar. A box or square means that the bar contains notes or other MIDI data. A dash means that the bar was recorded, but no notes were struck (a measure of silence). If the rightmost character on the line is an arrow pointing to the right, this means that the track continues beyond the right side of the screen. Use the arrow keys to move back and forth on a track, or up and down between tracks. If the track is looped, an L shows as the last character on the recorded portion of the track.

As you can see in figure 7.11, track 1 plays all the way through the song to bar 16 (under the arrow). Track 2 plays in every bar, and for some reason, plays on into bar 17.

Press the space bar again to watch the song being played. When a bar is being played, one of the small squares is highlighted. When you stop playing, you will see that you can move the measure highlight between tracks and back and forth with either the mouse or the arrow keys, enabling you to select a specific bar for a specific track and make changes. Most of the changes you can make are listed in the menu area at the bottom of the screen and are described later in this chapter.

Play the song one more time, this time watching the Bar:Beat indicator in the upper-right corner. The sour note is played in the 7th bar of the song. Stop the song and move the highlight to the 7th bar in track 1. Now press E to switch to the Edit screen.

The Edit screen, displayed in figure 7.12, shows what is being played by track 1 in the 7th bar. Each of the horizontal lines represents a different note being played during the 7th bar. In the Edit screen, you can modify the note being played in a bar, as well as its starting time and length.

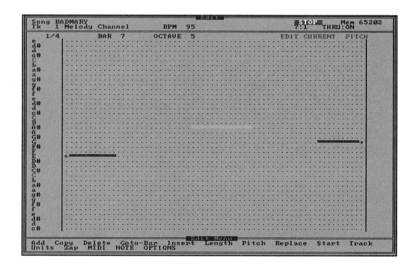

Fig. 7.12

The Edit screen.

Note that a blinking cursor shows up in the Edit screen, and you can move the cursor with the mouse or cursor-control keys. Be careful when using your mouse because SP Pro will sense horizontal motion and move your view to either the previous or next bar. SP Pro seems overly sensitive to mouse movement, some of which can be overcome by decreasing the sensitivity of your mouse. (Refer to the instructions that came with your mouse driver program to see whether you can reduce mouse sensitivity.)

Move the cursor to the horizontal bar in the middle of the screen. This is the culprit. An A♯ was played instead of the G that should have been played. You will notice that as the cursor touches the note line, the note itself sounds. Notice also that the note line changes color when touched by the cursor.

If you are using a mouse, move the cursor to the A♯ note bar until the bar changes colors; then press and hold down the left mouse button. Now you can drag the note bar up and down or left and right. As you drag the note bar up and down, you should hear the note change. Again, use caution when moving the note bar left and right with the mouse, or you will find yourself quickly in another measure of the song.

Drag the note bar down to the G line where it belongs, and with approximately the same start time. Release the mouse button and press the space key to begin playing the song at this bar. It should sound a little better now.

Stop play, and return to the 7th bar by moving the cursor to the left (watching the Bar:Beat indicator), or by pressing the G key and using the Goto-Bar menu option to move to bar 7.

Changing Note Length and Starting Time

In the Edit screen, you can change the length of a note by highlighting it and pressing L on the keyboard. Or you can click both the left and right mouse buttons to pull up the mouse menu, choose Length, and double-click.

The length of the note is changed in terms of the units set with the Units menu item. To make the note one unit shorter, press the minus (–) key. To make the note one unit longer, press the plus (+) key. In the case of Bad Mary, the Units are set to 16th beats; so to make the note 1/16 of a beat longer, press the plus key. To increase or decrease the time by four units, use the [and] keys. To change the note length by the smallest amount—a click—use the < and > keys.

You can adjust the starting time of a note by using the mouse or by selecting a note and then pressing S on the keyboard. You adjust the starting time upward or downward (sooner or later?) with the plus and minus keys, or by dragging the note horizontally with the mouse. Again, the adjustment is made in units, as set with the Units menu item. And as with the note length, you can use the [and] keys to change the start time by four units, or the < and > to change the time by clicks.

Now that you have fixed Mary's bad note, the next thing to do is look at bar 17 to see why it was recorded.

Deleting a Bar

Go back to the View screen by pressing the Esc key. Now move the highlight to the Drum Channel (track 2) and out to bar 17. Then press E to get back into the Edit screen.

What you should be seeing is a screen with no notes. This is what happens when you don't stop recording a song at precisely the same time you stop playing. SP Pro will continue to record even though you're not playing, and sometimes you will have empty bars left over at the end of a song. Because an empty bar takes up memory and disk space, you need to clean them up once in a while. Furthermore, if you loop a track—a rhythm track, for example—an empty bar will throw off your rhythm track.

Get back to the View screen by pressing Esc again. The highlight should still be on track 2's 17th bar. To delete the bar, press D. To quote a quasipopular figure of our time, "It's as simple as that."

Adding Your Own Track

Suppose for a moment that, although you are enamored of the song as it stands, you see some small possibility for improvement by adding your own track. You can do that, and here's how. For the following discussion, it is assumed that you have a MIDI keyboard attached to Sound Blaster. If you do not, you can insert notes from within the Edit screen, but it is neither easy nor convenient. Better yet, use the internal QWERTY Synth provided with SP Pro.

An internal MIDI keyboard is provided with SP Pro if you don't have one of your own. You can access this keyboard by pressing Shift-F1. A keyboard pops up on your screen, showing the PC keys that you can press to play specific notes. For example, middle C is the Q button on your keyboard. You are also given three options at the bottom of the keyboard window: change the octave of the keyboard from octave 1 (the lowest) to octave 7, change the duration of the note in units, and set the note velocity (how hard the note is struck) from a very soft 1 to a very hard 128. You change the values by highlighting the appropriate box and then pressing the plus or minus key. To get rid of the keyboard, press the Esc key.

If you are in the Edit or View screen, press Esc until you're back to the Main screen. Move the highlight anywhere within track 3. If you want, change the channel and program settings for track 3 so that you're adding a different instrument to the song.

Some musicians find it helpful to have a metronome going while they are playing, and to have someone do a lead-in, establishing the rhythm before playing. To start the metronome, you need to access the Options window by pressing O.

The Options window, shown in figure 7.13, lets you turn the metronome on and off and set the number of lead-in beats. In addition, you can adjust the time signature used in the song, decide whether benders or other MIDI controls can be included in the song, and set MIDI THRU to ON. All the options in the Options window are described in the next section.

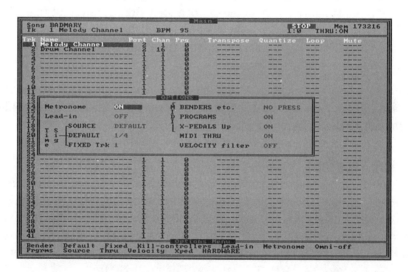

For the moment, all you need to do is turn on the metronome by positioning the highlight on the OFF indicator and then pressing the plus or minus key; either will work. Now move the highlight to the OFF indicator next to Lead-in. By pressing the plus key, you can select one of four lead-in options: 1 beat, 2 beats, 3 beats, or 4 beats. Press the plus key one more time, and the indicator goes back to OFF. Select a 4-beat lead-in and then press the Esc key. (The metronome and lead-in beats are sounded through your computer's speaker, not through the Sound Blaster system.) When you start playing or recording, a beginning beep will be sounded, followed by the four lead-in beeps.

Now you are ready to record. Recording is a two-step process. First, you must highlight the track you want to record on. Then you press R to indicate that you want to record a new track. You will see the word REC appear at the top of the screen. But you are not recording just yet. SP Pro waits until you press the space bar to begin recording. When you press the space bar, the lead-in beats will sound, playback will begin on the other two channels, and SP Pro will begin recording the new channel. Here is a recap of the steps:

1. Get ready.

2. Press R.

3. Press the space bar.

4. Position your hands over the keyboard.

5. Listen for the start beep followed by four lead-in beats.

6. Start playing!

If you make a mistake, just press the space bar to stop recording and then repeat the steps. You can record this track as many times as you like until you are satisfied. To play it back, press the space bar.

When you are satisfied, you need to save the new and improved song from the Files screen. Press F to open the Files screen. Then press S to save the file. You will be asked what you would like the file to be named. If you want to save the modified file with the current file name, just press Enter. If you want to rename the file (and I strongly suggest that you do), type a new file name and press Enter.

The Options Window

The Options window is used to set a number of SP Pro functions. You access this window by pressing O from the Main screen or pressing the F3 function key.

Refer again to figure 7.13. The left side of the Options window controls music timing, including the metronome. The right side of the window is used to set up the MIDI functions. The following items are in the Options window:

- *Metronome*. You can turn the metronome on and off by pressing the F2 key. Or you can call up the Options window and set Metronome to ON. To change the metronome setting, select Metronome with the arrow keys and press the plus or minus key. When set to ON, the metronome will sound a click every beat for the entire song.

- *Lead-in*. You use this field to sound a starting beep over the computer speaker, followed by a number of lead-in beeps before the song begins to play. The number of lead-in beeps can be set from 1 to 4. Lead-in beeps are most useful during the recording of a new track, giving the musician an opportunity to establish rhythm.

- *Time Sig*. The three time signature options—SOURCE, DEFAULT, and FIXED Trk—have to do with the timing applied to the song.

    SOURCE offers four possible sources of timing information:

    > CUR TRK—Uses the currently selected track's time signature.

    > FX TRK—Uses the track named in the Options window's FIXED Trk field for the song.

    > DEFAULT—Uses the value in the Options window's Time Sig DEFAULT field.

    > SMART—Lets SP Pro select the time signature from either the longest track or the currently selected track during playback. During record, SP Pro uses either the longest track or the setting in the DEFAULT field.

    You set the DEFAULT field to signatures in the following ranges: 1/2-8/2, 1/4-21/4, 1/8-32/8, and 1/16-32/16.

    You set the FIXED Trk field to any valid track number.

- *BENDERS*. You use this field to select what kind of MIDI events will be recorded. Recording controller and aftertouch data consumes file space. To record all MIDI events, set this field to RECORDED. To record all MIDI events except aftertouch, set this field to NO PRESS. To record only notes, program changes, and switch data, set this field to IGNORED.

- *PROGRAMS*. This field determines whether SP Pro allows a small amount of setup time for the MIDI instruments on-line to change their program numbers. When this field is set to ON, SP Pro delays the song slightly. When the field is set to OFF, all program changes are disabled (not transmitted), and the song begins the instant the space bar is pressed. When the field is set to DYNAMIC, only program changes embedded in the song are transmitted. The initial program changes are not transmitted.

- *X-PEDALS*. This field is used at the end of a song to either release damper pedals and reset pitch bend to 0 (ON), or to maintain the position of the damper pedal and pitch bend (OFF).

- *MIDI THRU*. This field turns MIDI THRU ON or OFF.

- *VELOCITY*. When this field is set to ON, SP Pro ignores all key velocity information from the instrument keyboard and sets velocity to the maximum value of 127. When this field is set to OFF, the velocity information is recorded.

In addition to the fields you can set within the Options window, a new menu is visible at the bottom of the screen, giving you control over several additional functions. All the fields described in the preceding list can also be set from this menu. Three additional options are available:

- *Kill-controllers*. You use this option to reset all the controllers in the MIDI network. You should use Kill-controllers only as a sort of "panic switch" when individual controllers get stuck. This option resets all controllers to zero and sets the master volume to 127.

- *Omni-off*. This option sends an Omni-off signal to all MIDI instruments, instructing them to respond only to the MIDI channel to which they are set, rather than to all channels.

- *HARDWARE*. This menu item brings up an additional window, used to report hardware information (see fig. 7.14).

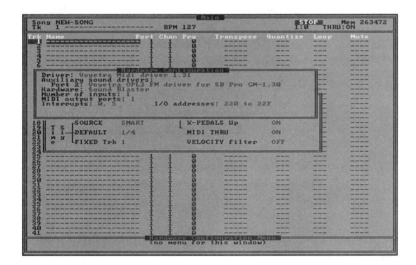

The Hardware Configuration window.

You use the Hardware Configuration window to report SP Pro's hardware configuration. When SP Pro is started, it examines the Sound Blaster hardware and stores that information as well as the version numbers of the software and firmware used to drive the hardware. All this information is reported in the Hardware Configuration window.

The View Screen and View Menu

The View screen, shown in figure 7.15, is very useful in getting a quick summary of which tracks play when. In addition, you can quickly move to a specific bar and track and then switch to the Edit screen to make modifications to the track. You reach the View screen by pressing V from the Main screen.

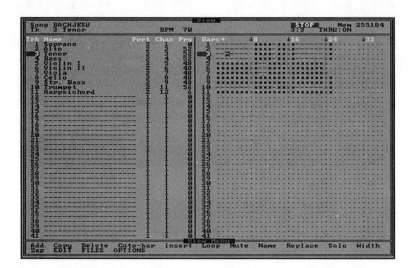

A set of characters, used on the right side of the screen, indicate the following:

A dot	Unrecorded bar
A box	Recorded bar containing MIDI notes and data
A dash	Recorded bar containing no MIDI data (silence)
M	Muted track
L	Looped track
Arrows	Track continued beyond the screen

In figure 7.15, for example, you can see that track 3 is recorded for the first 8 bars but doesn't actually play until the 9th bar. Likewise, the viola in track 7 is silent during bars 10 and 11. Track 12 was not recorded and consists entirely of dots.

Had any tracks in figure 7.15 been looped or muted, you would see an uppercase L or M following the last bar recorded for that track. Had any tracks run beyond the screen area to the right, a small arrow pointing to the right would be visible on the right edge of the screen.

You can move around in the song with the cursor-control keys or the mouse. The following movement commands are also available:

Home	Scrolls one screen to the left
End	Scrolls one screen to the right
Ctrl-Home	Jumps to the beginning of a track
Ctrl-End	Jumps to the end of a track
PgUp	Scrolls one screen up
PgDn	Scrolls one screen down
Ctrl-PgUp	Jumps to first track
Ctrl-PgDn	Jumps to last track

The menu items at the bottom of the View screen provide various functions. Many of these functions make use of SP Pro's three memory buffers. The buffer names are Temp, 0, and 1. You can use one buffer or all three at will. The following View menu options are available to modify the selected track:

Add	Inserts a number of blank bars into the current location. When you choose this menu item, you are prompted for the number of bars to be inserted. In addition, you can specify the time signature of the added bars.
Copy	Copies a range of bars into memory. You can use the Insert or Replace options to insert the bars into another part of the song. When you select this option, you are asked to provide the first and last bar numbers to be copied.
Delete	Deletes a range of bars. When you press D, you are prompted for the numbers of the first and last bars to be deleted. The deleted bars are placed into a memory buffer, and the bars to the right of the last bar deleted are shifted left. To delete a single bar without storing it in memory, press the Delete key on your computer keyboard.
Goto-bar	Jumps to a specific bar on the current track. You will be prompted to enter the bar number.

Insert	Inserts the contents of the memory buffer into the location pointed to by the cursor. When you insert buffer contents, all the bars to the right of the insertion point are shifted further to the right. To insert an empty bar into the current location, press the Insert key on your computer keyboard.
Loop	Inserts a loop command at the current bar and track.
Mute	Inserts a mute command at the current bar and track. To remove the mute, press the M key again.
Name	Names a recorded track. Tracks that have not been recorded cannot be named.
Replace	Replaces a range of bars with the contents of the memory buffer. The bars that are replaced are lost.
Solo	Inserts a solo command at the current bar and track.
Width	Expands the right side of the View screen to take up the entire screen, covering the track number, name, port, channel, and program information.
Zap	Copies a range of bars into a memory buffer. This command leaves behind empty measures. You are prompted for the number of the first and last bars to be zapped. Bars that are zapped into a buffer can be inserted elsewhere in the same track or another track with the Insert command.

The EDIT, FILES, and OPTIONS menu items were described earlier in this chapter.

The Edit Screen and Edit Menu

SP Pro's Edit screen has two additional variations: the MIDI Edit screen and the Note Edit screen. Both variations are discussed later in this chapter.

The Edit screen in figure 7.16 shows track 5, bar 1 of the song. Because the measure is 4/4, you can see the four beats of the measure marked by the heavy vertical lines, and the instrument is playing approximately a half note, a quarter note, and an eighth note.

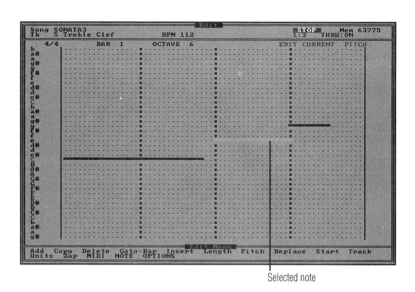

Fig. 7.16

The Edit screen
showing track 5,
bar 1 of a song.

Selected note

When a particular note is selected, it changes color, as indicated in the third
beat of this bar. After a note is selected, you can perform the following
functions. You will be prompted for information on the beginning and ending
bars in those cases where you are changing a range of bars:

Add	Inserts one or more blank bars before or after the current bar.
Copy	Copies a range of bars into the memory buffer.
Delete	Deletes a range of bars and places them in the memory buffer. Bars to the right of the deleted bars are shifted to the left.
Goto-Bar	Jumps to a selected bar number.
Insert	Inserts the contents of a memory buffer just before the current bar. Moves the existing bars to the right of the insertion point.
Length	Sets the length of the selected note. Use the following keys to adjust the note length:

	+ or −	Adjusts the length of the note by one time unit, as set with the Units menu item.
	[or]	Adjusts the length of the note by four time units.

	< or > Adjusts the length of the note by a single click. A click is 1/192 of a quarter note.
Pitch	Changes the pitch of a selected note. Use the + or – key to change the note up or down by a semitone. Use the [and] keys to move the note an octave at a time.
Replace	Replaces the current measure or measures with the contents of a memory buffer. The original notes are erased.
Start	Adjusts the starting time of a selected note. To adjust the starting time, use the following keys:

+ or –	Adjusts the starting time of the note by one time unit, as set with the Units menu item.
[or]	Adjusts the starting time of the note by four time units.
< or >	Adjusts the starting time of the note by a single click. A click is 1/192 of a quarter note.

Track	Jumps to the same bar in another track.
Units	Sets the time unit for cursor movement and note editing (see table 7.1).
Zap	Copies a range of bars into a memory buffer, leaving behind empty measures.
MIDI	Accesses the MIDI Edit screen.
NOTE	Accesses the Note Edit screen.
OPTIONS	Opens the Options window and Options menu.

The time units available for cursor movement and note editing are shown in table 7.1.

Table 7.1 The Edit Menu Time Units

Unit	Normal	Triplets
Quarter notes	4	4T
Eighth notes	8	8T
Sixteenth notes	16	16T
Thirty-second notes	32	32T
Sixty-fourth notes	64	64T
Single clicks	HIGH	N/A

The MIDI Edit Screen

As you learned in the preceding chapter, MIDI songs can be much more than just a sequence of notes. Because of the flexibility of MIDI, you can add interesting features to notes, such as pitch bending, adjusting a controller (a modulation wheel, for example), or changing the program number of a track partway through.

The MIDI Edit screen, shown in figure 7.17, enables you to add MIDI-specific effects to a song. You enable the MIDI Edit screen from the regular Edit screen by pressing the M key. There are several differences between the MIDI Edit screen and the normal Edit screen. One difference is the addition of a MIDI Line running along the bottom of the screen. The MIDI Line, labeled ML:, is used to display MIDI events. Another difference is the addition of a MIDI EVENT box just below the status area. The MIDI EVENT box shows you what events are being edited.

One seemingly peculiar thing about the MIDI Edit screen is that, although you can see the notes for the current track, you cannot edit the notes from within the MIDI Edit screen. That's because you use the MIDI Edit screen to add or change non-note data. Therefore, all the MIDI events you add to a song are shown only on the ML: line.

Table 7.2 shows the six possible MIDI events, referred to as *classes*, that can be placed on the ML: line. You choose classes by pressing the C key for Class and then cycling through the options by pressing the plus or minus key.

Fig. 7.17

The MIDI Edit
screen.

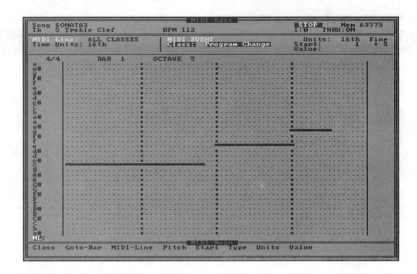

Table 7.2 MIDI Events (Classes)

Symbol	MIDI Event	Function
P:	Program Change	This event changes the program number for this track. By using the P: event, you can change the voice played by a track at any point during the song.
A:	Aftertouch	This event, also referred to as channel pressure, changes the keyboard pressure used during monophonic playback.
B:	Bender	This event allows you to add pitch bending.
T:	Tempo	This event lets you embed tempo changes within a track, even though SP Pro does not support embedded tempo changes.
K:	Key Aftertouch	This event changes the keyboard pressure for each note in a polyphonic playback.

Symbol	MIDI Event	Function
C:	Controller	Controller events are managed by the controller type. SP Pro supports 22 controller types (see table 7.3).

Table 7.3 lists the MIDI controller types that SP Pro recognizes.

Table 7.3 MIDI Controller Types

Number	Name	Possible Values
1	Mod Wheel	0-127
2	Breath	0-127
4	Foot Pedal	0-127
5	Portamento Time	0-127
6	Data Slider	0-127
7	Main Volume	0-127
8	Continuous Release	0-127
9	Parameter Number	0-127
10	Pan Position	0-127
64	Damper Switch	0 = Off, 127 = On
65	Portamento Switch	0 = Off, 127 = On
66	Sustenuto Switch	0 = Off, 127 = On
67	Soft Switch	0 = Off, 127 = On
68	2nd Release Switch	0 = Off, 127 = On
96	Data Plus	0 = Off, 127 = On
97	Data Minus	0 = Off, 127 = On
122	Local Control	0 = Off, 127 = On
123	All Notes Off	Normally 0

continues

Table 7.3 Continued

Number	Name	Possible Values
124	OMNI Mode Off	Normally 0
125	OMNI Mode On	Normally 0
126	Mono Mode On	0 (all voices to mono)
127	Poly Mode On	Normally 0

The MIDI EVENT box displays which MIDI event class is being edited and the current event's parameters. The following information is contained in the EVENT box:

Class   The event class, as listed in table 7.2.

Type   The controller type, shown only when the event class is set to Controller.

Pitch   The pitch value assigned to Key Aftertouch.

Units   The time units, as set with the Units menu item on the MIDI Edit menu.

Start   The starting time, in current units, of the current MIDI event.

Value   The value of the current MIDI event.

To insert a MIDI event in a song, select the appropriate event class (and the type, if necessary), move the event cursor to the point at which you want the insertion, and press the Insert key on your keyboard. To delete an existing event, highlight the event and press the Delete key. To modify the event, select it and then change the appropriate values at the top of the screen. You change values by entering the first letter of the value you want to change (for example, S for Start) and then using the plus and minus keys to scroll through the possible values.

The following menu items are available at the bottom of the MIDI Edit screen:

Class   Highlights the Class item at the top of the screen. Select the type of MIDI event you want by scrolling through the possible classes with the plus or minus key.

Goto-Bar   Jumps to a new bar within the current track.

MIDI-Line   Displays either one class or all classes of events on the MIDI line.

Pitch	Used with the Key Aftertouch event.
Start	Sets the starting time of a selected MIDI event.
Type	Selects which controller type is to be used (the Controller class must be selected).
Units	Controls cursor movement as described previously in the discussion of the Edit screen.
Value	Sets the value for the MIDI event.

Some of the events you can insert into MIDI songs may not be played by the Sound Blaster synthesizer but are passed on to any external MIDI units that may be capable of playing them. A stereo pan from left to right cannot be played on a standard monaural Sound Blaster. Sound Blaster and Sound Blaster Pro do not support embedded tempo changes. Although the events can be edited, they will not affect the tempo of a song played on Sound Blaster.

The Note Edit Screen

The Note Edit screen gives you extended capabilities to edit song notes (see fig. 7.18). In this screen, you can adjust note pitch, on and off velocity, and starting time. You access the Notes Edit screen by pressing N from the Edit screen.

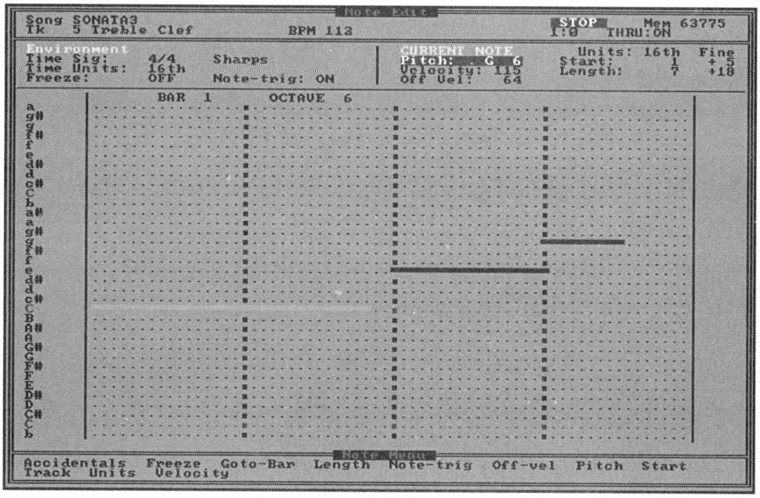

Fig. 7.18

The Note Edit screen.

The Note Edit screen displays an additional information box just below the status area. The information is divided into two areas: Environment and CURRENT NOTE.

The following data is provided in the Environment area:

Time Sig	Shows the time signature of the current bar.
Time Units	Shows the current time unit as set within the Edit screen.
Freeze	Displays the current setting of the Freeze menu item, which keeps the current pitch range visible at all times.
Note-trig	Displays the current setting of the Note-trig menu item. When Note-trig is set to ON, each note plays when it is highlighted.

The CURRENT NOTE area actually displays two kinds of information. If you have a note highlighted, it displays information about that note. If you do not have a note highlighted, however, you can use this area to create note information that is stored in an Insert Note buffer. When note information exists in this buffer, you can move the cursor to an appropriate location and then press the Insert key to insert the note into the song.

The following information is provided in the CURRENT NOTE area:

Pitch	Displays the note as a note letter followed by an octave number. If the Accidentals menu item is set to Numbers, pitch is displayed as a MIDI note number.
Velocity	Displays the note's velocity as a value ranging from 0 to 127.
Off Vel	Displays the note's off-velocity as a value ranging from 0 to 127.
Units	Displays the note's incremental time units, as set by the Units menu item on the Edit screen.
Start	Displays the note's starting time in units/clicks.
Length	Displays the note's length in units/clicks.

At the bottom of the Note Edit screen are the following Note Edit menu options:

Accidentals	Lets you select one of four possible note displays on the left side of the screen. The options are piano keyboard, sharps, flats, and MIDI note numbers. Press the A key to cycle through the options.
Freeze	When ON, shows the current pitch range when moving from bar to bar. When OFF, shows the range of notes in the current bar. You set this option to ON or OFF by pressing F.
Goto-Bar	Jumps to the specified bar number.
Length	Adjusts the currently selected note's length.
Note-trig	When ON, plays each note as it is highlighted.
Off-Vel	Adjusts the off-velocity for a note, in values ranging from 0 to 127.
Pitch	Sets the pitch for the note.
Start	Selects the starting time for the highlighted note. Two values are associated with the starting time. Under the Fine heading, the value is given in clicks, where each click is 1/197 of a quarter note. In figure 7.18, for example, the starting time is at the first 16th note plus 5 clicks. Clicks can be entered as either positive or negative numbers.
Track	Jumps to the same measure in a different track.
Units	Selects the time unit increment in which the cursor moves.
Velocity	Sets the current note's on-velocity, in values ranging from 0 to 127.

CHAPTER 8

Cakewalk Apprentice for Windows

Cakewalk Apprentice for Windows is the MIDI sequencer that has been shipped with the Creative Labs MIDI Kit and Wave Blaster since early in 1993. This chapter describes how to use Cakewalk Apprentice to create new MIDI files and edit existing MIDI files.

MIDI sequencers are programs that enable you to build a sequence of instructions for MIDI instruments. In the case of Cakewalk, you can send instructions to the Sound Blaster synthesizer (which can serve as a MIDI instrument), to an external MIDI instrument connected to Sound Blaster's MIDI connector, or to both. Cakewalk Apprentice for the Sound Blaster 16 and 16 ASP has the added capability of being able to embed Windows WAV files into a MIDI song. Although that capability is not currently available for Sound Blaster Pro or Sound Blaster V2.0, a new driver program is being developed that will allow this additional capability. In all other respects, Cakewalk Apprentice works on all current Sound Blaster products as described in the following pages.

Cakewalk Apprentice is a slightly reduced version of the popular Cakewalk Pro for Windows sequencer offered by Twelve Tone Systems, Inc. Cakewalk Apprentice is based on Version 1.0 of the Pro. At this printing, Twelve Tone Systems is about to release V2.0 of Cakewalk Pro.

I have always been a firm believer that the quickest way to learn how any computer software works is by playing with it. And I use "playing" in the literal sense. Have some fun! If what you're trying to do doesn't work right the first time, so what? Poke around in dark corners. Experiment. See what happens when you change things. You will learn faster and enjoy it too.

The Basic Song-Building Process

Typically, the process of building a song with a MIDI sequencer includes these basic steps:

1. Connect whatever MIDI equipment you are going to use as a note source. In other words, if you have a MIDI keyboard, connect the keyboard to Sound Blaster with the MIDI cables. If you do not have a MIDI keyboard, you can use SP Pro's internal synthesizer, which simulates a keyboard on your computer.

2. Select a tempo that works for your particular song and then turn on the metronome so that you can hear the beat.

3. Record the first track of the song. The first track can be the percussion, melody line, or background—it's entirely up to you. It can be as simple as a bass drum beating once every click of the metronome or, if you're an agile keyboardist, a syncopated background rhythm that will amaze your friends.

4. Record the 2nd, 3rd, or 17th track.

5. Go back and edit the whole song or edit individual tracks until you are happy with the way the song sounds. You can delete tracks, change the key of different tracks, and even change the instrument that plays on each track.

6. Save the song on disk. Actually, you will want to save the song several times throughout its development, or even different versions of the song.

The easy thing about MIDI recording is that the MIDI source you are using, whether it is an external MIDI keyboard or SP Pro's internal synthesizer, is capable of being an entire orchestra. To lay down a single bass drum track, for example, all you need to do is start the SP Pro recording and then press any key on the keyboard once for every click of the metronome. But, you say, that sounds like a piano! Yes, it does. However, because MIDI instruments are programmable, any instrument in the entire MIDI repertoire is available to you. You can change the programming so that the key you pressed sounds like a bass drum—or a glockenspiel, if you prefer.

When you're ready to lay down the second track, you have a choice of 128 different instruments to play, all from your MIDI keyboard.

Cakewalk Apprentice Installation

Cakewalk Apprentice is a Windows-based MIDI sequencer. Because it is a Windows application, it must be installed from Windows as instructed in the product documentation. Place the disk in the appropriate disk drive and then run the program SETUP.EXE from either Windows File Manager or the Control menu in the upper-left corner of any window.

One other part of the Windows environment that must be checked is the Windows MIDI Mapper in the Control Panel. Check that the MIDI Mapper is set to All FM, as shown in figure 8.1.

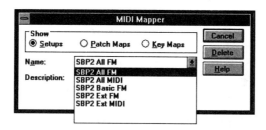

Fig. 8.1

The Windows MIDI Mapper must be set to All FM in order for Cakewalk Apprentice to work properly.

If you have the MIDI Mapper set to any of the MIDI options, Cakewalk will complain that the Microsoft MIDI Mapper is already in use.

Cakewalk Overview

Cakewalk opens with the main window shown in figure 8.2. From here, you record or load MIDI files and edit them, adding tracks and MIDI musical effects. Your screen is initially divided into the following areas:

Menu bar	The menu bar contains the pull-down menus used with Cakewalk. You access these menus by clicking with your mouse pointer, or by holding down the Alt key and pressing the underlined letter in the menu you want to pull down.

Control bar

The control bar contains timing information on the current song, as well as the record/playback control panel, and a gruesome-looking Panic button on the far right. The control bar functions are described a little later in this chapter. You can relocate the control bar to the bottom of the main window if you like.

Track/Measure

Cakewalk Apprentice has a number of windows, called *views*, that can be opened to show music data in a number of ways. The Track/Measure view provides detail on specific tracks in the song; this view is divided into two subwindows: the left window shows track detail that is described later, and the right window displays the measures that contain either music or MIDI instructions. For example, if a note were recorded on track 1 in measure 5 in figure 8.2, the square just below the 5 would be dark.

Fig. 8.2

The Cakewalk Apprentice main window showing the default Track/ Measure view.

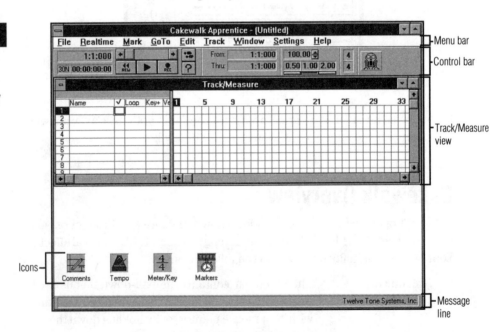

Icons

Several other windows are minimized and displayed near the bottom of the main window. Each of these is described later in this chapter.

Message line   The message line is at the bottom of the screen and is used to display any system messages that may appear.

Each of these items is discussed in greater detail later in this chapter. But first, you need to understand how Cakewalk views MIDI music.

Views

A MIDI song consists of many different elements: details about when a note is played on which track, how long the note lasts, how hard it is struck, whether its pitch is shifted while the note is being played (pitch bending), and so on. As a MIDI musician, you have to be interested in more than just the notes themselves. For example, sometimes you want to look at a MIDI song in terms of a musical staff, so you want to see the music as it would exist on a piece of sheet music. Sometimes you're interested in examining the MIDI events—the sequence of instructions passed to the MIDI instrument. Or you might want to see what's going on with just the MIDI controller effects.

Because of the different needs of a MIDI musician, Cakewalk Apprentice lets you look at your song in four different ways. You choose each view from the Window menu, as shown in figure 8.3.

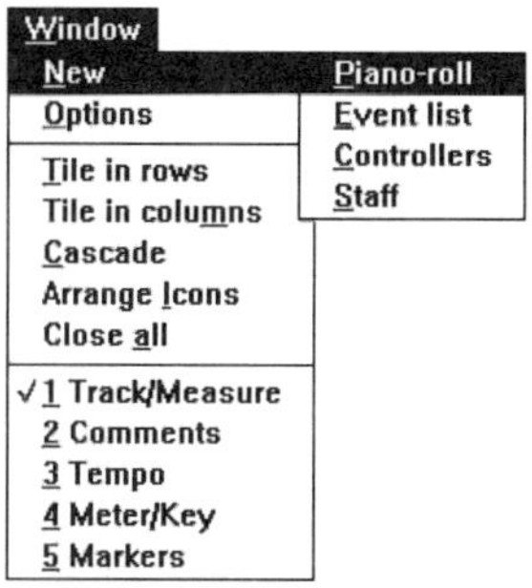

Fig. 8.3

Using the **Window New** command to choose a new view.

To examine a track using one of the views, you can point to the track number and then click the right mouse button. This opens a view selection box, and you can choose a new view for that track. Each of the views is described in the following paragraphs.

Track/Measure View

The Track/Measure view is the default view and appears whenever you start Cakewalk Apprentice. This view enables you to set the MIDI parameters for up to 256 different tracks, which can be thought of as the equivalent to the different tracks on a tape recorder. Figure 8.4 shows the Track/Measure view when a MIDI song is loaded into Cakewalk Apprentice. The Track/Measure view contains two window panes: the Track pane and the Measure pane.

Fig. 8.4

The Track/ Measure view.

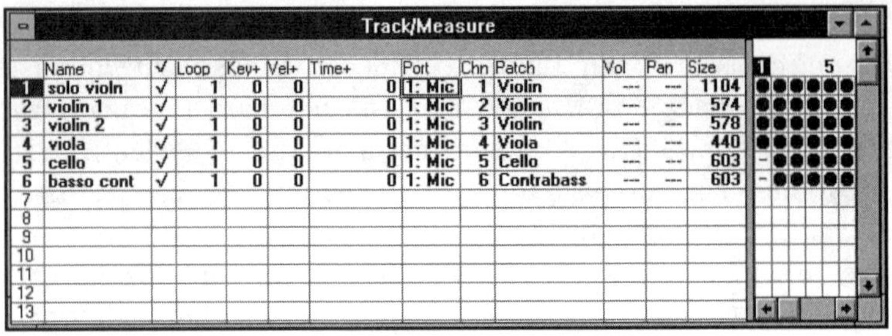

	Name	✓	Loop	Key+	Vel+	Time+	Port	Chn	Patch	Vol	Pan	Size		5
1	solo violn	✓	1	0	0	0	1: Mic	1	Violin	---	---	1104		
2	violin 1	✓	1	0	0	0	1: Mic	2	Violin	---	---	574		
3	violin 2	✓	1	0	0	0	1: Mic	3	Violin	---	---	578		
4	viola	✓	1	0	0	0	1: Mic	4	Viola	---	---	440		
5	cello	✓	1	0	0	0	1: Mic	5	Cello	---	---	603		
6	basso cont	✓	1	0	0	0	1: Mic	6	Contrabass	---	---	603		
7														
8														
9														
10														
11														
12														
13														

Track Pane

The left pane, called the Track pane, controls the parameters for up to 256 different tracks. The Track pane is organized like a spreadsheet, with each row representing a track, and the columns representing the parameters for that track. You can change the values inside each cell of the Track pane in a number of ways. You can point to the cell and select it by clicking the left mouse button once, entering a new value, and pressing Enter. Or you can point to the cell, and while holding down the left mouse button, move your mouse backward and forward. As you move the mouse, you will see all the possible values being scrolled back and forth within the cell. If your mouse is like mine, it is a bit too sensitive, and scrolling happens too quickly. If that is the case, you can usually adjust mouse sensitivity with the mouse driver either from DOS or from the Windows Control Panel. You can adjust the width of the track pane by pointing to the border between the two panes and, while holding down the left mouse button, dragging the border left or right.

You can control the following MIDI parameters from the Track pane:

Name   Each track is assigned a name of your choosing, up to 128 characters long, which means that you have enough space in the name cell to type a short description as well as the name. To enter a name in a cell, point to the cell, double-click the left mouse button, and begin typing.

✓   The status cell is used to indicate whether the track can be played (✓), is muted (m), or is archived (a). Cakewalk Apprentice allows you to temporarily silence selected tracks by muting them. To mute a specific track either before or during playback, simply point to the status cell for that track and click the left mouse button once. This action toggles playback from play (✓) to mute (m) and back again.

If a track is muted, Cakewalk still reads the MIDI data in the track, because you might decide to have a muted track play at any time. There is the chance of a performance penalty if you have a song with a lot of muted tracks. You can instruct Cakewalk to ignore a track completely by *archiving* the track, thus freeing up the computer time required to read the MIDI data in a track. Archiving simply instructs Cakewalk to ignore the track data during playback. An archive track will be loaded into Cakewalk and saved back to a file at the end of the session, but will not be played during playback unless you unarchive the track. To archive a track, select the status cell for the appropriate track and choose the **T**rack **A**rchive option.

Loop   The loop function is particularly useful in laying down rhythm tracks, or any other kind of repeating background sound. When you loop a track, Cakewalk will play to the end of the track and then go back to the beginning and play it again. Cakewalk allows you to set a loop number for each track. When loop = 1, the track is played once. When loop = 5, the track is played five times during playback. You can set the track to loop to a maximum of 9,998 times. If you want a track to loop until all the other tracks are done playing, set the loop value to 9999. To set the loop value, highlight the Loop cell for the appropriate track, type a new value, and press Enter.

Key+   Each note in a MIDI file is assigned a key number, or pitch. You can use the Key+ cell to temporarily alter the pitch of a note during playback by transposing it to a higher or lower pitch. Key+ enables you to shift the pitch of a particular track up or down by 127 semitones. For example, if you want to shift track 3, the second violin, upward by an octave, you highlight the Key+ cell for track 3 and then enter **12** (remember that an octave is made up of 12 semitones or half steps). To shift the track down an octave, enter **-12** (minus 12).

If you want to transpose a track permanently, you can edit the individual notes from the Piano-Roll or Staff view, or you can use the **E**dit Tra**n**spose option from the menu bar, which is described later in this chapter.

Vel+

Higher-quality MIDI keyboards have the capability to capture how hard a key is hit during a recording session, by measuring how fast the key is moving—its velocity—when it is struck. Each note in a MIDI song can have a velocity value attached to it. The Track/Measure view lets you adjust the velocity up and down during playback. A higher velocity means that the note is sounded as if the key were struck quickly, resulting in a loud initial sound. A lower velocity means that the note is sounded as though the key were pressed lightly, making a gentler sound. If you set the value of Vel+ to a higher number, velocity increases. A lower number means a lower velocity.

As with the Key+ value, velocity changes made in the Track pane are effective only during playback. To make permanent velocity changes, use the Piano-Roll or Event List view, both of which are described later in this chapter.

Time+

The Time+ cell enables you to start track playback earlier or later by "sliding" the track back and forth in time. The smallest value in the Time+ cell is a *tick*, and there are 120 ticks (0 through 119) in each beat. Time is entered here, and shown in the control bar, as three numbers separated by a colon, as in 2:3:050, which means 50 ticks into the third beat of the second measure. If, for example, you want to slide the beginning of a track out so that it starts at the third beat of the fourth measure, you enter **4:3:000** in the Time+ cell.

The Time+ cell can be used to delay the start of a looped track by a number of measures, beats, or ticks. For example, if you want to delay the start of a looping track for 4 measures, enter **4:1:000** in the Time+ cell and enter the number of loops you want played in the Loop cell. The starting delay will occur in only the first pass through the track. On the second and succeeding loops, the start delay is ignored.

You can set the next five columns (Port, Channel, Patch, Volume, and Pan) individually by selecting the cell and entering a new value; or by pointing to the cell with the mouse and, while holding down the left button, scrolling back and forth through the options. An alternative is to double-click any of the cells, which brings up the Track Parameters dialog box (see fig. 8.5).

The Track Parameters dialog box.

As you can see in figure 8.5, the Track Parameters dialog box also lets you set the Key+ and Vel+ values, which were just described. One of the most useful aspects of the Track Parameters dialog box is that you can call it up during playback and change any of the track parameters as the song is being played, listening to the effect of the change as it happens. If you like the change, click OK; the change will be saved, and the Track/Measure window reappears.

You can control the following additional MIDI parameters from the Track pane or the Track Parameters dialog box:

Port   This cell or *spin button* is used to select where you want a specific track to be played. In figure 8.5, for example, all the tracks are going to be played on port 1, the Microsoft MIDI Mapper, which is configured to use the Sound Blaster synthesizer as a MIDI instrument. What ports are available depends on which MIDI instrument drivers you have installed in your system, as well as the **S**ettings MIDI De**v**ices option in the menu bar.

In the setup used to write this book, I have Sound Blaster, of course, and a Casio MT-640 keyboard attached to the Sound Blaster MIDI port. The Windows MIDI Mapper is set up to use Sound Blaster as its MIDI instrument and is configured as SBPRO All FM. With this setup, I have two places where I can play MIDI music: on Sound Blaster itself as port 1 and on my Casio as port 2. You can select the output port by pointing to the Port cell and, while holding down the left mouse button, pushing your mouse back and forth to scroll through the options. Or you can double-click the Port cell, causing the Track Parameters dialog box to pop up, as shown in figure 8.5.

Chn

The Channel value is the specific MIDI channel on which you want the track played. You have the option of playing a track on any of the 16 channels available, as long as the MIDI instrument recognizes the selected channel. Sound Blaster can recognize all 16 channels. See Chapter 6 for a discussion of MIDI channels.

Patch

The Patch value is one of 128 different instrument sounds, or voices, that are available with general MIDI instruments such as Sound Blaster. The Patch names will vary slightly from vendor to vendor, but you can be fairly well assured that if you assign a violin patch to a track, it will sound like a violin on most MIDI-compliant instruments. See Chapter 6 for a discussion about MIDI patches.

Vol

The Vol setting is used to send a MIDI volume event to the MIDI instrument when song playback begins. A volume event sets the average starting volume for the track. MIDI songs can contain volume events within a track, but not all MIDI instruments respond to volume messages. Sound Blaster Pro and 16/16 ASP will respond, as will the Wave Blaster. Sound Blaster V2.0 will not, however. Nor will my Casio MT-640, which is not truly MIDI-compliant. If you decide to set the starting volume, you must also make sure that the track has its own assigned channel number so that the sequencer can issue the volume message to the correct channel.

Pan You use the Pan parameter when you're going to shift the stereo balance from left to right (or vice versa) during playback, using a MIDI pan event. Like the Vol setting, not all MIDI instruments respond to pan messages. The Pan parameter can be set from –1 (off) to 127. A value of 0 is full left, and a value of 127 is full right. Values from 1 to 126 are between full left and full right.

In addition to setting these track parameters in the Track Parameters dialog box, you can use the **C**onfigure button to select one of several preset patch tables for a number of instruments, as shown in figure 8.6.

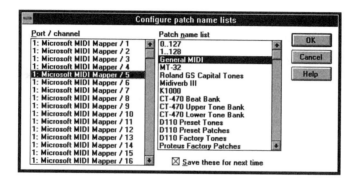

Fig. 8.6

The Configure Patch Name Lists dialog box.

On the left of this configuration box is a list of all the ports and channels that are currently active. On the right is a list of all the patch presets that come with Cakewalk Apprentice. Some MIDI instruments number their patches starting with 0 and going through 127, and others start with 1 and go through 128. The general MIDI patch list is shown in Chapter 6. And each of the MIDI instruments in the rest of the list has its own special patch list. For a description of patch lists and patch mapping, see Chapter 6.

In brief, a lot of MIDI instruments don't use the general MIDI patch number list. For example, in the general MIDI patch list, voice 40 is a violin. The MT-32 synthesizer, however, recognizes patch number 40 as an Echo Bell, while the Proteus synthesizer thinks patch 40 is a "Mythical Pad," and the Casio CT-470 will make an electric guitar sound. The **C**onfigure button in the Track Parameters dialog box lets you automatically assign the correct patch list to a specific port or channel. If, for example, I had a CT-470 attached to the Sound Blaster MIDI port, I could assign the CT-470's patch name list to that port so that when I scrolled through the patch list in the Track Parameters dialog box, I would see sound names appropriate to the CT-470.

Measure Pane

The right pane in the Track/Measure window is the Measure pane. You can widen the Measure pane to cover the width of the window by pointing to the dividing line between the two panes and, while holding down the left mouse button, dragging the edge of the pane to the left. Release the mouse button when you have the Measure pane as wide as you like.

You use the Measure pane to indicate which tracks contain MIDI information at what times during the song. Look at figure 8.7, which is a widened Measure pane of the Bach song, which is included on one of the shareware disks at the back of this book.

Fig. 8.7

The Measure pane showing which measures contain MIDI information for every track.

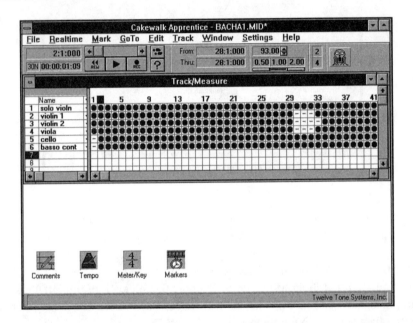

In the now-narrow Track pane, you can see the track number and name. Across the top of the Measure pane, you see a row of numbers that indicates measures in the song: measure 1, measure 5, measure 9, and so on. Each measure in the song is given a cell. This particular song has 172 measures. If a particular track is sending MIDI messages—a note to be played or a velocity change message, for example—the corresponding cell contains a black circle. If a track is not issuing MIDI messages at the moment but will in a later measure, the cell has a dash (-) in it. If no MIDI information is recorded on a track, the cell is empty.

In figure 8.7, you can see that tracks 1 through 4 begin playing immediately, but the cello and basso contra tracks don't begin playing until the second measure of the song. Later on, in measures 30 through 32, the first and second violins are silent, as is the viola. In fact, the second violin sits out measure 33 as well.

Notice on the left side of the control bar in figure 8.7 that the number 2:1:000 appears. This is the Now Time indicator, which reflects the position of a dark square at the top of the Measure pane. The Now Time is the current time in the song. The Bach piece has 172 measures, and the Now Time marker is positioned at the beginning of the second measure of the song. If you rewind the song and play it from the beginning, you will see the Now Time indicator showing the current measure, beat, and tick in the song as it is being played. In addition, you will see the Now Time marker in the Measure pane moving along as the song is being played, and the Measure pane scrolling from right to left. You can drag the Now Time marker to any measure in the song and begin playback from that point. To drag the marker, point to it with your mouse and, while holding down the left mouse button, drag the marker left or right.

Two other numbers of interest in the control bar are the From: indicator and the Thru: indicator. You use these two indicators when you are selecting specific measures to edit.

The Measure pane is useful for performing large edits on a song. While in the Measure pane, for example, you can copy specific measures from one track and place them in a new track, or insert them in an existing track. As an exercise, copy measures 1 through 12 of track 5, the cello track, into a new track. Begin by selecting track 5. Using the cursor keys on your keyboard, move the highlight indicator up or down until track 5 is highlighted (indicated by a blue background). Now you can select measures 1 through 12 by pointing to the measure 1 cell, holding down the left mouse button, and dragging the mouse pointer to the right until the measure 12 cell is highlighted. Now release the mouse button.

Notice that when you have a range of measures selected, the From: and Thru: indicators in the control bar show you that you have selected from measure 1:1:000 through measure 12:2:119. Now that you have the 12 measures selected, point to measure 1 with the mouse again and hold down the left mouse button. The mouse pointer changes to include a page indicator, and at the bottom of the screen, you see the message Drag selected measures to new position. While holding down the left mouse button, you can drag the 12 measures down into a new track, starting at any measure. Drag the measures to track 8, as shown in figure 8.8.

Dragging 12
measures to a
new track.

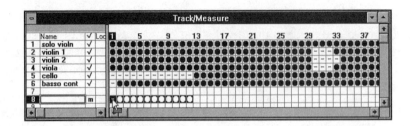

When you have the measures in place, release the left mouse button. Notice that the cells from which you dragged the measures have been filled with dashes, indicating that no MIDI events exist. Cakewalk has filled the empty measures with silence so that the remaining measures in track 5 will be played properly at the correct time.

You can also copy the measures instead of moving them, by holding down the Ctrl key while moving the measures. That places a copy of the measures in the new location instead of removing them from the original location.

Furthermore, you can cut or copy the measures, using **E**dit from the menu bar, and then paste the measures into a new location. If you paste the measures on top of existing measures, the existing measures are wiped out. If you want to insert new measures, you must make a hole for the insertion. First select all the measures to the right of the insertion point; then slide all the selected measures out in time to clear a number of measures, using the **E**dit **S**lide option from the menu bar, which is described later in this chapter.

If you want to duplicate an entire track, you use the cursor keys to select the track, and then choose **T**rack Clon**e** from the menu bar. This option, also described later in the section "Menu Bar," simply asks where you want the copy of the track placed.

The Track/Measure window is very useful for doing large-scale changes to music. For example, some musicians like to beef up a track by cloning or copying the entire track, creating two tracks that play the same notes on different channels, and thus doubling the sound of that track.

Piano-Roll View

The Piano-Roll view comes from the days of mechanical player pianos, when a roll of paper with cutouts representing the notes to be played would enchant you with the popular music of the day.

The old-fashioned Piano-Roll was indeed a roll of paper, punched with holes that represented each piano key that was to be played during the course of a song. If the key were to be struck and released quickly, a small hole was punched. If the key were to be struck and held down for a period of time, a longer hole was punched. Early in this century, hundreds of thousands of player pianos were sold each year.

The Piano-Roll view looks like the old paper version, as shown in figure 8.9.

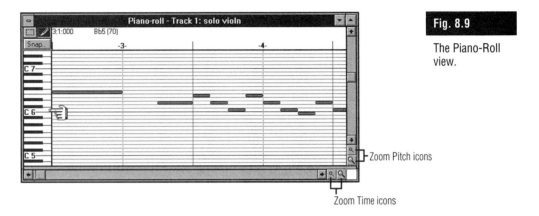

Fig. 8.9

The Piano-Roll view.

What you see in figure 8.9 are the third and fourth measures of track 1, the solo violin part. A playable piano keyboard runs up and down the left side of the window. When you position the pointing hand cursor over a key and press the left mouse button, that note will play.

The long bar stretching from the F key is indeed an F note played in the first beat of the third measure. The duration of the note is one beat. That is followed by a half-beat pause, and then the violin plays a D for a half beat; it then starts the fourth measure with an E note; and so on. Because the Meter indicator in the control bar shows that this track uses 2/4 timing (two beats to every measure, and the quarter note gets one beat), the first note in measure 3 must be a quarter note, the second must be an eighth note, and all the notes in the fourth measure are sixteenth notes. You can verify that with the Staff view, described later in this chapter.

Zooming the View

Notice the two sets of magnifying glass icons in the lower-right corner of the Piano-Roll window . The icons beneath the vertical scroll bar are the Zoom

Pitch icons. The icons to the right of the horizontal scroll bar are the Zoom Time icons. Clicking one of the larger icons zooms in, and clicking one of the smaller icons zooms out.

Using the Zoom Time icons in the lower-right corner, you can zoom in and out in time, showing more measures or fewer, as you like. In figure 8.10, the small magnifying glass was clicked several times to zoom out so that measures 1 through 11 are visible.

Fig. 8.10

Use the Zoom Time icons to show more or fewer measures.

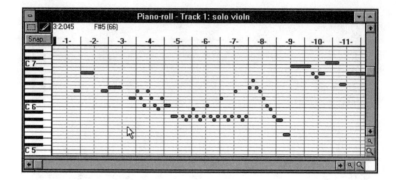

The Zoom Pitch icons work in the same way. Zooming in shows a smaller range of notes, and zooming out shows a larger range.

Velocity

In the Piano-Roll view, you can see also the velocity at which each note was struck (how hard the note was played). A second window pane is hidden at the bottom of the Piano-Roll view in figure 8.10. If you enlarge the window to full size and then drag the bottom border upward, as in figure 8.11, you will uncover the Velocity pane.

The Velocity pane indicates the keystroke velocity used when the recording was made. Each note has a corresponding vertical line indicating its velocity. In the case of the Bach piece used in figure 8.11, each note was struck with the same firmness; therefore, all the vertical bars are the same height. When the pointer is within the Velocity pane, the pointer changes shape to indicate that you can modify the velocity of each note, or a range of notes. To modify the velocity of a note, move the pointer to the top of the velocity indicator, hold down the left mouse button, and drag the indicator up or down. To modify a series of notes, you can draw a curve (see fig. 8.12).

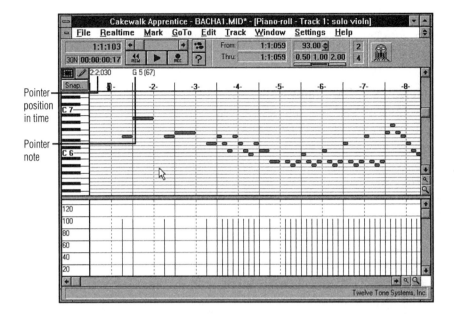

Pointer position in time

Pointer note

Fig. 8.11

The Velocity pane uncovered at the bottom of the Piano-Roll view.

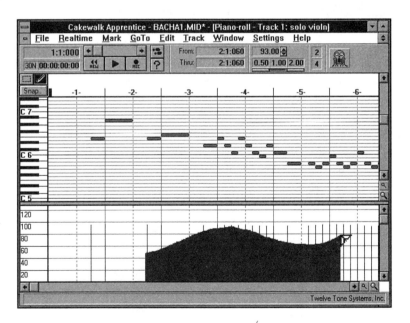

Fig. 8.12

Drawing a curve to change the velocity of a range of notes.

In figure 8.12, I pointed to a position just before the second note in the second measure, then held down the left mouse button, and drew the curve you see. When the mouse button is released, all the velocity indicators underneath the shaded area are adjusted to meet the top of the curve. In this way, the velocity of each note between the second beat of measure 2 and the first beat of measure 6 is changed.

Editing Notes in the Piano-Roll View

While working in the Piano-Roll view, you can change the pitch of a note, move its starting time, or change its duration. You can add a note, modify it, delete it, and play the track with your modifications. Start by noticing a few things in figure 8.11. In the upper Note pane, the mouse pointer is resting in the lower half of the pane. The pointer's position is reported near the upper-left corner of the Note pane by two values. Its position in time is 2:2:030, which means that the pointer is sitting on the second beat of the second measure, at tick number 30. The second value is G 5 (67). This means that the pointer is resting on a G note in the fifth octave, which happens to be MIDI note number 67. If you were to insert a note at that position, it would play a G starting in tick 30 of the second beat of the second measure. As you move the mouse pointer around, its current position is updated in the Note pane.

The other items to notice are in the upper-left corner of the Note pane. The Snap button is used to "snap" a note to the nearest significant time, whether the note is at the beginning or end of a beat or measure. If you were inserting a new note, for example, you would find it difficult to align the beginning of the note with the exact beginning of the measure. By clicking the Snap button and setting the snap value to something above 0, you can instruct Cakewalk to snap the note to the nearest border within that value (see fig. 8.13). Murky, huh? Try this. By setting the Snap-to value to 30, you are saying to Cakewalk, "When I insert this note and I'm within 30 ticks of the beginning of the measure, snap the note to the beginning of the measure for me." Or you are saying, "If I'm stretching this note out and I have the end of the note to within 30 ticks of the end of the beat, snap the note to the end of the beat for me." By the way, the default value of Snap-to is 30 ticks.

The Snap-to
dialog box.

The Snap function makes it possible to drop a new note near the correct position and to let Snap do the detail work. If, however, you want to set the beginning and end of each note to within 1/120 of the beat, just set the Snap-to value to zero.

The dotted box in the upper-left corner of the Piano-Roll window is the Select button. By clicking this box, you can select areas of the Piano-Roll to edit, as shown in figure 8.14.

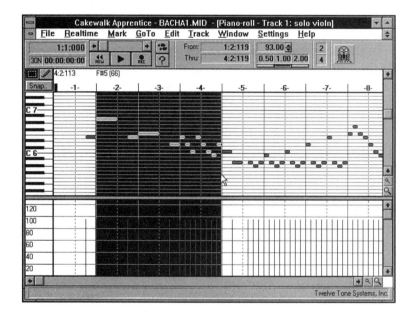

Fig. 8.14

Using the Select button to highlight areas to edit.

To select an area like that shown in figure 8.14, click the Select button, point the mouse to the beginning of measure 2, hold down the left button, and drag the highlight to the right. Once you have an area highlighted, you can use the **E**dit option in the menu bar to modify those measures. The **E**dit menu is described later in this chapter.

Changing a Note's Pitch, Starting Time, or Duration

The pencil icon in the upper-left corner of the Piano-Roll window is used to insert new notes or modify existing ones. You can also do something called "scrub" the notes in the measure. In figure 8.15, I've zoomed in on a few notes at the beginning of the song. When you click the pencil icon and point to the middle of a note (as in fig. 8.15), the note will sound, and the pointer will change to an up-and-down arrow. At this point, you can hold down the left mouse button and drag the note up and down until it is in the correct position.

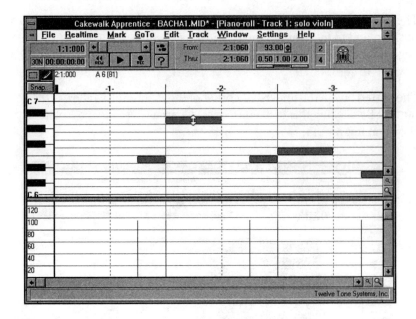

If you point to the left side of the note, as shown in figure 8.16, the pointer changes to a left-and-right arrow. This means that you can drag the note left or right to change its starting time. For example, if you wanted to move the start of this note out to begin half a beat later in the measure, you would point to the left side of the note, hold down the left mouse button, and drag the note to the right. Remember that you probably have Snap turned on, so if you can get the note within 30 clicks either side of the second half of the beat, Cakewalk will snap it to the correct position for you.

Pointing to the right side of the note allows you to lengthen or shorten the note. As before, you point to the right side, hold down the left mouse button, and drag the right side of the note left or right, to shorten or lengthen it, respectively.

You will notice that as you lengthen or shorten a note, it changes in 30-tick increments. If you want the note to change in smaller or larger increments, click the Snap button and change the Snap-to value to a smaller or larger number.

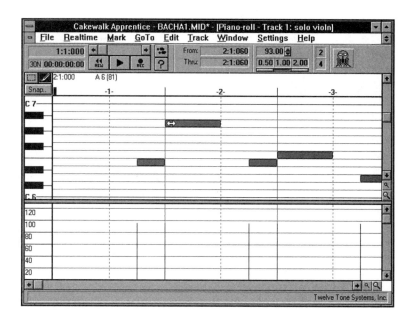

Fig. 8.16

Pointing to the left of the note enables you to drag it left or right, changing its starting time.

Inserting, Deleting, and Copying Notes

To insert a note, you point to the measure and pitch where you want the note, hold down the Ctrl key, and click the left mouse button. Cakewalk will insert a note at the position where you are pointing. The note will be based on the time signature—2/4 in this case, which results in the insertion of a quarter note one beat in length.

To delete a note, point to the note, hold down the left mouse button, and press the Del key. It doesn't matter which kind of arrow is showing at the moment you press the Del key.

To copy a note, point to the note you would like copied and, while holding down the Ctrl key, press and hold down the left mouse button. Drag the note to whatever pitch you would like the new note to play. The advantage of copying an existing note is that the new note inherits all the MIDI characteristics of the original note.

To achieve even finer control over some of the characteristics of a note, you can point to the note and then click the right mouse button. The Note Parameters dialog box appears (see fig. 8.17).

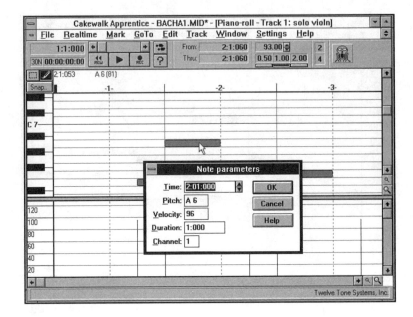

Fig. 8.17

The Note
Parameters dialog
box.

The Note Parameters dialog box lets you change the start time, pitch, velocity, duration, and output channel of the note you selected. As you click inside one of the boxes, a spin button appears, and you can spin through the appropriate values. Or you can highlight all or part of the value inside the box and then type a new value into the box.

Scrubbing Notes

The final act you can perform in the Note pane is to "scrub" the notes. As shown in figure 8.18, when you point to the left of the notes (in any area where there are no notes) and then hold down the left mouse button, a vertical scrub bar appears.

When you drag the scrub bar to the right or left, the notes over which the scrub bar passes are played. This is a handy feature when you've changed a note or two in a chord and want to hear how the chord sounds.

The Piano-Roll view is extremely useful in making changes to songs. You can even compose from this view if you are so inclined. The Piano-Roll view and the Staff view, described next, are certainly the most powerful music editing views.

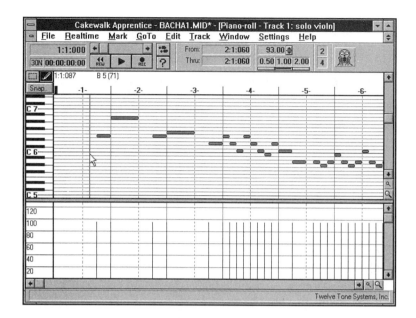

Fig. 8.18

The scrub bar.

Staff View

The Staff view looks at a song from the sheet music perspective. The Staff view window looks at MIDI notes as notes in a staff, in much the same way that musical notation software works.

However, as Twelve Tone Systems admits, Cakewalk Apprentice is not intended as a replacement for a full-featured music publishing software package. Cakewalk will not print the staff, nor does Cakewalk implement the many finer points of musical notation. Still, it is a useful music-editing tool.

When you activate the Staff view, Cakewalk looks at your track and decides whether it should present a bass clef, a treble clef, or both. By clicking the **L**ayout button in the Staff view window, you have the option of picking the clef, as shown in figure 8.19.

Using the **L**ayout button in the Staff window, you can pick a display for each selected track. In this example, only track 1 is selected.

In figure 8.19, you'll notice a column with the label (split). If you select both bass and treble clef displays, you can change the split point: the note at which the two staves split. The *split point* is the lowest note that should be displayed on the treble clef.

Fig. 8.19

The Staff View
Layout dialog box.

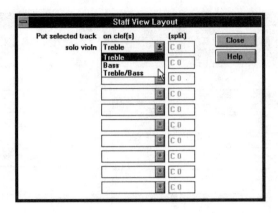

Adjusting Notation Appearance

When I play the keyboard, my general incompetence prevents me from striking and releasing a key at precisely the right time. Or one finger may get a little nervous and tromp on a key before another finger is off the key it's supposed to release. In other words, I have trouble keeping my fingers coordinated. If my actual keystrokes were displayed in a musical staff, there would be a terrible hodgepodge of 32nd notes, 64th notes, and ugly bridges. In other words, the view would be terribly complicated by my inaccurate keyboarding.

However, if I were a well-respected keyboard artist, I might be able to say, "I meant to play it that way." In either case, when the actual notes and durations are displayed in notation form—and accurately represent the times a key was held—it makes the staff much more complex to look at and use. Cakewalk Apprentice has three options that help clean up the display: Resolution, **F**ill, and Tri**m**. Each of these options alters the display of the notes, not the actual notes as recorded in the MIDI file. These are tools to simplify the view, and they do not in any way alter the length and overlapping of notes as you record them. To do that, you can edit the individual notes or use quantization to even everything out. For information on quantization and note parameter adjustments, refer to the **E**dit menu.

The Resolution pull-down button in the Staff window is used to reduce the amount of detail you see when looking at the Staff view. To demonstrate, I recorded a bit of drivel, as shown in figure 8.20. This is an attempt to play, in 4/4 time, a quarter note on the first and third beats of the measure. If I had done this ideally, you would see a quarter note, a quarter rest, a quarter note, and a quarter rest. If you examine 8.20, you can see what I really played.

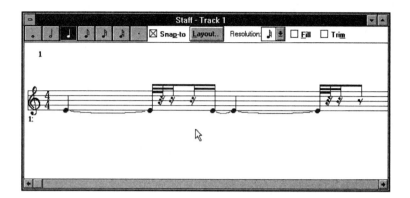

Fig. 8.20

With resolution set at its highest (show 1/32 notes), all note detail is displayed.

I managed to hit the E note at the beginning of the first beat but held it just a bit too long, and it ran 1/32 of a note into the second beat. Then I started the second note too soon and held it too long also.

I like the way that sounds, however. So I want to keep it but not look at it. How do I do that? Change the resolution. When you click the Resolution pull-down button, you have the option of one of four resolutions: you can show only 1/4 notes, 1/8 notes, 1/16 notes (the default), or 1/32 notes. In figure 8.20, resolution is set to the maximum 1/32 notes. In figure 8.21, resolution has been reduced to 1/8 notes.

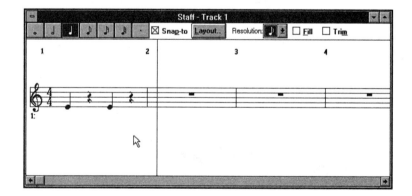

Fig. 8.21

When resolution is reduced to 1/8 notes, the display is considerably simpler.

Now you can see what I originally intended to play: note, rest, note, rest. Changing the display resolution is one way to clean up what might otherwise be a very messy notation.

The **F**ill box is used when you have a note that runs a bit shorter than you would like to see cluttering up the display. In figure 8.22, the note in the first beat is nearly, but not quite, a quarter note.

Fig. 8.22

Instead of displaying notes like this, use the **F**ill box to clean them up.

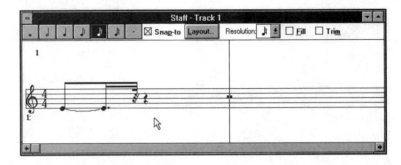

To clean up the display without editing the note, I clicked the **F**ill box. The result is shown in figure 8.23. The note 3/16 of a beat long, and just 1/32 of a full beat, has been filled out to a complete quarter note.

Fig. 8.23

Fill has, for display purposes only, filled out the note to a complete quarter note.

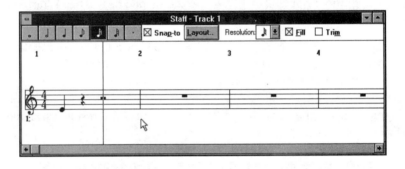

Again, the actual notes as recorded in a MIDI file have not been changed. Resolution, **F**ill, and T**rim** alter only the Staff view display, not the notes themselves. If you want to alter the note, you must edit it.

The final display option is T**rim**, which cuts off notes that have run a little long and are overlapping another note, as shown in figure 8.24.

Fig. 8.24

The quarter note is running a little long, overlapping the next note.

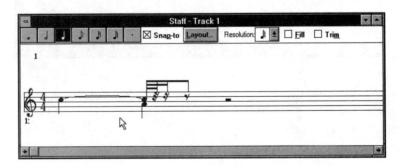

To clean up this kind of display, click **Trim**, which will trim the offending extension off the first note.

The Trim function trimmed back the duration of the first note so that it no longer bridged the second note.

All three of these functions can help with the display. However, if you are actually editing music by adding notes, or changing duration and starting times, you should turn off **Trim** and **F**ill, and use the highest resolution of display that is reasonable. For example, if you have a piece of 4/4 music and you insert a 1/8 note while Fill is enabled, the inserted 1/8 note will be displayed as a 1/4 note.

Editing Notes

Now you know how to modify what is displayed. How do you edit music in the Staff view? It is very much like editing music in the Piano-Roll view.

To move a note, point to the note with the mouse pointer and hold down the left mouse button. You can then drag the note up or down in pitch, and left or right in time. When you drag the note up or down to change its pitch, Cakewalk Apprentice automatically changes the pitch diatonically—using the current key signature to decide what the next higher or lower note is. To drag the note chromatically (in half steps, or semitones), hold down the left button and click the right button once. This will set the software to drag the note chromatically. The next time you select a note, this feature is automatically reset to make diatonic changes.

To delete a note, point to it, hold down the left mouse button, and press the Del key on your keyboard. To change the duration of the note, you can point to it and then click the right mouse button to bring up the Note Parameters dialog box (refer to fig. 8.17).

As in the Piano-Roll view, you can change the note's start time, pitch, velocity, duration, and channel from the Note Parameters dialog box.

To insert music, click the kind of note you want to insert at the top of the Staff view window. For example, to insert a dotted quarter note at the first beat of the second measure, click the quarter note icon, click the dot icon, point to the place you want to insert the note, hold down the Ctrl key, and click the left mouse button once. Again, to move the note, simply point to it and drag it while holding down the left mouse button.

The last part of the Staff view to be discussed is the box labeled Snap-to. When the Snap-to box is selected, notes that you insert in the music will be snapped to the nearest reasonable note boundary. For example, if you've clicked the quarter note icon and you insert a quarter note, Cakewalk attempts to insert the note to the nearest complete quarter-note boundary. In other words, in 4/4 time, the quarter note will be placed at the beginning of the beat, not halfway through the beat even if that is where you are pointing.

Event List View

You use the Event List view to look at the MIDI instructions being sent to the MIDI instrument. The Event List view, shown in figure 8.25, lists all MIDI events for the selected track, in the order in which they are sent to the MIDI instrument. If you have more than one track selected, the Event List view intermingles the data from both tracks, again listing them in chronological order.

Fig. 8.25

The Event List view.

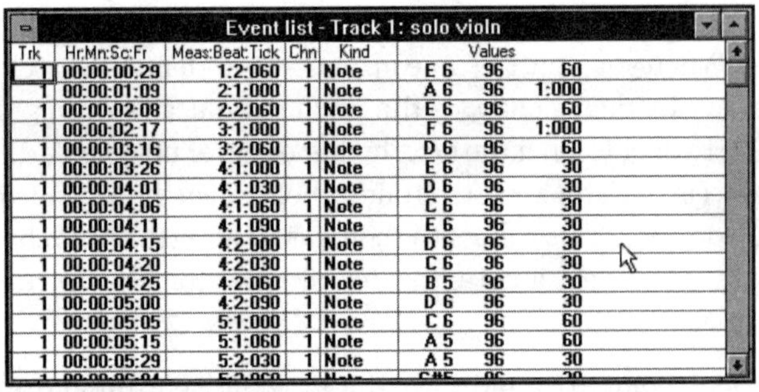

Trk	Hr:Mn:Sc:Fr	Meas:Beat:Tick	Chn	Kind	Values		
1	00:00:00:29	1:2:060	1	Note	E 6	96	60
1	00:00:01:09	2:1:000	1	Note	A 6	96	1:000
1	00:00:02:08	2:2:060	1	Note	E 6	96	60
1	00:00:02:17	3:1:000	1	Note	F 6	96	1:000
1	00:00:03:16	3:2:060	1	Note	D 6	96	60
1	00:00:03:26	4:1:000	1	Note	E 6	96	30
1	00:00:04:01	4:1:030	1	Note	D 6	96	30
1	00:00:04:06	4:1:060	1	Note	C 6	96	30
1	00:00:04:11	4:1:090	1	Note	E 6	96	30
1	00:00:04:15	4:2:000	1	Note	D 6	96	30
1	00:00:04:20	4:2:030	1	Note	C 6	96	30
1	00:00:04:25	4:2:060	1	Note	B 5	96	30
1	00:00:05:00	4:2:090	1	Note	D 6	96	30
1	00:00:05:05	5:1:000	1	Note	C 6	96	60
1	00:00:05:15	5:1:060	1	Note	A 5	96	60
1	00:00:05:29	5:2:030	1	Note	A 5	96	30
1	00:00:06:04	5:2:060	1	Note	C#6	96	30

Any of the MIDI events can be modified or deleted, and new events can be added. The Event List view provides the following information:

Trk   The track number you have selected.

Hr:Mn:Sc:Fr   The time at which the event occurs. Event time is provided in two formats. This format is SMPTE (Society of Motion Picture & Television Engineers) format and lists *hours:minutes:seconds;frames*. SMPTE timing is used to synchronize sound to television video or movie frames.

Meas:Beat:Tick	The time at which the event occurs, given as *measure:beat:tick*.
Chn	The channel to which the MIDI event is transmitted.
Kind	The kind of MIDI event. The possible MIDI events are described in the following discussion.
Values	The values assigned to each event.

If you look at the first event in the list in figure 8.25, you can see that the event started on the second beat of the first measure (1:2:060), was transmitted on channel 1, and was a note. In the Values column, the note was an E in the sixth octave, its velocity was 96, and its duration was 60 ticks.

To delete a MIDI event, click any item within the event and press the Del key. To insert a MIDI event, select the existing event above which you want to insert an event, and press the Ins key. Cakewalk Apprentice will copy the event you are pointing to, and you can edit the event if you want.

To change event parameters, double-click the appropriate parameter. In each case, excluding the event Kind, simply type a new parameter value. When you double-click Kind, a pop-up dialog box opens in which you can change the kind of MIDI event transmitted (see fig. 8.26).

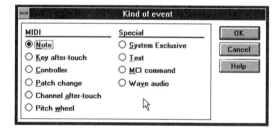

Fig. 8.26

The Kind of Event dialog box.

When the Kind of Event dialog box appears, you can click the appropriate button to change the event. You then need to change the parameter values for the event, as described here:

- **N**ote. A MIDI Note event has three parameters: pitch, velocity, and duration. Instead of entering the actual MIDI note number, you enter the note name and octave number. The velocity is a value ranging from 0 through 127. The duration is given in *beat:tick* format. If the note is shorter than one beat, only the tick value is given.

- **K**ey After-Touch. This MIDI event has two parameters: pitch and pressure. Refer to Chapter 6 for a description of key after-touch. Again, the pitch refers to the note name and octave number. The pressure value ranges from 0 through 127.

- **C**ontroller. The MIDI controller events have two parameters: the controller number, which ranges from 0 through 127; and the controller value, which also ranges from 0 through 127. Again, refer to Chapter 6 for more information on controller events.

- **P**atch Change. This event allows patch changes to be embedded in a MIDI song. There is only one parameter for the Patch Change event: the MIDI patch number or the MIDI patch name. Numbers are safer than names because names seem to vary from one implementation to the next.

- Channel **A**fter-Touch. There is only one after-touch parameter: the pressure amount, ranging from 0 through 127.

- Pitch **W**heel. The pitch wheel event has one parameter, which is the wheel position. The position can range from –8192 to 8192. A value of 0 centers the wheel.

- **S**ystem Exclusive. The System Exclusive event is not supported by Cakewalk Apprentice and is provided only to ensure compatibility with Cakewalk Professional for Windows. You may see a MIDI song with a System Exclusive event, but that event is not transmitted by Cakewalk Apprentice.

- **T**ext. This MIDI event has only one parameter: the text you want to include in the MIDI file. Text events are not played but simply give you a way to include comments. The Event List view does not support horizontal scrolling, so you are limited to viewing the amount of text visible in the window.

- **M**CI Command. This is an extension to MIDI to support Microsoft's Media Control Interface (MCI) driver, a part of the Multimedia Extensions for Windows 3.1. This event transmits a command to MCI. The event parameter is the MCI command itself. For example, the command

> **NOTE**
>
> The MCI and WAV events described here are not MIDI-compliant but are multimedia extensions added by Twelve Tone Systems, Inc. They function only with driver routines provided with Sound Blaster 16 and 16 ASP. As of this printing, driver routines that permit these functions are not available for Sound Blaster or Sound Blaster Pro. When Cakewalk Apprentice is run with Sound Blaster Pro, for example, all other sequencer functions work, including the capability to embed a WAV file within the MIDI file. Cakewalk cannot play the WAV event, however, and reports that it cannot do so. When Cakewalk Apprentice is running, it assumes control of the Sound Blaster card. The drivers provided with Sound Blaster and Sound Blaster Pro will not release the card even for other Windows events. For example, if Cakewalk Apprentice is minimized and you open Windows Media Player or Sound Recorder, neither can play WAV files because Sound Blaster is not available. The new driver under development for the other Sound Blaster cards will resolve this problem.

PLAY C:\WINDOWS\CHIMES.WAV causes the MCI driver to load the CHIMES.WAV file and play it. There is a delay during playback because the MCI driver must first be loaded and then play the appropriate file.

- Wave Audio. This nonstandard MIDI event is used to play WAV files. The event has one parameter, which is the WAV data that is loaded into the MIDI song. When you choose Wave Audio as an event, the dialog box shown in figure 8.27 appears.

Fig. 8.27

The Wave Event dialog box.

If a WAV event already exists, you can copy the WAV data from the event to the Windows Clipboard, allowing you to modify the data as you want or use it in another application. If WAV data is sitting in the Clipboard, you can paste the data into the MIDI file. You can also save the WAV data to a file. In this instance, you're inserting WAV data in the MIDI file, so the only option is to load the data from a WAV file. After the WAV data is loaded, the Values column in the Event List view contains the detail on the data.

In this case, the wave data is 4.06 seconds long at a playback sample rate of 22 kHz. It is an 8-bit monaural recording and uses 87K of space.

The advantage of embedding a WAV file inside a MIDI file is that playback is nearly instantaneous and does not require the loading of other files into memory. The downside is that an embedded WAV file will swell a typically small MIDI file enormously.

The Event List view is very useful if you want to modify the actual MIDI events in a song. If you do, you will probably be most interested in the remaining view, the Controllers view.

Controllers View

The MIDI specification has provisions for 120 controller events. Controller events are the electronic version of pressing the piano's soft or sustain pedals, or laying a modulation or tremolo effect on top of a note. Not all controller events are used, of course. Cakewalk Apprentice supports and lets you modify the following events listed in table 8.1.

Table 8.1 Events Supported by Cakewalk Apprentice

Event #	Description	Sound Blaster?
NA*	Pitch Wheel	Yes
NA*	Channel After-Touch	No
1	Mod Wheel	Yes
2	Breath	No
4	Foot Controller	No
5	Portamento Time	No
7	Main Volume	Yes
8	Balance	Yes (Pro, 16/16 ASP)
10	Pan	Yes (Pro, 16/16 ASP)
11	Expression	No
64	Pedal (sustain)	Yes (Pro, 16/16 ASP)
65	Portamento	No
66	Pedal (sostenuto)	No
67	Pedal (soft)	No
69	Hold 2	No
91	External Effects Depth	No
92	Tremolo Depth	No
93	Chorus Depth	No
94	Celeste (detune) Depth	No
95	Phaser Depth	No

*Not applicable

As you can see from the table, Sound Blaster supports some of these controller events but not others.

The Controllers view, shown in figure 8.28, is a graphical view because of the nature of these events. In this case, *graphical view* means that you can draw a shape in a window to control when and how an event will occur.

The Controllers view adds controller events to a track.

As an example, suppose that you want to add a tremolo effect to the second measure of a song, using the modulation (mod) wheel controller effect. You use the pull-down list box in the middle of the window to select the effect. Click the down arrow to the right of the box and scroll through the list until you find event 1, Mod Wheel. Then select it. (Note that another list box is available to force the effect onto another MIDI channel.) After you have selected the Mod Wheel, as shown in figure 8.29, there are several things to notice.

The Mod Wheel controller.

The point has been converted to its hang glider configuration, indicating that you will be drawing a shape instead of entering numbers or words. Across the top are the numbers indicating the measures, which you can zoom in on to show fewer measures, or out to show more measures. (To zoom in or out, use the magnifying glass icons in the lower-right corner.) On the left side of the window are the values to which a Mod Wheel can be set, ranging from 0 at the bottom to 127 at the top. As you move the pointer around within the window, you'll notice that its time position within the track is reported in the upper-left corner, as is the Mod Wheel value (17 in fig. 8.29).

NOTE

If you are tempted to select an area to delete or to copy a controller event with the **E**dit Cu**t** or **E**dit **C**opy option, don't. Unless you set up the Event Filter from the **G**oTo **S**earch option in the menu bar, you will end up deleting or cutting all the MIDI data from the selected area of the track. Using the erase button to erase the controller event data is quicker and safer.

The Select button and drawing pencil are shown in the upper-left corner of the window and are used in exactly the same way as in previous views. You use the Select button to select an area, setting the From: and Thru: time indicators in the control bar. You click the pencil icon to make a mark in the window. The icon that resembles a stop sign with a slash is the erase button, which is used to erase controller effects.

Now you can cause a modulation event in this track. Position the pointer at the zero value at the beginning of measure 2, hold down the left mouse button, and draw a curve upward and back down to zero by the end of the measure, as shown in figure 8.30.

Fig. 8.30

Drawing the shape of a modulation event in a track.

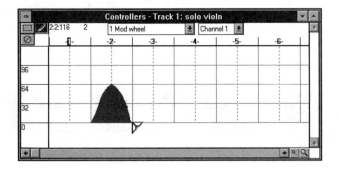

As you are drawing the shape, the area beneath the pointer will be a solid color, which will turn into a series of vertical lines as soon as you release the mouse button. That's all there is to it! Now, when you play the song, a tremolo effect will start at the beginning of measure 2, peak about the middle, and then dampen at the end of the measure. The higher you draw, the more intense the effect. If you don't like the shape or want to extend the effect, click the erase icon, hold down the left mouse button, and scribble over the event. When you release the mouse button, the event will be gone.

Once you've achieved the effect you want, you can close this view and go back to the Event List view for this track and see the event embedded in the MIDI instructions. For this composition, by drawing a shape, I added 63 MIDI controller events to the song to accommodate the effect I wanted, and managed to achieve this in a few seconds. As always, your mileage will vary, and the number of events you add to a song to modify it will undoubtedly be different.

Now that you are familiar with the ways in which you can look at and alter MIDI data, it's time to go back to the top of the screen and explore the control and menu bars.

Control Bar

If you've read through the preceding descriptions of the Cakewalk views, going through the control bar will be slightly anticlimactic, but worthwhile just the same. The control bar is used to indicate timing points in a song, to control recording and playback, and to set tempo. Oh yes, the ghoul is used to escape any horrible conditions in which you may find yourself.

Timing Indicators

Starting at the left of the control bar, note that there are two timing indicators, one above the other, as shown in figure 8.31.

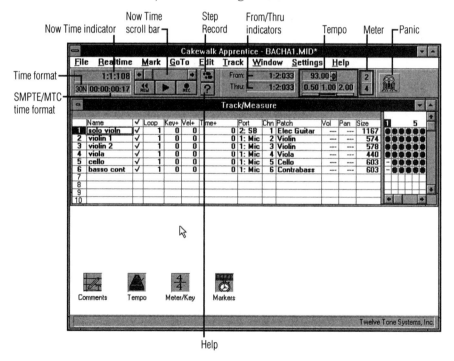

Fig. 8.31

The control bar.

Help

Cakewalk Apprentice uses two concepts of musical time. The first is the relatively common *measure:beat:tick* time, as displayed in the upper timing indicator at the far left. The second is time in terms of the SMPTE standard, which refers to *hours:minutes:seconds:frames* and is displayed in the lower timing indicator at the far left. The SMPTE time format is used to synchronize sound and video or film. You use the Time Format button, labeled 30N in figure 8.31, to change the SMPTE time format, as shown in figure 8.32. You can select one of four SMPTE synchronization rates.

The Time Format dialog box.

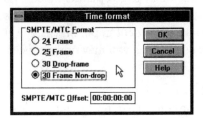

It is well beyond the scope of this book to address video or film sound synchronization, beyond saying that 24 frames per second is the standard U.S. theater movie frame rate, and 30 frames per second is the U.S. television broadcast frame rate. The offset box allows playback to be delayed in order to ensure proper synchronization among all the relevant pieces of equipment.

Next on the control bar are the playback, rewind, and record buttons. If you have loaded a song, click the playback button (▶) to play the song. Cakewalk does not rewind automatically; therefore, you must click the rewind button before playing again. You use the record button to start recording, and it activates the internal metronome unless you have silenced it through the **S**ettings menu.

Above the record and playback buttons is a scroll bar that controls the "Now Time." The now time concept is a somewhat overly complicated way of saying, "At the current time in the music." Now Time starts at measure 1, beat 1, and goes forward as the music is being played. Or you can use the Now Time scroll bar and scroll to a specific point in the music to begin recording or playback, and that time becomes the Now Time. In other words, use the Now Time scroll bar to move back and forth in the song.

Step Recording

One of the most interesting features of Cakewalk Apprentice is its support of a method of recording called Step Record. The philosophy behind Step Record is that not everyone is an extremely talented keyboard artist, but that should not prevent a person from recording music. Step Record allows you to record the notes in a song one at a time, at your own speed, instead of trying to play a song exactly as you would expect an expert keyboardist to play it. You don't have to be able to play two notes in a row to rhythm. When you click the Step Record button (displaying footprints), the dialog box shown in figure 8.33 appears.

Fig. 8.33

The Step Recording dialog box.

You are working in Step Record mode all the time this dialog box is open. When you close the box, Cakewalk Apprentice reverts to its standard recording method.

To record, you must have a MIDI keyboard attached to Sound Blaster's MIDI port, of course. You cannot use Cakewalk's recording facilities with the Sound Blaster FM Organ, for example, nor does Cakewalk have the facilities to use your computer keyboard as a MIDI keyboard.

The process of Step Recording includes the following steps:

1. Use the default tempo and meter. You can change them later if you like. Defaults are 4/4 time and 100 beats/minute.

2. Click the footprints to start Step Recording.

3. Choose a step size. The step size relates to the chosen meter. If you choose a **W**hole step size, each note you record will take a whole measure. If you choose a **Q**uarter step size, each note takes a quarter measure.

4. Choose a note duration. You can choose the duration independently or tie it to the step size by clicking the **F**ollow Step Size button at the bottom of the right column.

5. For now, leave the Au**to** Advance box selected.

6. Play the first note. The time indicator near the bottom of the box will be increased an amount in relation to the step size.

7. If the note you played is OK, play the next note. But if you made a mistake, click the Delete button and try again.

8. When you have played all the notes for this session, click Keep, and the dialog box closes. Your song is now in memory and can be played back and edited.

You can choose several options in the Step Recording dialog box. The first is to set a custom step size by clicking the **O**ther box on the left. This opens a dialog box that lets you set the step size in ticks. Remember that a beat has 120 ticks. You can do the same thing with note duration. By clicking the Othe**r** box on the right, you can set note duration by ticks.

The **A**dvance button and Au**to** Advance check box are used to determine how you advance to the next step while recording. If the Au**to** Advance box is checked, each time you play a note, you will advance to the next step. If A**uto** Advance is not checked, you must click the **A**dvance button each time you're ready to advance to the next step. The mechanical advance feature is particularly useful if you have to build chords based on only being able to play one note at a time. The reason is that when Au**to** Advance is turned off, each note that you play before clicking **A**dvance is recorded as if you had played all the notes simultaneously.

To skip a step, click the **A**dvance button. You can also use the **P**attern box to set up Cakewalk to automatically skip a step in a repeated fashion. For example, to record a note in step 1 and step 2, skip step 3, and record in step 4 again, type **12.4** in the box. The period tells Cakewalk to automatically advance past the third step at the completion of step 2. If you want to skip every other step, you type **1.** in the **P**attern box.

In the middle of the control bar are the From: and Thru: indicators (refer to fig. 8.31). They reflect any area you might have selected for editing in one of the views. Conversely, you can enter From and Thru values directly into these boxes to perform large-scale editing tasks. The values are given in the Cakewalk *measure:beat:tick* format.

Tempo Controls

Next come the tempo controls. Tempo, in beats per second, can be changed with the spin buttons in the control bar. Just below the Tempo indicator are three more boxes with narrow buttons just beneath them. These are the tempo ratio buttons. You can use these buttons to alter the tempo quickly. Look once more at figure 8.31. The tempo is set to 93.00 beats per minute. The leftmost tempo ratio box is set to 0.50, the middle box is set to 1.00, and the right box is set to 2.00. If you click the button below the 0.50 box, the tempo will immediately be cut by 50 percent. If you click the button below the 2.00 box, the tempo will be doubled to 186 beats/minute. If you want a less radical change, you can assign new values to the tempo ratio buttons by clicking the number itself. The Tempo Ratio dialog box then appears, as shown in figure 8.34. Again, use the spin buttons to set the tempo ratio value to whatever you like.

Fig. 8.34

The Tempo Ratio dialog box.

The next part of the control bar is the Meter/Key indicator, which displays the meter as one number above another. The key is not visible until you click the indicator. At startup, Cakewalk Apprentice sets the meter to 4/4 time, in the key of C. You can change the meter and key by clicking the Meter/Key indicator. The Current Meter/Key dialog box is displayed (see fig. 8.35).

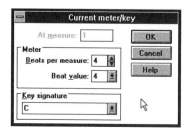

Fig. 8.35

The Current Meter/Key dialog box.

In this dialog box, you select the meter with two spin buttons: the top button sets the beats per measure, and the lower button sets the beat value (which note gets one beat). In this case, there are four beats per measure, and each quarter note is assigned one beat.

To change the current key, click the **K**ey Signature box, as shown in figure 8.36. The scroll list that appears supports keys ranging from 7 flats to 7 sharps, which should be sufficient for most western music.

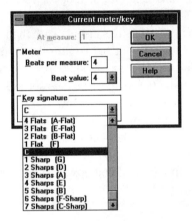

You come at last to the icon representing Edvard Munch's painting "The Scream." With any sequencer, you can find yourself in some situations in which the synthesizer ends up making a nonstop screech. This typically happens when a feedback loop is accidentally created whereby part of a tone is fed back into the synthesizer, creating a self-generating loop of noise. Clicking "The Scream" will send a note-off message to all the MIDI instruments and controllers.

Comments, Tempo, Meter/Key, and Markers Icons

The Comments icon gives you the ability to add text notes to a MIDI file. When you double-click the Comments icon, the window shown in figure 8.37 appears.

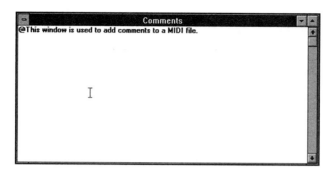

Fig. 8.37

Attaching a text note to your MIDI file.

The Comments window is a straightforward text-entry window, much like the Windows Notepad. When the Comments window is opened, the **E**dit menu changes, disabling most editing functions except undo, cut and copy to clipboard, and paste. When you open a Comments window, the text is attached to the MIDI file and can be viewed by double-clicking the Comments icon. If you would like to have the Comments window open automatically each time a file is opened, simply place the "at" (@) character as the first character in the window, as shown in figure 8.37.

The Tempo icon shows you a graphical view of tempo changes that might be embedded in a song. Not all MIDI sequencers support embedded tempo changes, although Cakewalk Apprentice certainly does. This does mean, however, that if you share with someone else a MIDI file you have created that contains embedded tempo changes, they may not be able to experience the changes.

When you double-click the Tempo icon, the window shown in figure 8.38 is opened. The Tempo window closely resembles the Controllers view and the Velocity pane of the Piano-Roll view. It is graphical in use and contains the magnifying glass icons to zoom in and out, except that in this case a zoom factor (50% in fig. 8.38) is shown in the upper-right corner of the window. The Tempo window graphically shows tempo changes in a song.

The tempo of the Bach song does not change; therefore, the tempo is shown as a straight line at 93 beats/minute. Suppose that you want to increase the tempo to 145 beats/minute halfway through the second beat of the first measure. To do that, click the pencil icon in the upper-left corner and then position the pointer at the exact time and tempo value you want, using the pointer values shown in the upper-left corner. In this case, the values should read 1:2:060 145.00, as shown in figure 8.39. Then click the left mouse button once.

Fig. 8.38

The Tempo window.

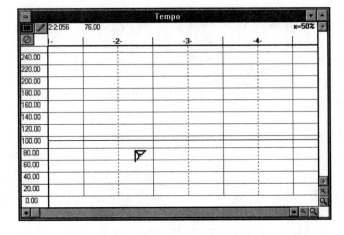

Fig. 8.39

A steady tempo is shown as a straight line.

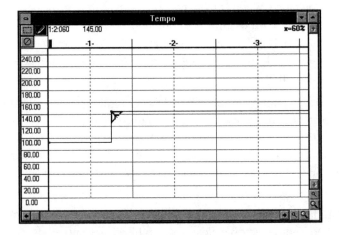

When you click the left mouse button, Cakewalk automatically changes the tempo of the song from that point forward. To change the tempo back at some future time, you must make the same kind of change.

Suppose that you want to slowly reduce the tempo to its original beat. This is called a *ritardando*, or gradual slowing of the tempo, although not very gradual in this example. Referring to figure 8.40, point the cursor to where you would like the change to start (the beginning of the second beat in measure 2 here).

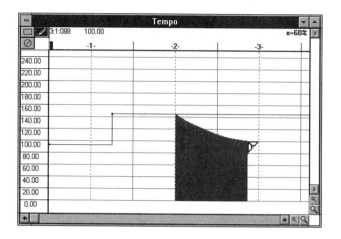

Fig. 8.40

Altering the tempo by sweeping the cursor up or down over time.

Hold down the left mouse button and sweep the cursor down and to the right, as shown in the preceding figure. When you have the cursor at the correct tempo, release the mouse button. When you release the mouse button, a line is left behind, indicating the tempo change—in this case, down to 100 beats/minute.

You can change the tempo in the other direction, creating an *accelerando*, in exactly the same way. When the tempo change is to your satisfaction, you can close the Tempo window. Or, if you don't like the change and want to erase it, click once the erase icon (the stop sign with a slash). Then, while holding down the left mouse button, erase the changes. The tempo will return to its former state. As stated before, not all sequencers can support embedded tempo changes.

The Meter/Key icon calls up a window that lets you change the meter and key on measure boundaries. You can cause a meter or key change at the beginning of measure 16, for example. Figure 8.41 shows the Meter/Key window and a dialog box that appears when you choose **A**dd or **C**hange.

As you can see, the Bach song has just one meter and key signature. At measure 1, the meter is 2/4, in the key of C. To add a change, click **A**dd, which brings up the Current Meter/Key dialog box. If you click in the At **M**easure box, a spin button appears, and you can select the measure at which you want the change to begin. Clicking in the **B**eats per Measure box results in another spin button, letting you scroll through the possible selections. The Beat **V**alue box enables you to select a note type for every beat, and the **K**ey Signature box lets you set a new key for display. If you have multiple meter or key changes (or both), and you want to delete one, simply highlight the change you want to delete; then click the **D**elete button.

Fig. 8.41

The Meter/Key window in which you keep track of meter and key changes.

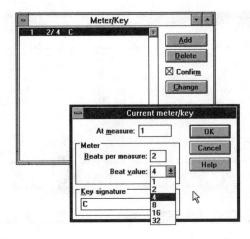

NOTE

Changing the key in the Current Meter/Key dialog box does not actually change the MIDI note values stored in the file. You must use the **E**dit Transpose option in the menu bar to change the data. Changing the key signature in the Current Meter/Key dialog box simply changes the way the music is portrayed in the Piano-Roll or Staff view.

The last icon at the bottom of the screen activates the Markers window, as shown in figure 8.42. This window lets you add markers (similar to bookmarks) to a MIDI file.

Markers are used to connect text to specific points in the song, in much the same way that bookmarks are used to add commentary to points in a book. When you open the Markers window, a list of all the current markers is provided. You can use the **A**dd, **D**elete, and **C**hange button to add, delete, and change markers, respectively. When you add or change a marker, the Marker dialog box appears, as shown in figure 8.42. Click in the **N**ame box to type the text you want. (The marker text cannot be scrolled left or right in the Markers window, so keep it short.) In the **T**ime box, enter the *measure:beat:tick* time that you want to associate with the marker. If you check the **L**ock to SMPTE box, the **T**ime box will be converted to use SMPTE time, in *hours:minutes:seconds:frames*. This figure shows a marker added to measure 5, beat 2.

Fig. 8.42

The Markers window and the Marker dialog box.

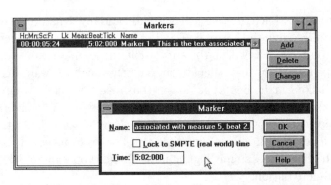

You can use markers as places to go to from the menu bar, using the **G**oTo menu. Finally, if you want to add large amounts of text to specific points in a song, use the Comments window, or add a MIDI text event to the file.

Menu Bar

If you've read all the preceding pages about Cakewalk Apprentice, the menu bar should now be a snap to use. There are nine menu bar items, most of which are duplications of functions and effects that can be accomplished from the various views and windows. The rest of this chapter describes the pull-down menus accessed from the menu bar.

File Menu

The **F**ile menu is used to start new songs, save modified songs, or load existing songs into Cakewalk.

Cakewalk Apprentice uses two file formats; standard MIDI files are loaded and saved with the MID or MFF extension, and Cakewalk work files are stored with the WRK extension. The difference between work files and MIDI files is that when you save a song in WRK format, all the non-MIDI Cakewalk functions that temporarily change keys, key velocity, channel, and tempo can be saved in the file. Those temporary changes cannot be saved in a MIDI file because the MIDI specification makes no provision for them. Please keep in mind that changes made with the **E**dit menu are permanent and are stored as MIDI data. However, changes made with the Controllers view, for example, are temporary and can be saved only if you save the file as a work file with the WRK extension.

Cakewalk Apprentice has a feature that enables you to establish a startup configuration. If, when initializing itself, Cakewalk finds a file named $DEFAULT.WRK in the working directory, it loads that file's music parameters (meter, tempo, and so on) and then sets the current file name to (*Untitled*), allowing you to record a song and then save it with the file name of your choice. To create $DEFAULT.WRK, click **N**ew, set the various parameters however you like, click Save **A**s, and save the file as $DEFAULT.WRK. Then, whenever you start Cakewalk, it automatically loads your favorite parameters.

The following options are available on the **F**ile menu:

New	Clears the current song from memory—after asking whether you want to save the song if it has changed—and prepares Cakewalk to record or load a new song.
Open	Loads a MID or WRK file into memory.
Save	Saves the current song with the current file name. If this is a new song, Cakewalk prompts you for a file name.
Save **A**s	Saves the current song with a new file name. You are prompted to enter an appropriate file name, keeping in mind the differences between the extensions MID and WRK, as just described.
Merge	Loads a song into Cakewalk's scrap buffer, a memory area similar to the Windows Clipboard. Any song data that is cut or copied is moved into the scrap buffer. When you use the **M**erge option, the file you are prompted for is loaded into the scrap buffer and is available for you to paste anywhere you like.
	Note: **M**erge cannot load Cakewalk for DOS 1.x files. You must use the **O**pen command to load these files, and then use **S**ave to save them. The DOS 1.x files will be saved in the current format, and you can then load them into the scrap buffer with **M**erge.
Extract	Saves in a disk file the current contents of the scrap buffer (see **M**erge). **E**xtract can be used to save music data that has been cut or copied into a file. For example, while using the Piano-Roll view, you select three measures and use **E**dit to cut them from the song. You can then use **E**xtract to save the cut measures into a file. Keep in mind that the scrap buffer holds only the most recently cut or copied information.
Exit	Leaves Cakewalk. If a file is loaded into Cakewalk and has been modified, you are asked whether you want to save the song.

Realtime Menu

The **R**ealtime menu duplicates the functions of the play, rewind, and record buttons on the control bar.

Because these functions are precisely the same as those described previously, you can refer to the discussion of the control bar. In summary, **P**lay begins playing the currently loaded song at the Now Time position. To rewind the song and reset the Now Time indicator to the beginning, choose Rewind. To record music at the Now Time position, choose **R**ecord. Choose **R**ecord again to stop recording. S**t**ep Record brings up the Step Record window described earlier in this chapter.

Mark Menu

Whenever you want to perform editing (such as cutting, copying, pasting) on a range of music, you have to mark the beginning point and the end point, called From: and Thru:, respectively. You can select From: and Thru: points in a variety of ways, most commonly through the Piano-Roll view, Staff view, and the Track/Measure view's Measure pane. Or you can select points from the **M**ark menu.

When you choose **F**rom Value or **T**hru Value, you are prompted to enter a point in the music, in the Now Time format used by Cakewalk. You use a spin button to select the appropriate time in the music. The other **M**ark menu items perform the following tasks:

From = Now	Sets the From: marker to the current Now Time.
Thru = Now	Sets the Thru: marker to the current Now Time.
From = **S**tart	Sets the From: marker to the beginning of the song.
Thru = **E**nd	Sets the Thru: marker to the end of the song.
Select **A**ll	Sets the From: marker to the beginning of the song, and the Thru: marker to the end of the song.
Un-select All	Clears the From: and Thru: markers.

GoTo Menu

To move around in a song, you can scroll through the song from within one of the views, or you can use the **G**oTo menu.

You can use one of the following ways to shift the Now Time to any point in the song:

Time	Choosing this option brings up a dialog box and spin button that enables you to enter a specific time in the *measure:beat:tick* format to jump to.
From	Jump to the current value in the From: indicator.
Thr**u**	Jump to the current value in the Thru: indicator.
Beginning	Go to the beginning of the song.
End	Go to the end of the song.
Previous Measure	Back up to the previous measure.
Next Measure	Jump to the next measure.

With the **S**earch option, you can search the currently selected track for one or more MIDI events. When you choose **S**earch, the rather complex Event Filter dialog box appears, as shown in figure 8.43. This dialog box enables you to narrow the editing actions to a specific range or kind of event.

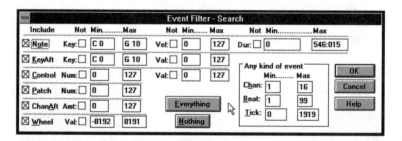

The Event Filter is indeed a filter in that it allows you to focus many editing actions on selected MIDI events, filtering out and ignoring other events. A *filter* sets a number of conditions before allowing an action to take place. If you said, for example, "I never eat chicken except on Tuesdays in August," you would be creating a filter. Chicken is not OK unless the following conditions are met: it must be Tuesday *and* it must be the month of August. If offered chicken on a Wednesday, you would refuse. Wouldn't you?

The Event Filter performs the same kind of filtering action on MIDI events. You could say, for example, "Search for every instance in this song where a pedal event occurs." Or you could say, "Find every place where the note C# is played." Or even, "Find any event sent to MIDI channel 5 on the third beat of every measure." Because MIDI events have ranges of data associated with them (every MIDI voice patch has a number between 0 and 127, for example), you can tell the filter not only to notice whether a MIDI event occurs, but whether the event's parameters fall within a specified range. All of these elements are called filter criteria.

Filter criteria can be set in the negative sense as well. You can instruct the Event Filter to search for a specific event, or you can instruct the filter to search for everything *except* that specific event. Referring to figure 8.43, notice at the bottom of the Event Filter dialog box the two buttons labeled **E**verything and **N**othing. These buttons automatically set up the simplest search criteria: turn on all the filter options (**E**verything), or turn them all off (**N**othing). Unless you are modifying a previous search and just need to change the criteria slightly, it's usually easier to start fresh. If you want to search for a very specific event and believe you can describe it with all the appropriate parameters, click **N**othing. If, however, you want to look at a fairly broad range of MIDI events, it might make more sense to start with **E**verything turned on and then deselect the criteria that aren't important.

The Event Filter is set up to use six MIDI events as criteria:

Note	Patch
Key After-touch	Channel After-touch
Controller	Pitch Wheel

You may recall that each of these events has a specific set of parameters that is used to define the event. The Event Filter dialog box enables you to select an event for filtering by clicking the check box to the left of each event's abbreviated name. If a check mark appears in that box, the corresponding event will be used as part of the filter criteria.

Following the event name is a tricky little column of check boxes labeled Not. The Not box sets up the reverse criteria mentioned earlier. To understand how the Not box is used, you should go through a regular search. Using the Note event as an example, you could establish the following criteria:

Find every note that has a pitch of C in octave 5, with a velocity of 0 to 66, and a duration of 3 beats.

To perform this search, check the Note Include box and then click the Min box to set the minimum value you're looking for. If you were searching for any note between C and D#, for instance, then C would go in the Min box, and D# would go in the Max box. However, because you're not searching for a range of notes, but rather a specific note in a specific octave, you would enter **C 5** in both the Min and Max boxes. Moving on to the velocity, you do have a range of values that you're interested in, so you would enter a **0** in the Min box and a **66** in the Max box. Finally, you are interested only in notes with a duration of 3 beats, so you enter **3** in both the Min and Max boxes. In figure 8.44, you can see that I chose **N**othing and then entered the appropriate values for this search.

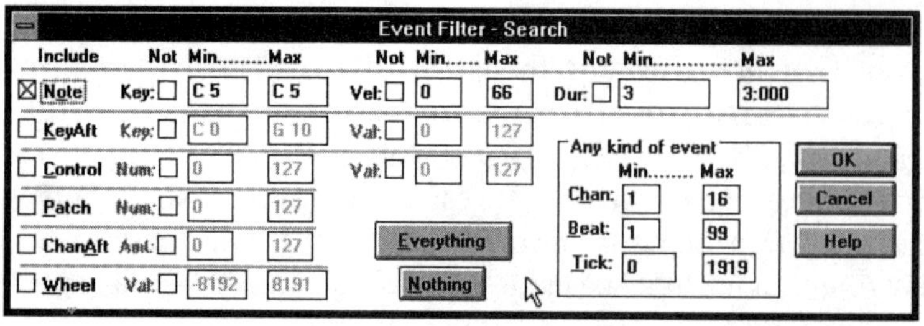

Fig. 8.44

Searching for a specific note.

If you clicked OK now, **S**earch would begin looking through your song for any C in the fifth octave, with the velocity and duration ranges set as in figure 8.44. Would it find any? Maybe. But a lot of MIDI songs have note velocity set to a fixed value, and the duration can be all over the place. What if you wanted to ignore the velocity and duration? In that case, set the Min value to the absolute minimum, and the Max value to the absolute maximum. Now your search criteria says the following:

Find any C in the fifth octave, with any velocity and any duration.

In most instances, you probably don't care about many of the criteria, so you can leave them at their minimum and maximum values.

What does all this have to do with the Not box? Quite a bit, actually. Imagine if you will (apologies to the late Rod Serling) a situation in which you have a song that sounds great except that in a couple of places you think you hear a note that shouldn't be there—a peeping, high-pitched sort of note when all the rest of the song is being played in the middle registers. One way to find that note is to identify the range of notes that should be playing, and then search for any note that is *not* within that range. If you knew that all the notes in the song should fall between a D in the third octave and a D in the fifth octave, and you don't care about any of the other criteria, you could set up the search as shown in figure 8.45. This search criteria simply says, "Find any note that is not between D 3 and D 5."

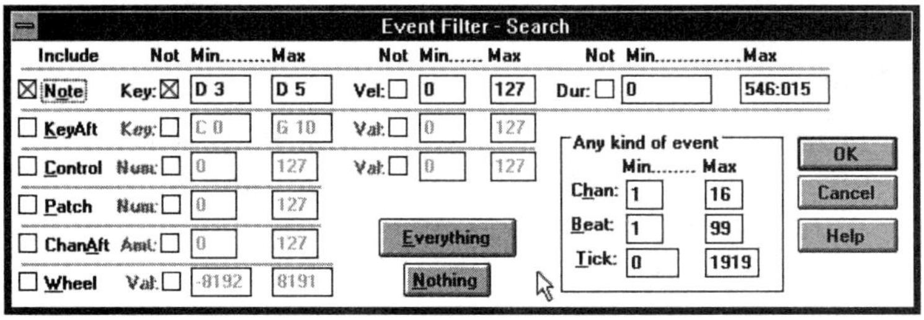

Fig. 8.45

Searching for a note outside a specific range of notes.

The one remaining element of the Event Filter dialog box is the section labeled Any Kind of Event. The three items here let you focus your search even more intently. You can search only for events that are sent to a specific channel, or that happen during a particular beat or range of beats. As an example, suppose that you want to search for any note outside the range of D 3 to D 5 and sent to channel 5. All you would have to do is set the Min and Max values for Chan: to 5 and start the search. This feature is particularly useful if you're creating a MIDI song that you would like to have comply with Microsoft's basic and extended MIDI channel limitations.

There you have it. You can apply the same kind of criteria and thinking to each of the MIDI events in the Event Filter dialog box. Just keep in mind the following:

- Search for anything within a range by setting the minimum and maximum values.

- Search for anything outside a range by setting the minimum and maximum values and then clicking the Not box.

- Search for a specific value by entering the same value in both the Min and Max boxes.

- To ignore a parameter, set the minimum and maximum values to their extreme limits.

- To reset all parameters to their extreme limits, click **E**verything or **N**othing.

- To search for a note in any octave, replace the octave number with a question mark.

The final option under **G**oTo is Search Ne**x**t, which finds the next occurrence of the criteria described in the Event Filter dialog box.

Edit Menu

The **E**dit menu enables you to modify a note or a range of notes in one or more tracks. These are the global editing functions. Typically, editing changes are made on time ranges specified by the From: and Thru: indicators in the currently selected tracks.

Most of the editing commands take advantage of the Event Filter, described in the previous pages. You should refer to that discussion to understand how the Event Filter works in association with editing commands.

Cakewalk uses a buffer in which to store information that is cut or copied from a song. If you cut or copy song data from three tracks at once, all three tracks are placed in the scrap buffer. Should you paste the contents of the scrap buffer elsewhere in the song, the song data is put back into the track from which it came, but in the new location. Information cut or copied from track 2 will be pasted back into track 2—unless, of course, you use the Paste to **O**ne Track command, described a little later.

Copy

The **C**opy command copies the selected song information into the scrap buffer. You use the Copy dialog box, shown in figure 8.46, to copy a range of measures or other MIDI data, specified in the **F**rom: and **T**hru: boxes.

Fig. 8.46

The Copy dialog box.

You can set the From: and Thru: indicators manually or by selecting a From: Thru: region from one of the views. You can set these indicators also by using the following keystrokes:

Key	Indicator
F9	From: = Now Time
Ctrl-F9	From: = beginning of the song
F10	Thru: = Now Time
Ctrl-F10	Thru: = end of the song

When you call up the Copy dialog box, the **F**rom: and **T**hru: boxes are already set to the most recent selection. You can manually change these values by clicking the text box and using the spin button to set the correct time, or by highlighting the values and directly typing the new values.

You use the Copy What section of the Copy dialog box to select what information is to be copied. To copy MIDI events from within the range, make sure that the **E**vents box is checked. To copy tempo changes in addition to MIDI events, click the Tem**p**o Changes box. If meter and key changes exist in the currently selected track, you can copy those too.

Note that a check box is marked **U**se Event Filter. If you want finer control over what you are copying, you can use the Event Filter to set a criteria for copying data. See the previous discussion on the **G**oTo menu for information on using the Event Filter.

Cut

The Cu**t** option is nearly identical to the **C**opy option, with one exception. The exception addresses the question, what do you do with the hole left behind? When you chop music out of a song with Cu**t**, Cakewalk fills the space left behind with silence. The measures will be preserved, but no MIDI information will be contained in them. If you would rather have Cakewalk remove the silence by sliding the rest of the song back to the left to fill the void, check the **D**elete Hole box.

Paste

This command pastes the contents of the scrap buffer into the Now Time insertion point. **P**aste gives you the option of placing multiple copies into the song, as shown in figure 8.47.

Fig. 8.47

The Paste dialog box.

When the Paste dialog box is opened, the **T**o Time: box contains the current Now Time as the insertion point. You can change the insertion point by clicking the box and either entering a new value directly or using the spin button to set a new value.

The **R**epetitions: box can be set to copy multiple copies into the insertion point.

You use the Existing Material section of the Paste dialog box to define how you want to handle music data that already exists at the insertion point. You can **B**lend the existing material and the material from the buffer, Re**p**lace the existing material with the new material, or **S**lide the existing material to the right to make room for the new material.

The last section of the Paste dialog box enables you to decide what to paste from the scrap buffer. If you check the **E**vents box, only MIDI events are pasted. The Tem**p**o Changes box lets tempo information be pasted at the insertion point. Any existing meter or key information is pasted when you check the **M**eter/Key Changes box. You can check any combination of boxes; if no boxes are checked, nothing is pasted.

Paste to One Track

You use this command if you have copied or cut multiple tracks into the scrap buffer but want to paste all the information into a single track. Paste to **O**ne Track is identical to **P**aste, with the addition of one box used to select the track to paste to.

Quantize

Some people believe that the **Q**uantize option is useful in cleaning up small recording problems such as not starting a note at exactly the beginning of the beat, or holding a note just a few ticks too long. Others believe that **Q**uantize bleeds the life out of a performance, making it sound dull and mechanical. Both groups are correct.

Using the Quantize dialog box, shown in figure 8.48, you can go through your song, checking to see whether note start time and duration are on some even multiple of a number of ticks. The number of ticks depends on the resolution you have selected. **Q**uantize adjusts note start times and durations to align them with current meter timings.

Fig. 8.48

The Quantize dialog box.

The resolution can range from whole notes to 1/32 triplets. If, for example, **R**esolution were set to 1/8 notes, the start time for each note in the selected time range would be adjusted to begin on 1/8 note multiples. A finer resolution would be achieved if you adjust the notes to start on 1/32 note boundaries.

You can quantize note start times and duration by checking the appropriate box in the Change section. The **P**ercent Strength: number is used to sort of "fudge" note times back and forth. When this number is set to 100, each note is perfectly aligned. When the number is set to 75, each note is moved 75 percent of the way to where it should be. The strength number can range from 1 through 100.

At the bottom of the Quantize dialog box, the **F**rom: and **T**hru: indicators are already loaded. You can change these times if you want. You can also use the Event Filter by checking the **U**se Event Filter box. Quantization is not very useful in adjusting non-note data, so the Event Filter is of limited use.

Length

You use the **L**ength option to expand or reduce the starting time and/or duration of notes within the selected time frame (see fig. 8.49).

Fig. 8.49

The **L**ength dialog box.

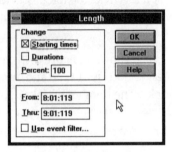

When the **S**tarting Times box is checked in the Length dialog box, the starting time for each note in the selected region is stretched out or reduced in time by the amount in the **P**ercent: box. If **P**ercent is set to 200, the start times are twice as far apart. If **P**ercent is set to 50, the time between notes is cut in half. The same holds true for note duration if the **D**urations box is checked.

As with all other editing commands, the music region to be lengthened is given in the **F**rom: and **T**hru: boxes, and these values may be changed. In addition, you can use the Event Filter to help select which events to operate on.

Slide

The **S**lide command adjusts the MIDI event times in or out, depending on the amount you've selected in the **A**mount box in the Slide dialog box (see fig. 8.50).

Fig. 8.50

The **S**lide dialog box.

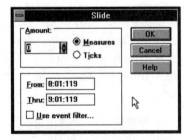

In this dialog box, you can set whether the amount is measured in **M**easures or **T**icks by clicking the appropriate button. The amount can be a positive or negative number. Suppose that you had a riff on one track that you wanted to come in just a little bit later. Select the appropriate measures, click Ticks, and set the amount for 30. Those notes will begin 30 ticks later than they did originally.

Changes made with **S**lide are permanent and are saved as MIDI timing data.

Transpose

You use the Transpose option to adjust all the notes within the selected region up or down in pitch (see fig. 8.51). Transpose makes permanent changes to the MIDI data.

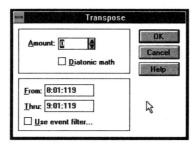

Fig. 8.51

The Transpose dialog box.

You have the option of transposing the notes diatonically or chromatically. If you check **D**iatonic Math, the notes are adjusted upward or downward relative to the current key signature, ensuring that the transposed notes will be in key. If you don't check **D**iatonic Math, the notes are adjusted chromatically, a half step at a time.

Again, you can use the Event Filter to select specific events to be adjusted.

Controller Fill

The Controller fill command in some ways duplicates the function of the Controllers view; both are used to insert controller changes in a song. The Controller Fill command, however, can generate only straight-line changes from one time to another (see fig. 8.52).

To insert a controller action, make sure that the appropriate time range is selected, and then scroll through the **W**hat list until the appropriate controller event is selected. Set MIDI **C**hannel to the right channel number and assign the **B**egin and **E**nd values for the event.

Fig. 8.52

The Controller Fill
dialog box.

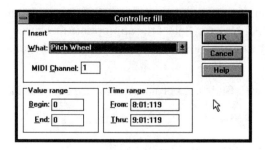

Track Menu

You use the **T**rack menu to change track parameters in the Track/Measure view. Most of the **T**rack menu options are duplicates of those described previously in the Track/Measure view discussion. Only the five additional commands are described here.

The S**o**lo and **U**n-solo commands are actually better used as keyboard short-cuts. To mute all other tracks except the currently selected track, press the slash (/) key. This feature is particularly useful to isolate the notes in one track when playing back a song. If multiple tracks are selected, all the selected tracks will play. To turn solo off, press the backslash (\) key.

You use the Clon**e** command to copy the contents of one track onto another track (see fig. 8.53). You have the option of copying just the MIDI event data, the parameters shown in the Track/Measure view, or both. Clon**e** automatically assumes that you will want to copy the data to the next available empty track, but you have the option of setting a track number.

Fig. 8.53

The Clone dialog
box.

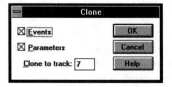

The **W**ipe and K**i**ll options remove all events from a track, leaving behind track parameters (**W**ipe), or deleting everything from a track, including track parameters (K**i**ll). Neither of these commands can be recovered from when invoked. Thus Cakewalk warns you, as shown in figure 8.54, that **W**ipe and K**i**ll cannot be undone.

Fig. 8.54

A warning
message issued
when you choose
Wipe or **K**ill.

When you just want to remove the notes and other MIDI events from a track—
leaving the name, port, channel, patch name, and other track parameters
intact—use **W**ipe.

Window Menu

The **W**indow menu controls the environment—what windows are open and
how they are organized on the screen. This menu, shown in figure 8.55, is
divided into three parts.

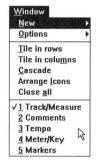

Fig. 8.55

The **Window**
menu.

The bottom portion of the menu is used to activate one of four minimized
windows (icons) at the bottom of the screen. The menu in this figure shows
that the Track/Measure view is already open because Track/Measure has a
check mark beside it. To open the other windows, either double-click the icon
or choose them by name from the **W**indow menu.

The central portion of the **W**indow menu has to do with how the windows are
organized on your screen. Because these are standard Windows functions,
they are not discussed here.

The upper portion of the **W**indow menu has two commands. The **N**ew
command is simply another way of opening one of the views. You can activate
any of the views by holding down the right mouse button while in one view, or
selecting a view with the **N**ew command.

From the **N**ew pop-out menu, you can open the **P**iano-Roll, **E**vent List, **C**ontrollers, or **S**taff view.

The **O**ptions command has three functions that enable you to set Cakewalk preferences.

In most Windows applications, you must click in a window to activate it. When you choose **A**uto-activate, Cakewalk has the unique capability to automatically activate the window where the pointer is located. The **C**ontrol Bar at Bottom option relocates the control bar to the bottom of the screen. And the **D**OS F6 View Keys option is for users who are familiar with the DOS version of Cakewalk and want to use the F6 key as they do in DOS to bring up or close views. When **D**OS F6 View Keys is enabled, the standard Windows Ctrl-F6 function is disabled. You can make the following view changes with the F6 key:

F6	Close the active Piano-Roll or Event List view and open the Track/Measure view.
Ctrl-F6	Open or activate the Event List view.
Alt-F6	Open or activate the Piano-Roll view.

Settings Menu

With the **S**ettings menu, you set up the various MIDI parameters used to create and play back MIDI songs. The **S**ettings menu controls the MIDI environment.

The **S**ettings menu is divided into two functional areas: metronome control and MIDI control.

Metronome

When you choose **M**etronome, the Metronome dialog box appears (see fig. 8.56). You can control when and how the metronome works.

The metronome uses both the PC speaker and Sound Blaster when operating. The PC speaker beeps as usual, while Sound Blaster issues an approximation of the closed hi-hat sound.

In the General section of the Metronome dialog box, you can determine whether the metronome should sound during **P**layback, **R**ecording, or both. You can also turn on the **A**ccent effect, which adds an accent to the first beat of the measure. The **C**ount In value is the number of count-in clicks you hear before recording or playback begins. The **U**se PC Speaker box enables you to use or not use the PC speaker as a metronome sound.

The MIDI Note section of this dialog box sets up the Sound Blaster metronome. You can change each of the boxes to use a different port, channel, key, velocity, and duration of the metronome tick. To disable the MIDI metronome, set **V**elocity to zero.

MIDI Devices

The MIDI De**v**ices command brings up the Select MIDI Devices dialog box, shown in figure 8.57. You select the appropriate MIDI devices from this window.

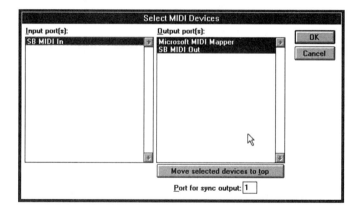

Fig. 8.57

The Select MIDI Devices dialog box.

MIDI input and output ports are shown in the two scrolling lists. What appears in the lists depends entirely on what MIDI drivers are installed in your system. At a minimum, you should see the three ports listed in figure 8.57. Select the three ports shown in the figure and click OK. Each output device is then available from the Track/Measure view, and you can set that device by double-clicking the Port entry in that view.

Some MIDI systems use synchronization signals to keep all the instruments together. Check the **P**ort for Sync Output box to select the appropriate synchronization port.

Patch Names

You use the **P**atch Names command to associate a MIDI patch list with each port and channel used. See the discussion about the Track/Measure view earlier in this chapter for a detailed description of how to configure patch names.

MIDI Thru

The MIDI Thr**u** command controls how Cakewalk Apprentice routes MIDI signals from the master keyboard. There are three Thru mode options, as shown in figure 8.58. Refer to Chapter 6 for information on MIDI Thru.

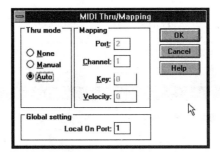

You can turn MIDI Thru off by clicking the **N**one button. If you click **M**anual, MIDI Thru is enabled. You can then control the destination of the MIDI data in terms of output Por**t** and **C**hannel, whether the MIDI data should be transposed to a higher or lower **K**ey, and whether the **V**elocity data should be transposed to a higher or lower value. If you choose **A**uto mode, the mapping automatically tracks the currently selected track in the song.

Some MIDI keyboards contain an internal synthesizer to play music. In other words, these MIDI controllers do not have to be connected to a separate, external synthesizer. This becomes a problem in some instances because the MIDI keyboard may play a note at the same time the note is supposed to be played on Sound Blaster. Many modern MIDI keyboards with internal synthesizers have a function called Local Control. When Local Control is set to on, your keyboard synthesizer will play when you press the keys, and at the same time that MIDI instructions are being sent to Sound Blaster. When Local Control is set to off, your internal synthesizer is disabled, even though the MIDI instructions are being passed on to Sound Blaster.

A problem can arise if Local Control is set to on. First you play a note, your keyboard's internal synthesizer plays the note, and Cakewalk then routes the MIDI instruction for playing that note back into your MIDI keyboard. When that happens, an effect called "note doubling" occurs. It sometimes sounds as if you struck a key twice, or that a key is bouncing. If possible, you should set Local Control to off on your MIDI keyboard to avoid this phenomenon. If you cannot do this, however, you can indicate to Cakewalk which port your keyboard is connected to, and Cakewalk will try to avoid sending data back to your internal synthesizer.

If your MIDI keyboard has the capability to turn Local Control off, set the Local On Port value to 0. If you cannot turn off Local Control, set the Local On Port value to the port number of your keyboard.

MIDI Out

The MIDI **O**ut command controls when and what kind of MIDI synchronization instructions are issued, and resets and configure controllers. When you choose MIDI **O**ut, the MIDI Out dialog box appears (see fig. 8.59).

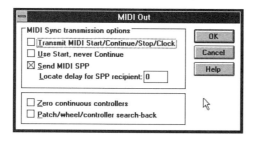

The MIDI Sync Transmission Options allow Cakewalk Apprentice to get all MIDI instruments in sync so that they all start and play at the same time. The **T**ransmit MIDI Start/Continue/Stop/Clock check box enables Cakewalk to issue these MIDI commands. Try running without checking this box to improve performance slightly. If you find that you are having synchronization problems, check this box.

The **U**se Start, never Continue option forces Cakewalk always to restart a song from the beginning, even if you've paused midway through a song, or you've set the Now Time pointer to be somewhere other than at the beginning. Some drum machines have synchronization problems when you start from the middle of a song.

Send MIDI SPP causes Cakewalk Apprentice to send the MIDI Song Position Pointer (SPP) data before beginning playback. The SPP number indicates where playback should begin. When this box is checked, Cakewalk sends the SPP message, waits the amount of time loaded in the **L**ocate Delay for SPP Recipient box, and then begins playback. The delay unit is 1/18 of a second, and the delay gives devices that receive the SPP time to respond to the message.

The **Z**ero Continuous Controllers box causes Cakewalk to reset the pitch wheel, pedals, and modulation wheel to their zero positions at the end of playback. For example, you may experience "stuck notes" when you stop playback. That may be because the sustain pedal event is still in the on position, and the last note played is being sustained indefinitely. Checking this box allows Cakewalk to directly turn off all such effects.

The **P**atch/Wheel/Controller Search-back box enables Cakewalk to set these three items to the correct position when you start playback from somewhere other than the beginning of the song. When this box is checked, Cakewalk searches backward from the Now Time marker until it finds the most recent settings for the current patch, wheel, and other controller events used in the song. When these three items are properly configured, playback begins. You need to use this option only if you have altered any of these items during the course of a song.

Time Format

Using the Time **F**ormat command is identical to clicking the Time Format indicator in the control bar. Time **F**ormat is used to establish synchronization messages to be used when MIDI songs are merged with video or movies. See the earlier discussion about the control bar for more information about Time Format.

Cakewalk Pro

As stated at the beginning of this chapter, Cakewalk Apprentice is a junior version of Cakewalk Pro for Windows. Cakewalk Pro works with any device that provides a Windows Multimedia Extensions driver, whereas Cakewalk Apprentice works only with Sound Blaster. The Pro version also provides the following enhancements:

- You can record multiple takes for one track and then keep the one you like best.

- You can select specific areas in a song that will be replaced during playback by new material. You do this by setting a punch-in time (when the replacement material is started) and a punch-out time (when play switches back to the original MIDI song).

- Cakewalk Pro supports automatic looping through an area in a song.

- The Pro version can send MIDI system-exclusive messages.

- You can write your own editing commands, using the Cakewalk Application Language.

These and many more enhancements are available with the new Cakewalk Pro for Windows Version 2.0.

Thanks for Bach!

Here's a final word on this chapter. From the beginning, you have probably noticed that the word *violin* is misspelled in track 1 of the Bach song used as an example. Why, you must be asking yourself, wasn't that corrected? There is what I believe to be a good reason for this error. Many musicians who go through the effort to convert classic pieces like this into MIDI songs sometimes leave a little signature behind. That's because many songs are released into the public domain, yet the musician would like to see how many times the song pops up and in what forums. Therefore, a typo will be left in the song, or a couple of notes will be slightly out of place. I do not know for a fact that the musician who transcribed the Bach piece did leave that misspelling there for this purpose. But if he did, I would like to say, "Hello, and thanks for giving us this music to work with."

> **NOTE**
>
> The MIDI file of the Bach A minor concerto is part of a two-disk set of "The Violin Music of J.S. Bach." It includes five violin concertos, six sonatas for violin and piano, and six sonatas and partitas for violin solo (including the famous "Chaconne"). The set is available for $29.95. Please add shipping: U.S. $2.50, foreign $5. Please specify your computer. To order, contact:
>
> Dietrich Gewissler
> 92 Smith Street
> Howell, NJ 07731
> Telephone: (908) 364-8719

CHAPTER 9

Windows and Sound Blaster

Microsoft Windows 3.1 is the first widely available multimedia computer environment for Intel-based personal computers. The multimedia extensions to Windows are just now being exploited (in the positive sense of the word) to our common benefit.

Multimedia as a concept is a little disconcerting or even confusing to some. It shouldn't be. After all, multimedia is simply the presentation of information through sound, video, and text. If there were some way to generate smell, it too would be added to the multimedia pot.

A personal computer with a sound board, Windows 3.1, and adequate computing horsepower is a fully qualified multimedia engine. (A 33 MHz 80386 or later PC is a must because video puts a severe load on the computer chip.) You can watch video clips, watch television (provided you purchase Creative Labs' Video Blaster), hear music, read text—what's left?

The Windows environment enables developers to blend sound, video, and text more easily in a cohesive manner—thanks to a couple of capabilities provided by Microsoft. One is called Media Control Interface (MCI), and the other is Object Linking and Embedding (OLE). The MCI package is a way for software applications to access multimedia equipment, such as CD-ROM players. By using MCI, software developers don't have to write their own control software, and all applications can access the equipment in a consistent manner.

OLE is important because it allows one application to embed copies of, or link to, files created by other applications. Therefore, a document that you prepare using Word for Windows can include sound, video clips, drawings—even a spreadsheet. Then when you click the sound icon, that sound file is played.

If the embedded object is a spreadsheet, clicking the spreadsheet icon opens the file and the source application.

If you are a Windows user, you might be wondering whether sound will make your life better. Initially, it will probably only make your life more entertaining. If you are running Windows 3.1 and you have Sound Blaster installed in your computer, you've probably already experienced the entertaining aspects of sound on your computer. Many users, for example, have found Clint Eastwood's voice the perfect complement to exiting Windows. But the future is bright for sound to make your life more productive, and Windows is a good vehicle for that improvement.

The Windows 3.1 environment includes several application packages that deal with sound. The first part of this chapter discusses those packages. The chapter also covers some Windows applications provided with Sound Blaster and then briefly describes several shareware packages that have proven to be useful, entertaining, or both.

Windows Control Panel

The Windows Control Panel is where all the drivers and controls are set up for Sound Blaster. Figure 9.1 shows the Control Panel.

Fig. 9.1

The Windows 3.1 Control Panel.

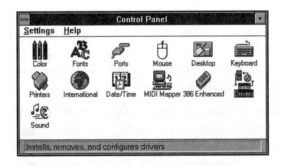

Three of the applications in the Control Panel window are essential for sound: Drivers, Sound, and MIDI Mapper. You use Drivers to install low-level hardware drivers into the Windows environment. Sound enables you to attach WAV files to different Windows events, and MIDI Mapper is used to configure the Windows Media Player to reproduce MIDI files with the appropriate programs (voices).

Drivers

When you install new hardware such as Sound Blaster into your computer, and you want Windows to detect and use the hardware, you must install driver routines. Likewise, if you've written software that uses several Windows resources differently than they're typically used, you must write and install a different driver. In most cases (as with Sound Blaster), the application's installation routine takes care of setting up the drivers. However, if you are going to install an updated driver, you will need to use the Drivers application. The Drivers application, shown in figure 9.2, takes care of properly installing drivers into the Windows environment. To open the Drivers window, click the Drivers icon in the Windows Control Panel.

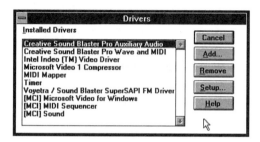

Fig. 9.2

The Windows Drivers application.

Figure 9.2 shows the drivers that are installed on my system. Whether or not you have a sound card, Windows installs both the MIDI Mapper and the Timer driver. In addition, this system includes two Sound Blaster drivers, as well as a driver for the Sound Blaster FM chips from Voyetra. Other versions of Sound Blaster will have different drivers. Again, the Sound Blaster installation process usually takes care of installing drivers for you.

The three drivers that begin with [MCI] are multimedia drivers from Microsoft. MCI stands for Media Control Interface—an interface developed by Microsoft that allows software applications to control and use a variety of hardware, including CD-ROMs and Sound Blaster.

Remember that whenever a new piece of hardware is added to the system, a new driver is probably needed. Or you might be sent an update of a driver program that must be installed. To add new drivers to the environment, you use the **A**dd button. The Add dialog box appears (see fig. 9.3).

Fig. 9.3

The Add dialog
box.

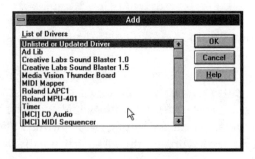

The list in the Add dialog box includes all the drivers Windows has detected. To add a driver to the active list, simply highlight the driver name and click OK. The new driver is then added to the Installed Drivers list.

Presumably, when you installed Sound Blaster, everything worked just fine. But occasionally, you will discover that the settings you picked during installation cause conflicts with other hardware. For example, you may have to change the I/O address to something other than 220H. Rather than reinstall all the software after making a hardware change, you can make the change and then use the **S**etup button in the Drivers window to update Windows so that all the applications that use Sound Blaster know where to look for it. Figure 9.4 shows the Setup options.

Fig. 9.4

The SOUND
BLASTER PRO
Setup dialog box.

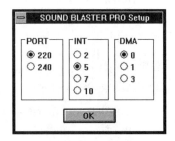

For example, when the Sound Blaster driver is selected, Setup tells you what it believes are the port address, interrupt number, and DMA channels. If these items are incorrect, you can change them.

Most software and hardware that you buy includes an installation routine which automatically installs the appropriate drivers. Seldom do you have to install drivers yourself.

Sound

The Sound application, shown in figure 9.5, is used to assign sounds to Windows events. To access the Sound application, you choose Sound in the Windows Control Panel.

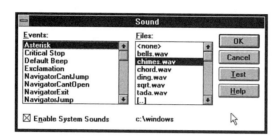

Fig. 9.5

The Windows
Sound application.

Microsoft considers Windows an "event-driven" environment. That is, you cause things to happen by pointing the mouse and clicking a button, or by typing a character. Pointing, clicking, and typing are all *events*. There are other events as well. Starting Windows is an event, as is leaving Windows. Pushing the wrong key at the wrong time is an event.

Windows lets you assign sounds to events. Look at figure 9.5; you might ask yourself, "What is a Critical Stop? How can an Asterisk be an event?" Neither Critical Stop nor Asterisk is an event in itself. Windows provides these event names for the applications that run within Windows. One software developer might use the Default Beep whenever you point the mouse outside an active area and click a button. Another developer might use Question if your request wasn't clear. In other words, there are no hard-and-fast rules about which sound events are caused by what actions. Software suppliers are free to do as they please. Some shareware suppliers provide a list of additional events to be displayed in the Sound application.

To assign a sound to an event, highlight the event in the left box and then highlight the sound in the right box. The sound must be in a WAV file. To hear your choice, click the **T**est button.

You can assign sound files from anywhere in your file system. To move out of the C:\WINDOWS directory, double-click the [..] line in the **F**iles box. Use this method to browse through your file system until you find just the WAV file you want.

After you're happy with your sound assignments, click OK. If you are tired of hearing sounds, shut off the sounds by clicking the Enable System Sounds box (the x is removed). When you assign sounds, remember that you should attach short—rather than long—sound files to events. Ten seconds of dialog every time you click the wrong button can become tedious quickly, unless, of course, you have nothing better to do than listen to sound files.

MIDI Mapper

The MIDI Mapper, shown in figure 9.6, can be one of the more complicated applications dealing with sound. If you're unclear about MIDI terminology, review Chapters 6 and 7.

To summarize, MIDI songs are composed of messages that are issued to the MIDI instrument. The messages are sent over channels and contain information about the patch (program or voice) to be used to play a note.

Three things can go wrong when it comes time to play a MIDI song, and all of them have to do with the synthesizer for which the song was recorded. If the synthesizer that the song was composed for was not General MIDI-compliant, you can run into these problems:

- The channel assignments used to record the song disagree with General MIDI standards.

- The patch assignments used to record the song disagree with General MIDI standards.

- The key in which the song was originally recorded is not the key in which the song plays on a MIDI-compliant instrument.

As you can see, Murphy is hard at work here. As a prime example, table 9.1 lists the differences between what my Casio MT-640 thinks are MIDI patch assignments and the general MIDI patch assignments actually supported by MIDI-compliant instruments.

Table 9.1 Casio MT-640 versus General MIDI

	Casio	MIDI
Channels	1-4	1-16
Percussion Channel	4	16 (16 or 10 for Windows)
# Patches	20	128
Patch 0	Piano	Piano
Patch 11	Funky clavichord	Vibraphone
Patch 12	Jazz guitar	Marimba
Patch 16	Chorus	Hammond organ

As table 9.1 shows, when a song is composed to play on the Casio, it's probably going to sound different on a General MIDI instrument. A pretty guitar song tends to sound like someone beating on a log with a stick.

You also must deal with where the MIDI song will be played. Basically, you have two options: the song can be played on Sound Blaster's synthesizer, or the song can be routed to an external synthesizer or synthesizers attached to Sound Blaster's MIDI connector. Some sequencers can play on both Sound Blaster and an external MIDI instrument.

If you're using a General MIDI instrument and don't care about Microsoft's multimedia guidelines, you don't have to worry about the MIDI Mapper. However, Microsoft has complicated the issue somewhat by bending the General MIDI guidelines and creating new rules regarding the placement of the percussion channel.

General MIDI guidelines state that channel 16 is used for percussion and that channels 1 through 15 are used for melodic sounds. Microsoft divided the MIDI world into two groups: basic and extended. Microsoft's Basic MIDI guideline says that only four channels are used; channels 13 through 15 are used for melodic sounds, and percussion uses channel 16. Microsoft's Extended MIDI guideline says that 10 channels are available; channel 10 is used for percussion sounds, and channels 1 through 9 are used for melodic sounds.

In short, a song composed to Microsoft MIDI standards may not sound just right when played on a General MIDI instrument because channel 10 is playing a percussion track instead of a melody track. This stipulation is particularly true with drum machines that typically pay attention to messages sent only over channel 16.

A song composed for a General MIDI instrument with percussion transmitted on channel 16 will need channel 16 mapped to channel 10 to be compliant with Microsoft Extended MIDI.

Windows MIDI Mapper is extremely useful if you find yourself working with MIDI songs or instruments that do not comply with the General MIDI specification for channel use and patch numbers. MIDI Mapper enables you to modify an existing setup or patch map, or create a new one for your specific needs. In either case, MIDI Mapper resolves nearly all the compatibility issues that arise in the MIDI world.

Setups

So now you must deal with three different kinds of MIDI: General MIDI, Microsoft Basic MIDI, and Microsoft Extended MIDI. A MIDI song can be played in six different places in six different ways, each requiring its own mapping.

Microsoft tried to help by providing canned setups that resolve some of these issues. Notice that the MIDI Mapper window includes a pull-down box that lists five different setups, as shown in figure 9.7. The names on your screen may vary slightly depending on your Sound Blaster card.

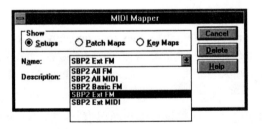

Fig. 9.7

The Name Box for selecting a Microsoft default channel, patch, or key map setup.

When you select a setup and click the **E**dit button, a new window opens that lists all the characteristics of that setup. Here are descriptions of the setups listed in figure 9.7:

- *SBP2 All FM*. This setup routes all 16 MIDI channels to the Sound Blaster synthesizer chip(s), as shown in figure 9.8.

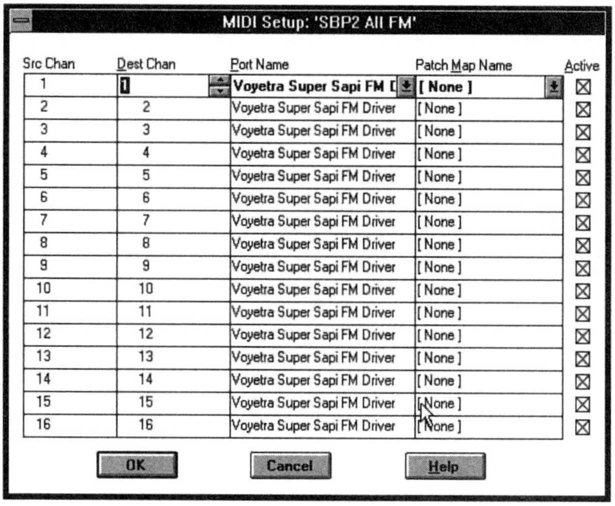

Fig. 9.8

The All FM setup.

This setup assumes that channel 16 is used as the percussion channel per General MIDI guidelines. The source channel (the channel originally used in the song) is mapped to the same channel number. You can also see that the Voyetra driver for the Sound Blaster card is being used and that no patch map names have been assigned to the various channels. Patch maps are described a little later in this chapter. You can assign a patch map name by double-clicking in the table cell corresponding with the channel you want to map, and selecting a map name from the list that appears.

You can modify the setup by clicking the spin arrows for the destination channel, port name, and patch map name.

- *SBP2 Basic FM*. The Basic FM setup, shown in figure 9.9, is used to play Microsoft Basic MIDI songs.

  In this setup, only channels 13 through 16 are active, which complies with the Basic MIDI guidelines. This setup includes no channel mapping and no patch maps.

- *SBP2 Ext FM*. The extended FM setup, shown in figure 9.10, is used to play Microsoft's Extended MIDI songs.

  In this setup, some channel mapping occurs. Only channels 1 through 10 are activated, and source channel 10 is mapped to destination channel 16. Again, no patch maps are used.

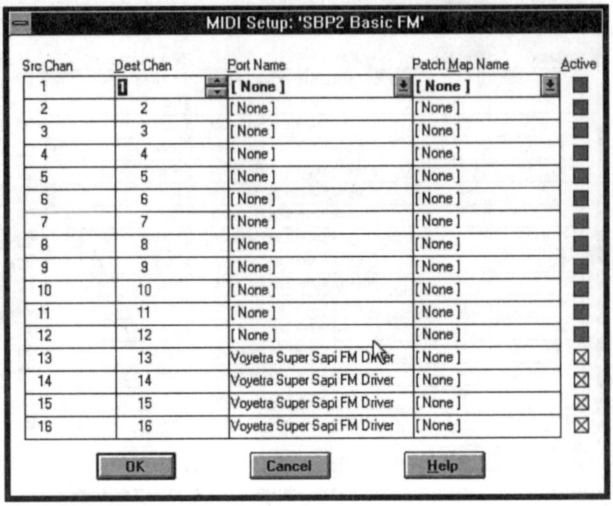

Fig. 9.9

The Basic FM setup.

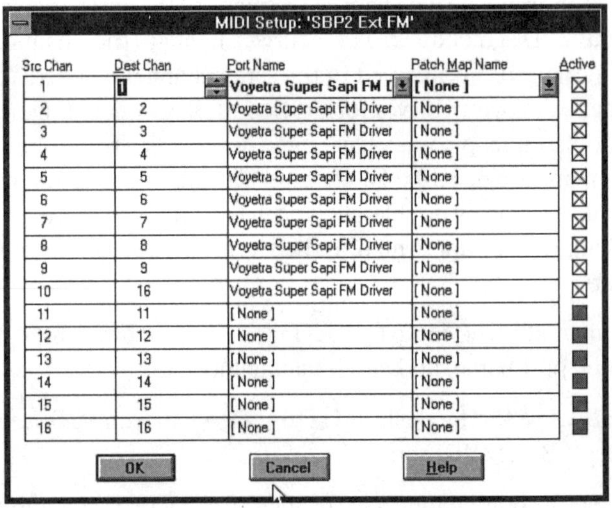

MIDI Setup: 'SBP2 Basic FM'

Src Chan	Dest Chan	Port Name	Patch Map Name	Active
1	1	[None]	[None]	■
2	2	[None]	[None]	■
3	3	[None]	[None]	■
4	4	[None]	[None]	■
5	5	[None]	[None]	■
6	6	[None]	[None]	■
7	7	[None]	[None]	■
8	8	[None]	[None]	■
9	9	[None]	[None]	■
10	10	[None]	[None]	■
11	11	[None]	[None]	■
12	12	[None]	[None]	■
13	13	Voyetra Super Sapi FM Driver	[None]	☒
14	14	Voyetra Super Sapi FM Driver	[None]	☒
15	15	Voyetra Super Sapi FM Driver	[None]	☒
16	16	Voyetra Super Sapi FM Driver	[None]	☒

OK   Cancel   Help

Fig. 9.10

The Extended FM setup.

MIDI Setup: 'SBP2 Ext FM'

Src Chan	Dest Chan	Port Name	Patch Map Name	Active
1	1	Voyetra Super Sapi FM D	[None]	☒
2	2	Voyetra Super Sapi FM Driver	[None]	☒
3	3	Voyetra Super Sapi FM Driver	[None]	☒
4	4	Voyetra Super Sapi FM Driver	[None]	☒
5	5	Voyetra Super Sapi FM Driver	[None]	☒
6	6	Voyetra Super Sapi FM Driver	[None]	☒
7	7	Voyetra Super Sapi FM Driver	[None]	☒
8	8	Voyetra Super Sapi FM Driver	[None]	☒
9	9	Voyetra Super Sapi FM Driver	[None]	☒
10	16	Voyetra Super Sapi FM Driver	[None]	☒
11	11	[None]	[None]	■
12	12	[None]	[None]	■
13	13	[None]	[None]	■
14	14	[None]	[None]	■
15	15	[None]	[None]	■
16	16	[None]	[None]	■

OK   Cancel   Help

- *SBP2 All MIDI.* The All MIDI setup, shown in figure 9.11, closely resembles the All FM setup.

  Again, no channel mapping occurs. All 16 channels are used. The Port Name has changed to SB MIDI Out, however, indicating that the MIDI messages will be routed to the external MIDI instrument.

- *SBP2 Ext MIDI.* The last setup, shown in figure 9.12, is for playing Microsoft Extended MIDI songs on an external MIDI instrument.

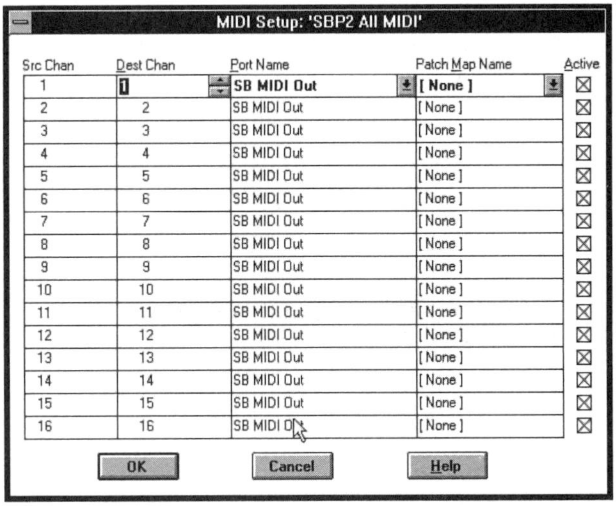

Fig. 9.11

The All MIDI setup.

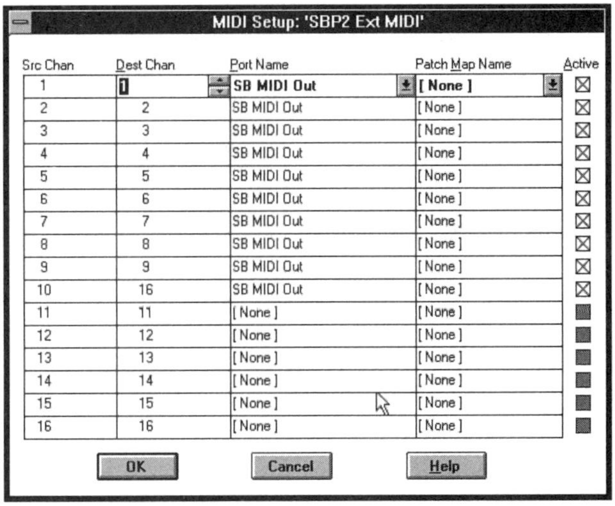

Fig. 9.12

The Ext MIDI setup.

In this setup, the source channel 10 has been mapped to channel 16 for play on a General MIDI instrument. If the external MIDI instrument were configured to send percussion over channel 10 when recording, you would need to change the channel mapping to map the source channel 10 to the destination channel 10.

Patch Maps

The Patch Map function of MIDI Mapper is used to reassign program (patch) numbers. Again, some MIDI instruments do not comply with the current standard patch numbers. There are 128 melodic patch numbers (see table 6.11 in Chapter 6) and 20 percussive patch numbers (see table 6.12 in Chapter 6).

To open a patch map, click the **P**atch Maps button in the MIDI Mapper window. Five standard patch maps are provided with Windows, as shown in figure 9.13.

Five standard patch maps are provided with Windows.

The MT32 and MT32 Perc maps are for the Roland MT32 synthesizer. The Prot/1 and Prot/1 Perc maps are for the Proteus synthesizer.

Look at the patch map for the MT32 by highlighting MT32 and then clicking **E**dit. The patches, shown in figure 9.14, are fairly significant.

The patch map for the Roland MT32.

MIDI Patch Map: 'MT32'

1 based patches

Src Patch	Src Patch Name	Dest Patch	Volume %	Key Map Name
0	Acoustic Grand Piano	13	100	[None]
1	Bright Acoustic Piano	0	100	[None]
2	Electric Grand Piano	0	100	[None]
3	Honky-tonk Piano	7	100	[None]
4	Rhodes Piano	5	100	[None]
5	Chorused Piano	6	100	[None]
6	Harpsichord	17	100	[None]
7	Clavinet	21	100	[None]
8	Celesta	22	100	[None]
9	Glockenspiel	101	100	[None]
10	Music Box	101	100	[None]
11	Vibraphone	98	100	[None]
12	Marimba	104	100	[None]
13	Xylophone	103	100	[None]
14	Tubular Bells	102	100	[None]
15	Dulcimer	105	100	[None]

OK   Cancel   Help

The column labeled Src Patch gives the General MIDI patch number. Src Patch Name is the name of the General MIDI patches. The **D**est Patch is the patch number recognized by the instrument that will play the song. For example, if you have a General MIDI song that features a glockenspiel and you would like to have the song play correctly on a Roland MT32, you must map the General MIDI patch number 9 to the Roland MT32 patch number 101. If you use an MT32 with percussion, though, the patch map is pretty standard.

Different MIDI instruments seem to play different sounds at different volume levels. MIDI Mapper lets you adjust the volume level for each patch. Finally, if the target instrument has different percussion instrument assignments than those suggested by General MIDI, you can use the key map.

Key Map

The key map (shown in fig. 9.15) is used to compensate for MIDI instruments that can play percussion on channel 16 but use different patch numbers from those specified by General MIDI.

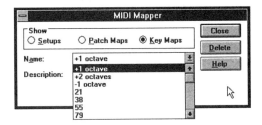

Fig. 9.15

The key map used to map General MIDI percussion sounds to different patch numbers.

The scroll box in figure 9.15 has a fairly substantial number of key patches. Each key patch shown consists of a number of different individual instrument patches. For example, if you select the +1 octave patch and click the **E**dit button, the key map for +1 octave is shown, as in figure 9.16. The standard General MIDI percussion patch numbers appear in the left column, and the names appear in the next column. The third column lists the patch numbers that are recognized by the target instrument.

In figure 9.16, the Src Key number is a MIDI patch number. You can change the destination number, thereby mapping a general MIDI instrument sound to a MIDI number for a nongeneral MIDI instrument. For example, the general MIDI hand clap sound is key number 39. You may have a MIDI drum machine that plays hand clap sounds on key number 50. This key map maps key 39 to key 50 so that the MIDI song that expects a hand clap sound gets a hand clap sound on the nongeneral MIDI instrument. Likewise, nonpercussion sounds (notes) may have to be mapped up or down an octave to play correctly.

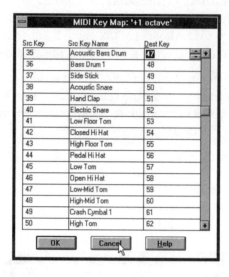

	MIDI Key Map: '+1 octave'	
Src Key	Src Key Name	Dest Key
35	Acoustic Bass Drum	47
36	Bass Drum 1	48
37	Side Stick	49
38	Acoustic Snare	50
39	Hand Clap	51
40	Electric Snare	52
41	Low Floor Tom	53
42	Closed Hi Hat	54
43	High Floor Tom	55
44	Pedal Hi Hat	56
45	Low Tom	57
46	Open Hi Hat	58
47	Low-Mid Tom	59
48	High-Mid Tom	60
49	Crash Cymbal 1	61
50	High Tom	62

OK   Cancel   Help

Microsoft Windows Sound Applications

The title of this section is slightly misleading. Microsoft provides two sound applications with Windows: Sound Recorder and Media Player. Most of the major applications that currently run on Windows, however, support sound using OLE and MCI.

The following sections describe Sound Recorder and Media Player and then discuss how a sound file can be embedded in a text document.

Sound Recorder

Sound Recorder, shown in figure 9.17, is used to record, modify, and play back WAV files. To start Sound Recorder, double-click the Sound Recorder icon in the Accessories window.

Sound Recorder is actually a fairly versatile WAV file editor. With it, you can record sounds as well as modify existing sound files until they're unrecognizable.

Fig. 9.17

Windows Sound
Recorder.

Windows comes with a set of four files for use with the Sound application in the
Control Panel. One of those files, CHIMES.WAV, is a pleasant little chime
sound. If you want to try Sound Recorder, double-click the Sound Recorder
icon and choose **F**ile **O**pen. If you followed the standard Windows installation
procedure, the file CHIMES.WAV is in the WINDOWS directory and immediately visible. Load CHIMES.WAV into Sound Recorder by highlighting the file
name and clicking OK. The name of the sound file appears in the window
header when the file is successfully loaded. At this point, all you see on-screen
is a straight horizontal line—green if you have a color monitor.

Click the center Play button; you hear the chime sound and see a rough
approximation of its waveform. As you can see in the window, the chime sound
is approximately 0.72 seconds long. Now choose the Effect**s** menu from the
menu bar. The menu that appears contains all the modifications you can make
to a sound file. You can increase or decrease volume, slow or speed playback,
add an echo, or play the file backward. For this exercise, click D**e**crease Speed
once. Then choose Effect**s** and click D**e**crease Speed a second time. Then do
it a third time.

At this point, the sound file playback takes about 5.76 seconds. Play the sound
by clicking the Play button. Because you have slowed down the speed of the
sound, you can hear how the chime sound is constructed—a series of five bell
sounds with a significant pitch change between each sound. When I listen to
this file at this speed, I find that I really like the last two tones. They sound like
two very large bells being struck by soft hammers.

Play the file again, this time making note of when the fourth bell sounds. It
seems to be struck somewhere between 1.5 and 2 seconds into the recording.
Using the mouse, point to the slider beneath the display graph in the window;
while holding down the left mouse button, slide the slider back and forth until
the Position is at about 1.5 seconds. Now press Play again. You should be close
to the beginning of the strike on the fourth bell. Through experiment, I found
that if I position the slider at 1.69 seconds, and then click the Play button,

Sound Recorder plays the precise sound I want. Try positioning the slider at 1.69 seconds and then choose **E**dit from the menu bar. You have the option of deleting all the sounds before the current Position, or all the sounds after the current Position. Choose Delete **B**efore Current Position. The program asks you to confirm the deletion. Now click Play again. You hear a pretty fair approximation of two large bells being struck.

If you want to keep the bell sound, choose **F**ile **S**ave. Then save the file with a file name of your choosing.

Two other options are available from the **E**dit menu: the **I**nsert File option lets you merge two files, and the **M**ix with File option lets you mix two files. To try mixing two files, begin with the newly created bell sound loaded into Sound Recorder. Choose **E**dit and then **M**ix with File. When the file dialog box opens, select the original file, CHIMES.WAV. Sound Recorder opens the chimes file and mixes it with the bell file so that both are played simultaneously. Now click the Play button. If you like what you hear, save the mixed file. If you don't, try something completely different. Play with it!

Media Player

Media Player, shown in figure 9.18, is just what its name implies: a media player. Media Player can play WAV sounds, MIDI files, and media clip files that have the AVI extension. To start Media Player, double-click the Media Player icon.

Fig. 9.18

Windows Media Player.

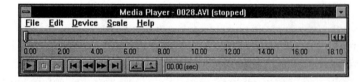

Microsoft Video Playback

The AVI file format is supported in Windows for media clips with sound. AVI files contain both video frames and a sound track. When an AVI file is loaded, a small window opens that displays one frame of the video, as shown in figure 9.19. Depending on the configuration you have selected, the media clip can be played in the small window, or the screen can be blanked and the clip played in the center of the screen in a larger size.

Fig 9.19

Media Player can play media clips in this small window.

If you have a CD-ROM player and received a copy of *The Software Toolworks Multimedia Encyclopedia* with Sound Blaster, you can access a large number of AVI files. The video clips stored on the encyclopedia disk are in AVI format and can be played by Media Player. If, for example, your CD-ROM is installed as drive D:\ you can choose **D**evice from the menu bar, choose **V**ideo for Windows, choose **F**ile from the menu bar, and search the D:\001AVI and \002AVI directories on the CD-ROM.

When you play an AVI file from CD-ROM, you generally see a few frames, the display pauses, and then a few more frames. The playback is even more disruptive when it includes an audio track. What you are experiencing is how slowly data is read from CD-ROM and transferred across most CD-ROM-to-computer interfaces. The data rate is too slow to show live-action video as it is being read in real time from the CD-ROM. To approximate real-time playback, without annoying interruptions, move the AVI file to your hard disk, which has a much higher data transfer rate.

The AVI Video Playback Options dialog box contains several options for playing AVI files (see fig. 9.20).

Fig. 9.20

The Video Playback Options dialog box.

The Video Mode area is where you select whether the video is played back in a small window (refer to fig. 9.19) or on as much of the screen as possible. The **F**ull Screen option rarely displays a video using the entire screen simply because of the memory and disk space requirements. You can double the size of the displayed image by clicking the **Z**oom by 2 box. You will, however, see some image degradation.

The "waveform device" referred to in the Video Playback Options dialog box is your Sound Blaster. If you check this box, Media Player waits until Sound Blaster is available before playing a video sequence that contains sound. In other words, if you are using Sound Blaster to play a little background music and you open an AVI file to play, Media Player waits until Sound Blaster is not being used before playing the video clip.

The next option involves how video data is stored in AVI files. Not every video frame is stored in its entirety. *Key frames* are the only complete frames. Frames between key frames depend on data in the key frames to complete an image. If you check the Always Seek to **N**earest Key Frame option, you are telling Media Player that when you scroll through a video sequence, you want to stop only at complete key frames. If you do not check this box, you can stop at the incomplete intermediate frames, although they will look strange.

Video sequences sometimes have an associated audio track. Because video contains so much more data than the audio track, the video and audio may get out of sequence because Windows can't display the video as fast as Sound Blaster can play the audio. The **S**kip Video Frames If Behind option enables Media Player to skip some video frames in order to keep the audio synchronized with the video.

Finally, Media Player creates a buffer in memory that it fills before displaying an image on-screen. Using this buffer somewhat slows the display, however. You can turn off the buffer by choosing **D**evice, **C**onfigure, and then **D**on't Buffer Offscreen, allowing the image to be sent directly to the screen without buffering. When you don't buffer, though, image degradation often occurs—even though frame data is displayed more quickly—because Media Player uses this buffer to reconstruct partial frames from data in key frames.

MIDI Playback

Media Player can act as a rather simple MIDI player, able to play one MIDI song at a time. To play a MIDI song, choose **D**evice from the Media Player menu bar and then choose **M**IDI Sequencer. From there, choose **F**ile **O**pen and find your favorite MIDI file. The front panel controls in the Media Player dialog box act just like the controls on your CD player. MIDI Mapper determines where the MIDI messages are directed—either to Sound Blaster or to an external MIDI instrument.

WAVE Playback

Finally, Media Player is capable of playing WAV files. Just as with the MIDI songs, you choose **D**evice **S**ound. Then open your favorite WAV file from the **F**ile menu.

Neither MIDI nor WAV playback is particularly impressive; in fact, far superior WAV editors and MIDI sequencers are available for the Windows environment. Cakewalk Apprentice, described in Chapter 8, is a superior MIDI sequencer.

Using Media Player to Create OLE Objects

You can use Media Player to create OLE Objects that are linked or embedded in other application documents. For example, to embed a WAV file in a Word for Windows document, simply use Media Player to open the WAV file, and then choose **E**dit **C**opy Object. Exit Media Player, start Word for Windows, and open the document in which you want to embed the sound file. Position the insertion point where you want the sound embedded, choose **E**dit, and then choose **P**aste. Your computer grinds away for a while, and then a Media Player icon appears in the document; the name of the WAV file appears below the icon. To play the WAV file, click the icon.

In fact, you don't need Media Player to embed sound files in other applications that support OLE. When using Word for Windows, for example, you can choose **I**nsert from the menu bar and then **O**bject. You are given your choice of a wide range of objects that can be embedded. If you choose Sound from the list shown in figure 9.21, Windows opens Sound Recorder. From there, you can load the appropriate WAV file, open Sound Recorder's **E**dit menu and copy the sound, exit Sound Recorder, and choose **P**aste from the Word for Windows **E**dit menu.

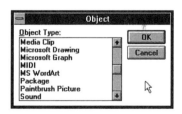

Fig. 9.21

The Insert Object dialog box within Word for Windows.

When the WAV file is embedded in your document, the Sound Recorder icon appears on-screen (see fig. 9.22). Double-click the icon to play the sound file.

A Sound Recorder icon within a Word for Windows document.

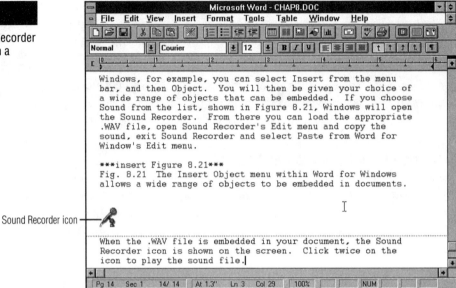

Sound Recorder icon —

Inside the Word window (Microsoft Word - CHAP8.DOC):

Windows, for example, you can select Insert from the menu
bar, and then Object. You will then be given your choice of
a wide range of objects that can be embedded. If you choose
Sound from the list, shown in Figure 8.21, Windows will open
the Sound Recorder. From there you can load the appropriate
.WAV file, open Sound Recorder's Edit menu and copy the
sound, exit Sound Recorder and select Paste from Word for
Window's Edit menu.

insert Figure 8.21
Fig. 8.21 The Insert Object menu within Word for Windows
allows a wide range of objects to be embedded in documents.

When the .WAV file is embedded in your document, the Sound
Recorder icon is shown on the screen. Click twice on the
icon to play the sound file.

The capability to embed sound files in documents or spreadsheets is something of an answer in search of a question. But there's little doubt that in Bill Gates' paperless office of the future, you're going to hear your boss's comments on your document rather than read her terrible handwriting.

Sound Blaster Windows Applications

Sound Blaster comes with many valuable Windows applications—several of which are described in the following sections. This chapter does not cover Talking Scheduler and HSC Interactive; these two packages are left to your exploration and imagination.

Soundo'LE

The Soundo'LE application is sort of an enhanced Sound Recorder (see fig. 9.23). The biggest differences are that you have significantly more control over the quality of the sound you will record, and you can record sources other than a microphone.

Fig. 9.23

The Soundo'LE application from Creative Labs.

The Soundo'LE window has the now-standard CD buttons and a slider bar to move back and forth through the sound file. In addition, the Sound Blaster Pro and 16/16ASP versions include a stereo display that graphically shows the sound levels for both stereo channels.

When you click the **O**ptions menu item, you see two options: Recording Settings and Mixer Settings. The Recording Settings option allows you to select one of three sample rates, the option to record in stereo (depending on the sound source), and the sample rate (see fig. 9.24).

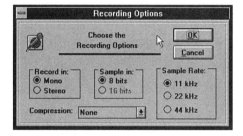

Fig. 9.24

The Recording Options dialog box.

The Mixer Settings options, shown in figure 9.25, are quite useful. You can set volume levels for the six sound sources available with Sound Blaster Pro. You can test the analog sound levels that are being fed to Sound Blaster's analog-to-digital converter, and you can select high frequency, low frequency, or no filtering.

Another function of the Soundo'LE application is that, just as with Sound Recorder, you can copy a sound file and embed it in another application document. Soundo'LE is OLE-compatible—hence, its rather strange name.

SBP Mixer

The SBP Mixer is simply a stand-alone version of the Mixer Options described under Soundo'LE.

Fig. 9.25

The Sound Blaster
Pro Mixer Control
dialog box.

Multimedia JukeBox

Multimedia JukeBox, shown in figure 9.26, is really a MIDI file jukebox. With
Jukebox, you can queue up a series of MIDI files to be played one after the
other. In the left box, you select the directory in which the MIDI files are held;
you then highlight each file you want played and click the Queue button. If you
want all the files in that directory played, click the Q All button.

Fig. 9.26

The JukeBox
dialog box.

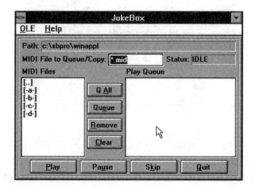

The OLE item in the menu bar is the JukeBox's version of Edit/Copy. If you
want to embed a MIDI song in a document, load the song into JukeBox, choose
OLE, and then choose Copy MIDI File as Object. Then open the appropriate
application document and paste the MIDI song.

Creative WaveStudio

The Creative WaveStudio application is an advanced WAV sound editor. As
shown in figure 9.27, WaveStudio can open multiple WAV files and enable you
to edit those files, cutting or copying sound data from one file and pasting it
into another file.

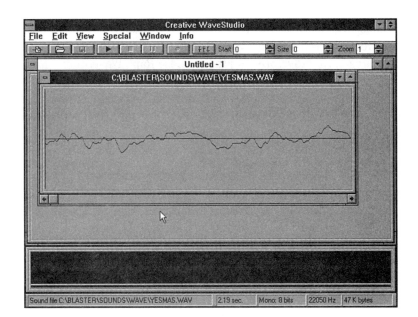

Fig. 9.27

The Create
WaveStudio
application.

WaveStudio displays the sound file as a complete waveform at the bottom of
the screen, with a zoomed window in the middle so that you can see detailed
waveform information. In addition, WaveStudio has a nice set of sound effect
functions, as shown in figure 9.28.

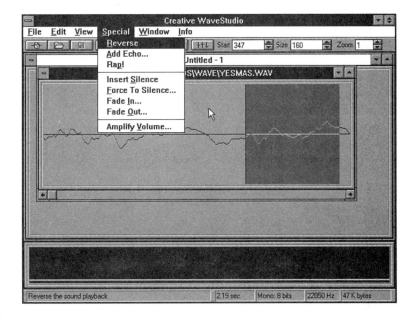

Fig. 9.28

Advanced
WaveStudio
sound effects.

If you choose **S**pecial from the menu bar, you see a menu of fun functions. Most of the effects are self-explanatory but Ra**p**! is unique. When you highlight a specific area in the waveform and then choose Ra**p**!, WaveStudio duplicates the selected area and inserts the copy into the sound file immediately following the source. Suppose that you have a sound file containing speech. You can highlight a word, choose **S**pecial Ra**p**!, and have the word repeated again during playback. This technique was used in the "Max Headroom" television show a few seasons back to make Max appear to get stuck on a word.

The Insert **S**ilence item does what you'd think: inserts a block of silence into a sound file at the position you request, moving the sound data out in time so that no sound is lost. **F**orce to Silence, however, silences specific areas of sound. Finally, Fade **I**n and Fade **O**ut do as they imply. Fade **I**n is particularly useful for getting rid of that bothersome snap that sometimes begins WAV files.

Creative WaveStudio is well worth the time you might spend learning to use it. The program enables you to clean up WAV files, as well as be a little creative.

CHAPTER 10

Programming Sound Blaster

This chapter serves as an overview of programming the Sound Blaster cards and covers register functions and drivers for the DSP chip, FM synthesizer, and mixer. In addition, the new Sound Blaster 16/16 ASP Advanced Signal Processor device driver is discussed.

If you are serious about writing software for Sound Blaster, order the Developer Kit from Creative Labs. The kit contains a hefty book as well as sample software and libraries for use with these languages:

Microsoft Assembler V4.0

Microsoft C V5.0

Borland's Turbo C V2.0

Microsoft QuickBasic V4.5

Microsoft Basic PDS V7.0

Borland's Turbo Pascal V6.0

This chapter does not contain instructions on how to write software. Nor is it tutorial in nature. If you are already familiar with software program development, the information included in this chapter will be sufficient for you to make good use of the driver routines provided with Sound Blaster, as well as access the low-level functions on Sound Blaster cards.

Overview

This chapter discusses five versions of Sound Blaster:

Sound Blaster V1.5

Sound Blaster V2.0

Sound Blaster Pro V2.0

Sound Blaster 16

Sound Blaster 16 ASP

The Sound Blaster V2.0, Pro, and 16/16 ASP cards use the same Yamaha OPL 3 synthesizer chip for FM sound synthesis. Only the Pro, 16, and 16 ASP cards have a mixer chip, which has been enhanced for the 16 and 16 ASP versions.

The 16 and 16 ASP cards have an enhanced DSP chip for improved analog-to-digital (ATD) conversion at either 8-bit or 16-bit resolution. The MIDI port on the 16 and 16 ASP has been modified and now can work as both the standard Sound Blaster MIDI port and an MPU-401 compatible MIDI port. Finally, the 16 ASP has the new Advanced Signal Processing (ASP) chip on-board for high-speed real-time data compression and speech recognition.

Sound Blaster 16 and 16 ASP have modified driver programs, including two new drivers to sample and play back WAV files. And the 16 ASP has a new driver for the ASP functions.

Finally, the 16 and 16 ASP are able to support four different interrupts over a single interrupt (IRQ) line.

Sound Blaster I/O

Over the years, the various Sound Blaster versions have used a range of I/O addresses. Versions 1.5 and 2.0 have provisions for the addition of a C/MS chip set, but the C/MS chips are not standard; therefore, commands issued to the C/MS chips listed in the following tables are applicable only if the chips are present.

Sound Blaster V1.5

Sound Blaster V1.5 could use one of six selectable base addresses, as listed in table 10.1. The function of each address is shown in table 10.2.

Table 10.1 Sound Blaster V1.5 I/O Addresses

Base Address	Address Range
210H	210H-21FH
220H	220H-22FH
230H	230H-23FH
240H	240H-24FH
250H	250H-25FH
260H	260H-26FH

The V1.5 I/O ports use port addresses $2x$0H through $2x$FH, where x is the number of the selectable base I/O address (refer to table 10.1).

Table 10.2 Sound Blaster V1.5 I/O Functions

Address	Description	Access
200H-207H	Analog Joystick Port	Read/Write
2x0H	C/MS Music Voice 1-6 Data	Write
2x1H	C/MS Music Voice 1-6 Register	Write
2x2H	C/MS Music Voice 7-12 Data	Write
2x3H	C/MS Music Voice 7-12 Register	Write
2x6H	DSP Reset	Write
2x8H*	FM Music Status	Read
2x8H*	FM Music Register	Write
2x9H*	FM Music Data	Write
2xAH	DSP Read Data	Read
2xCH	DSP Write Data or Command	Write
2xCH	DSP Write Buffer Status (Bit 7)	Read
2xEH	DSP Data Available Status (Bit 7)	Read

*Note: *FM music registers can also be accessed through I/O port address 388H and 389H.*

Sound Blaster V2.0

Version 2.0 of Sound Blaster uses one of two possible base I/O addresses: 220H and 240H. Selection of the base address is done by jumper.

Table 10.3 lists the V2.0 I/O addresses and functions.

Table 10.3 Sound Blaster V2.0 I/O Functions

Address	Description	Access
200H-207H	Analog Joystick Port	Read/Write
2x0H	C/MS Music Voice 1-6 Data	Write
2x1H	C/MS Music Voice 1-6 Register	Write
2x2H	C/MS Music Voice 7-12 Data	Write
2x3H	C/MS Music Voice 7-12 Register	Write
2x6H	DSP Reset	Write
2x8H*	FM Music Status	Read
2x8H*	FM Music Register	Write
2x9H*	FM Music Data	Write
2xAH	DSP Read Data	Read
2xCH	DSP Write Data or Command	Write
2xCH	DSP Write Buffer Status (Bit 7)	Read
2xEH	DSP Data Available Status (Bit 7)	Read

*Note: *FM music registers can also be accessed through I/O port address 388H and 389H.*

Sound Blaster Pro/16/16 ASP

Sound Blaster Pro, 16, and 16 ASP use 24 consecutive I/O addresses. The Sound Blaster Pro address range starts at a base of either 220H or 240H, whereas the 16/16 ASP can use a 220H, 240H, 260H, or 280H base address. Table 10.4 lists the register addresses for the Pro, 16, and 16 ASP.

Table 10.4 I/O for Sound Blaster Pro/16/16 ASP

Address	Description	Access
200H-207H	Analog Joystick Port	Read/Write
Base+0H	Left FM Music Status	Read
Base+0H	Left FM Music Register	Write
Base+1H	Left FM Music Data	Write
Base+2H	Right FM Music Status	Read
Base+2H	Right FM Music Register	Write
Base+3H	Right FM Music Data	Write
Base+4H	Mixer Chip Register	Write
Base+5H	Mixer Chip Data	Read/Write
Base+6H	DSP Reset	Write
Base+8H*	FM Music Status	Read
Base+8H*	FM Music Register	Write
Base+9H*	FM Music Data	Write
Base+AH	DSP Read Data	Read
Base+CH	DSP Write Data or Command	Write
Base+CH	DSP Write Buffer Status (Bit 7)	Read
Base+EH	DSP Data Available Status (Bit 7)	Read
Base+10H	CD-ROM Data	Read
Base+10H	CD-ROM Command	Write
Base+11H	CD-ROM Status	Read
Base+12H	CD-ROM Reset	Write
Base+13H	CD-ROM Enable	Write

*Note: *Mono FM music registers can also be accessed through I/O port address 388H and 389H.*

Advanced Signal Processor

Creative Labs provides a device driver named ASP.SYS that controls access to the ASP. No low-level programming information is available at this printing.

Services to the driver are invoked through a far call to the driver entry point. Function arguments are pushed onto the stack in the C calling convention, from right to left. Creative Labs provides a header file with the developer's kit to ease this kind of access. Because a low-level access method cannot be provided at this time, the following is a brief description of the functions of ASP.SYS:

Acquire ASP	Assigns a handle to the ASP.
Release ASP	Releases ASP and frees the handle.
Download into ASP	Downloads a set of ASP-specific software for execution.
Start Execution	Begins execution of the downloaded code.
Stop Execution	Halts execution of the downloaded code.
Set Parameters	Configures ASP to expect mono or stereo data, and in 8-bit or 16-bit chunks.
Get Parameters	Reports the current configuration of the ASP.

At this time, Creative Labs provides ASP code for real-time data compression and decompression and for voice recognition.

Digital Signal Processing

The Sound Blaster DSP chip handles all analog-to-digital, digital-to-analog, and compression tasks. In addition, the DSP is used to process MIDI commands and control the MIDI port. Sound Blaster and Sound Blaster Pro support 8-bit D-to-A and A-to-D conversion, whereas the 16 and 16 ASP support 8-bit or 16-bit conversion.

The Sound Blaster and Sound Blaster Pro DSP uses two data transfer modes: direct (under application control) and single-cycle DMA. The DMA mode also supports data compression. DMA is achieved with an 8237 DMA controller chip. In addition, two transfer speeds are used: normal and high. The difference is that during high-speed transfer, the DSP will not accept any interrupts for commands until transfer is complete.

The Sound Blaster 16/16 ASP DSP supports a transfer mode called auto-initialized DMA, which removes the delay at the end of every transfer block experienced by the older single-cycle DMA mode. Auto-initialized DMA uses a stationary DMA buffer to perform double-buffering.

Sound Blaster 16/16 ASP Interrupt Sharing

The Sound Blaster 16 and 16 ASP is capable of supporting four different DSP interrupts using a single IRQ line. Those interrupts are the following:

8-bit DMA-mode voice I/O or Sound Blaster MIDI interrupts

16-bit DMA-mode voice I/O

MPU-401 MIDI interrupts

The interrupt service routine (ISR) uses the Interrupt Status register within the new mixer register map (see the section "Sound Blaster 16/16 ASP Mixer" later in this chapter). The Interrupt Status register is at address 82H and is structured as follows:

D7	D6	D5	D4	D3	D2	D1	D0
X	X	X	X	X	MPU-401	16-bit DMA Voice I/O	8-bit DMA Voice or SB MIDI

The states of D3-D7 are undefined. Bits D0-D2 are set to 1 if the corresponding interrupt has occurred. Note that 8-bit DMA Voice and Sound Blaster MIDI interrupts share the same status bit and therefore cannot be distinguished.

To acknowledge an interrupt, perform a read from the corresponding I/O address as

```
in al,dx
```

where register *dx* contains one of the following values:

2xEH	8-bit DMA voice I/O or Sound Blaster MIDI (x = 2, 4, 6, or 8 depending on Sound Blaster base I/O address)
2xFH	16-bit DMA Voice I/O (x = 2, 4, 6, or 8 depending on Sound Blaster base I/O address)
3x0H	MPU-401 (x = 0 or 3 depending on MPU-401 base I/O address)

Sampling Rate

The sampling rate supported by the various Sound Blaster cards depends on transfer mode, compression, and the card. Table 10.5 lists the possible sample rates.

Table 10.5 DSP Sample Rates

Card	Transfer Mode	Rate
Input:		
SB 16/16 ASP	Stereo/High Speed	5 kHz-45 kHz
SB PRO	Mono/Normal	4 kHz-23 kHz
	Mono/High Speed	23 kHz-44.1 kHz
SB V2.0	Mono/Normal	4 kHz-13 kHz
	Mono/High Speed	13 kHz-15 kHz
SB V1.5	Mono/Normal	4 kHz-13 kHz
Output:		
SB 16/16 ASP	Stero/High Speed	5 kHz-45 kHz
SB PRO	Mono/Normal	4 kHz-23 kHz
	Mono/High Speed	23 kHz-44.1 kHz
SB V2.0	Mono/Normal	4 kHz-23 kHz
	Mono/High Speed	23 kHz-44.1 kHz
SB V1.5	Mono/Normal	4 kHz-23 kHz

Without compression, all Sound Blaster and Sound Blaster Pro output data is in 8-bit words. Using Adaptive Delta Pulse Code Modulation (ADPCM), data is output in smaller words with different sample rates, as shown in table 10.6.

Table 10.6 DSP Output Sample Rates with Compression On (Sound Blaster and Sound Blaster Pro Only)

Transfer Mode	Rate
Mono/Normal, 4-bit ADPCM	4 kHz-12 kHz
Mono/Normal, 2.6-bit ADPCM	4 kHz-13 kHz
Mono/Normal, 2-bit ADPCM	4 kHz-11 kHz

Using the Voice Drivers

Two loadable drivers are used to program the Sound Blaster and Sound Blaster Pro DSP:

CT-VOICE.DRV   Voice memory driver to store or play back voice files from within memory

CTVDSK.DRV   Voice disk double-buffering driver to record or output voice files larger than available memory

Versions of these drivers provided with Sound Blaster 16 and 16 ASP have been modified to some extent and use version numbers 3.00 and higher. Those changes are identified and described in the following text.

NOTE

New Version 3.00 drivers now use a block type (9) for recording. See Appendix B for a description of the new block type.

In addition, two new drivers are provided with Sound Blaster 16 and 16 ASP:

CTWMEM.DRV   Windows WAV format driver stores or plays back WAV files from within memory.

CTWDSK.DRV   Windows WAV format driver stores or plays back WAV files from disk.

These two drivers are nearly identical in all aspects to CT-VOICE and CTVDSK. Differences that exist are noted in the text.

You use the following procedure to load all drivers:

1. Allocate a memory buffer starting at offset zero of a segment.

2. Load the driver into the buffer.

3. Invoke the driver functions. Functions can be invoked by using the libraries provided with the Developer Kit, or by making a FAR CALL to the offset zero of the memory segment.

You can verify that the driver has been properly loaded by checking for the text string CT-VOICE starting at offset three of the segment.

To properly use the drivers, you must establish an unsigned integer variable called ct_voice_status. This status variable is used by your application to read driver status. The address of the ct_voice_status word is issued to the driver with driver function 5.

The following sections describe accessing the drivers by using the FAR CALL instruction. In all nonreserved calls, the BX register contains the driver function number. All registers excluding AX and DX are saved and restored during an access.

CT-VOICE.DRV

Table 10.7 summarizes the available function calls.

Table 10.7 CT-VOICE Driver Functions

Function (BX=)	Description
0	Get Driver Version
1	Set Base I/O Address
2	Set DMA Interrupt
3	Initialize Driver
4	Turn DAC Speaker ON/OFF
5	Set Status Word Address
6	Start Voice Output
7	Start Voice Input
8	Stop Voice I/O
9	Terminate Driver
10	Pause Voice Output
11	Continue Voice Output
12	Break Voice Output Loop
13	Set User-Defined Trap
14	Start Voice Output from Extended Memory

Function (BX=)	Description
15	Start Voice Input to Extended Memory
16	Set Recording Mode (SBPRO Only)
17	Set Recording Source (SBPRO Only)
18	Set Recording Filter (SBPRO Only)
19	Set DMA Channel (SBPRO Only)
20	Get Card Type
21	Reserved
22	Filter ON/OFF (SBPRO Only)
23-25	Reserved
26	Get Voice Sampling Rate
27	Read Filter Status (SBPRO Only)
28*	Get Environment Settings
29*	Get Parameter
30*	Set DMA Buffer
31*	Set I/O Parameter
32*	Get I/O Parameter
33*	Input into Conventional Memory
34*	Input into Extended Memory
35*	Output from Conventional Memory
36*	Output from Extended Memory
37*	Stop Voice I/O
38*	Pause Voice Output
39*	Continue Voice Output
40*	Break Voice Output Loop

*Note: *Available only with driver V3.00 and later (Sound Blaster 16/16 ASP)*

Function 0—Get Driver Version
Fetches the version number of the loaded driver.

Entry	BX = 0
Exit	AH = major version number
	AL = minor version number

Function 1—Set Base I/O Address
Sets the base I/O address used by the driver. The base I/O address should be captured from the BLASTER environment variable.

Entry	BX = 1
	AX = base I/O address
Exit	none

The default base address is 220H and is assumed if this function is not called. If this function is called, it must be the first function called.

Here are the available I/O addresses:

Card	Address
SBPRO	220H or 240H
SB V2.0	220H or 240H
SB V1.5	210H, 220H, 230H, 240H, 250H, or 260H

Function 2—Set DMA Interrupt
Sets the interrupt number used by the driver. The interrupt is issued by the Sound Blaster card at the end of a DMA transfer.

Entry	BX = 2
	AX = DMA interrupt number
Exit	none

The default interrupt number is 7 and is assumed if this function is not called. If this function is called, it must be called immediately following function 1.

These are the available interrupts:

Card	Interrupt
SBPRO	2, 5, 7, or 10
SB V2.0	2, 3, 5, or 7
SB V1.5	2, 3, 5, or 7

Function 3—Initialize Driver

Initializes the driver and checks the Sound Blaster card for correct installation and operation. This function must be invoked before all remaining functions, excluding function 19.

Entry	BX = 3	
Exit	AX = 0	driver initialized successfully
	1	incorrect driver version
	2	I/O read/write failure
	3	DMA interrupt failure

If the default address or interrupt vector is changed, this function is called following functions 1 and 2.

Following initialization, output to Sound Blaster's speaker jack is turned on.

Function 4—Turn DAC Speaker ON/OFF (Sound Blaster Only)

Following initialization, Sound Blaster's speaker jack is turned on. The speaker must be turned off during voice input and before your application exits.

Entry	BX = 4
	AL = 0 OFF
	nonzero ON
Exit	none

This function has no impact on Sound Blaster Pro or 16/16 ASP.

Function 5—Set Status Word Address

Loads the address of ct_voice_status into the driver.

Entry	BX = 5
	ES:DI = ct_voice_status address
Exit	none

The address is a 2-byte value.

Function 6—Start Voice Output

Using the DMA controller, outputs data in the VOC format to the speaker. When the function is called, the value of ct_voice_status is set to 0FFFFH, and control is immediately returned to your application.

Entry   BX = 6
        ES:DI = address of output buffer

Exit   AX = 0   if successful
               nonzero   if failure

The ES:DI address must point to the start of the voice data block and not the start of the voice file. See the VOC file format description in Appendix B.

To monitor transfer progress, check the contents of ct_voice_status. This status location contains one of three values. ct_voice_status is initially set to 0FFFFH and remains nonzero until the end of the voice buffer is reached, or until the transfer process is terminated with a call to function 8, Stop Voice I/O.

At completion, ct_voice_status is set to 0.

If the driver encounters a Marker sub-block, the value of the Marker is loaded into ct_voice_status.

Function 7—Start Voice Input
Begins DMA transfer for voice input. When the function is called, the value of ct_voice_status is set to 0FFFFH, and control is returned to your application.

Entry   BX = 7
        AX = sampling rate in Hertz
        DX:CX = length of input buffer in K
        ES:DI = address of input buffer

Exit   AX = 0   if successful
               nonzero   if failure

The sampling rate values depend on the Sound Blaster card being programmed:

Card	Sample Rate
SBPRO	4000-44100 Hz mono
	22050 or 44100 Hz stereo
SB V2.0	4000-15000 Hz mono
SB V1.5	4000-13000 Hz mono

Voice input is terminated when the input buffer becomes full, or when your application calls function 8, Stop Voice I/O. When either of these conditions occur, ct_voice_status is set to 0.

Only two stereo sample rates are supported by Sound Blaster Pro: 11025 Hz and 22050 Hz. Stereo sampling is started by assigning AX a value twice the desired stereo rate. To record at 11025 Hz, call function 7 with AX = 22020. To record at 22050 Hz, call function 7 with AX = 44100.

For Sound Blaster Pro, functions 16, 17, 18, and 22 should be invoked prior to recording.

Function 8—Stop Voice I/O
Ends any I/O processes and sets ct_voice_status to 0.

Entry	BX = 8
Exit	none

Function 9—Terminate Driver
Terminates the current session and initializes the Sound Blaster card.

Entry	BX = 9
Exit	none

This function turns off the speaker. Call function 9 before exiting your application.

Function 10—Pause Voice Output
Pauses voice output and resumes with a call to function 11.

Entry	BX = 10	
Exit	AX = 0	if successful
	1	if voice output not active

When function 10 is called, ct_voice_status retains its last value.

Function 11—Continue Voice Output
Used with function 10; continues voice output following a pause.

Entry	BX = 11	
Exit	AX = 0	if successful
	1	if voice output not paused

Function 12—Break Voice Output Loop

Stops voice sub-block repeats. See Appendix B for the file format.

Entry	BX = 12	
	AX = 0	leave voice loop at end of current cycle
	1	leave voice loop immediately
Exit	AX = 0	if successful
	1	if voice loop not active

The VOC file format supports sub-block voice data looping. Function 12 can stop looping prior to the embedded looping factor.

Function 13—Set User-Defined Trap

Provides the driver with the address of a trap routine that will be called before processing each voice data sub-block.

Entry	BX = 13
	DX:AX = user trap routine address
Exit	none

On entry to the trap routine, ES:BX points to the first byte of the new voice data sub-block. The first byte of the sub-block contains the block type. ES:BX is a 32-bit address if the voice data is in extended memory.

The trap routine must do the following:

- Perform a far RET.

- Save all registers, including flag registers, except the carry register.

- Clear the carry flag if the current voice data sub-block is to be processed by the driver. Otherwise, the carry flag must be set.

- Clear the carry flag if the current voice data sub-block is Type 0, Terminate.

To disable the trap routine, invoke function 13 with DX and EX equal to 0.

Function 14—Start Voice Output from Extended Memory

Same as function 6, except that voice data is in extended memory.

Entry	BX = 14
	DX = extended memory handle
	DI:SI = offset of extended memory block

Exit   AX = 0 if successful
         nonzero if failure

This function requires an extended memory handle in register DX. The offset is the start of the voice data block.

Function 15—Start Voice Input to Extended Memory
Same as function 7, except that voice data is stored in extended memory.

Entry   BX = 15
      DX = extended memory handle
      AX = sampling rate in Hertz
      CX = length of buffer in kilobytes
      DI:SI = offset of extended memory block

Exit   AX = 0 if successful
         nonzero if failure

Because voice data is being stored in extended memory, a memory handle is required. The application can start recording at any offset within the allocated extended memory.

The stored data contains only raw data as a voice data block; you should insert a file header block before saving the data to a file.

For Sound Blaster Pro, functions 16, 17, 18, and 22 should be invoked prior to recording.

Function 16—Set Recording Mode (Sound Blaster Pro Only)
Sets stereo or mono recording mode.

Entry   BX = 16
      AX = 0 mono
         1 stereo

Exit   AX = previous recording mode

Function 17—Set Recording Source (Sound Blaster Pro Only)
Selects sound source.

Entry   BX = 17
      AX = 0 microphone (default)
         1 CD
         2 microphone
         3 line-in

Exit   AX = previous source

Function 18—Set Recording Filter (Sound Blaster Pro Only)
Selects which filter will be used during sampling.

Entry	BX = 18	
	AX = 0	low filter (default)
	1	high filter
Exit	AX = previous filter status	

To avoid having input filtered, use function 22 to turn off the filter.

Function 19—Set DMA Channel (Sound Blaster Pro Only)
Loads the DMA channel number into the driver.

Entry	BX = 19	
	AX = 0	channel 0
	1	channel 1
	3	channel 3
Exit	none	

If you use this function, you must call it after functions 1 and 2.

Function 20—Get Card Type

Entry	BX = 20	
Exit	AX = 1	Sound Blaster V1.5
	2	Sound Blaster Pro
	3	Sound Blaster V1.5

Function 22—Filter ON/OFF (Sound Blaster Pro Only)
Turns off input and output filtering.

Entry	BX = 22	
	AX = 0	recording
	1	output
	CX = 0	ON
	1	OFF
Exit	AX = previous filter status	

This function uses the AX register to determine whether input or output filtering occurs, and uses register CX to turn filtering on and off. Use function 27 to determine filter status.

Function 26—Get Voice Sampling Rate

Retrieves the sampling rate as set by function 7.

Entry	BX = 26
	AX = 0 recording
	1 output
	DX = 0 mono
	1 stereo (Sound Blaster Pro only)
Exit	DX:AX = Maximum:Minimum sampling rate

The values returned in DX:AX must be multiplied by 10 to derive the actual sampling rate.

Function 27—Read Filter Status (Sound Blaster Pro Only)

Retrieves the filter status as set by function 22.

Entry	BX = 27
	AX = 0 recording
	1 output
Exit	AX = 0 ON
	1 OFF

Function 28—Get Environment Settings (Driver V3.00, Sound Blaster 16/16 ASP Only)

Passes the BLASTER environment string to the driver. This function must be used before function 3.

Entry	BX = 28
	ES:DI = far pointer to BLASTER string
Exit	AX = 0H if successful
	1H far pointer is null or points to empty string
	2H base I/O address not specified or out of range
	4H IRQ number not specified or out of of range
	8H 8-bit DMA channel not specified or out of range
	10H 16-bit DMA channel not specified or out of range

Function 29—Get Parameter (Driver V3.00, Sound Blaster 16/16 ASP Only)

Retrieves information on the current driver and sound card.

Entry	BX = 29
	AX = parameter type
	ES:DI = far pointer to a double-word parameter storage location
Exit	AX = 0 if successful
	nonzero if failure

The parameter type must be one of the following constants:

Value	Definition
0x0001	*Driver version.* The driver version word contains the minor version number in byte 0, and the major version number in byte 1.
0x0002	*Card type number.* This value stores the card type number supported by the driver.
0x0003	*Card name.* This value is a far pointer to an ASCIIZ string containing the name of the supported sound card.
0x0004	*Number of input channels.* 1 if mono; 2 if stereo.
0x0005	*Number of output channels.* 1 if mono; 2 if stereo.
0x0006	*Driver size, less the embedded DMA buffer.* The size in bytes of the driver, less the embedded DMA buffer. Used with 0x0009 and function 30 to create larger external DMA buffer.
0x0007	*Number of I/O handles supported.* The number of I/O handles supported by the driver.
0x0008	*Driver build number.* The least significant word (LSW) contains the build number of the driver. The most significant word (MSW) is set to zero.

Value	Definition
0x0009	*Size of embedded DMA buffer.* This value is the current size of the embedded DMA buffer. Buffer size is given in units of 2K per half-buffer. For example, a value of 2 means that the embedded DMA buffer is 4K/half-buffer, or 8K total.
0x000A	*Sampling rate limits.* When requesting the sample rate limits, you must specify which limit is to be retrieved by placing a parameter in the double-word location pointed to by ES:DI, according to the following:

Byte 0   Set to 0 to retrieve minimum sampling rate; set to 1 for maximum sampling rate.

Byte 1   Set to 1 to retrieve mono sampling rate; set to 2 to retrieve stereo sampling rate.

Byte 2   Set to 0 to retrieve ADC sampling rate; set to 1 to retrieve DAC sampling rate.

Byte 3   Always set to zero.

Byte 3 must always be set to zero. On return, the location pointed to by ES:DI will contain the sampling rate limits.

Function 30—Set DMA Buffer (Driver V3.00, Sound Blaster 16/16 ASP Only)

Allocates a DMA buffer and assigns an I/O handle.

Entry   BX = 30

AX = handle

ES:DI = 32-bit linear address of DMA buffer, which must reside in lowest 1M of memory

CX = buffer size in units of 2K per half-buffer (value can range from 1 through 16)

Exit   AX = 0   if successful
                      nonzero   if failure

The DMA buffer must not straddle a physical page (64K) boundary. If the buffer does not start on a 16-byte paragraph boundary, you must allocate an additional 16 bytes because the driver will do an internal paragraph adjustment.

The valid range for the buffer size is from 1 through 16. An invalid size causes an error code to be returned.

Function 31—Set I/O Parameter (Driver V3.00, Sound Blaster 16/16 ASP Only)

Sets the value of an I/O parameter.

Entry   BX = 31
                      AX = I/O handle
                      DX = parameter type
                      DI:SI = parameter value

Exit   AX = 0   if successful
                      nonzero   if failure

The parameter type must be one of the following:

Value	Definition
0x0001	*Voice status word address.* Set this parameter to the far address of the status word. A status word address must be assigned before starting any voice I/O. When the status word is checked, a value of 0 indicates that voice I/O has stopped; any other value indicates that voice I/O is active.
0x0003	*Sampling rate for recording.* Use this parameter to specifiy the recording sampling rate. If no value is assigned, the default rate of 11,025 Hz is used. The acceptable sampling value range is from 4,000 through 44,100 Hz. If an invalid sampling rate is specified, the nearest valid rate is used. Do not double this number for stereo recording.
0x0004	*Mono or stereo.* Use this parameter to set the recording mode. When the parameter is set to 1, record in mono. When the parameter is set to 2, record in stereo. The default is 1.

Value	Definition
0x0005	*Left-channel source.* This parameter selects the source for left-channel recording input. The default is the microphone. To select another source, use one or a combination of the following values:

Value	Definition
0x0003	Microphone
0x0004	CD audio right channel
0x0008	CD audio left channel
0x0010	Line-in right channel
0x0020	Line-in left channel
0x0040	MIDI right channel
0x0080	MIDI left channel

You can mix input sources by performing a logical OR on the required sources. For example, to use both the microphone and MIDI right channel as the left-channel source, set this parameter to 0x0043.

Value	Definition
0x0006	*Right-channel source.* This parameter selects the source for right-channel recording input. The default is the microphone. To select another source, use one or a combination of the following values:

Value	Definition
0x0003	Microphone
0x0004	CD audio right channel
0x0008	CD audio left channel
0x0010	Line-in right channel
0x0020	Line-in left channel
0x0040	MIDI right channel
0x0080	MIDI left channel

continues

continued

Value	Definition
	You can mix input sources by performing a logical OR on the required sources. For example, to use both the microphone and MIDI right channel as the right-channel source, set this parameter to 0x0043.
0x0007	*Recording voice format.* This parameter selects the format in which voice data is recorded:

CTVDSK.DRV

Value	Definition
0x0000	8-bit PCM
0x0004	16-bit PCM
0x0006	a-LAW
0x0007	m-LAW
0x0200	Creative ADPCM

CTWDSK.DRV

Value	Definition
0x0001	PCM
0x0006	a-LAW
0x0007	m-LAW
0x0200	Creative ADPCM

Value	Definition
	The default format is 8-bit PCM. If you select another format, you must also set the bits-per-recorded-sample parameter. Data recorded in a-LAW, m-LAW, or Creative ADPCM is compressed and decompressed in real time on Sound Blaster 16 ASP.
0x0008	*Bits per recorded sample.* This parameter sets the bits per sample value:

Value	Definition	
	CTVDSK.DRV	
	Format	*Value*
	8-bit PCM	8
	16-bit PCM	16
	a-LAW	8
	m-LAW	8
	Creative ADPCM	4
	CTWDSK.DRV	
	Format	*Value*
	PCM	8 or 16
	a-LAW	8
	m-LAW	8
	Creative ADPCM	4

Function 32—Get I/O Parameter (Driver V3.00, Sound Blaster 16/16 ASP Only)

Gets the value of an I/O parameter.

Entry	BX = 32
	AX = I/O handle
	DX = parameter type
	ES:DI = far pointer to double-word parameter location
Exit	AX = 0 if successful
	nonzero if failure

The parameter type to be fetched is one of the following:

Value	Parameter
0x0001	Voice status word address
0x0003	Recording sampling rate

continues

continued

Value	Parameter
0x0004	Mono or stereo
0x0005	Left-channel source
0x0006	Right-channel source
0x0007	Recording voice format
0x0008	Bits per recorded sample

See function 31 for more information regarding the content of the I/O parameters.

Function 33—Input to Conventional Memory (Driver V3.00, Sound Blaster 16/16 ASP Only)

Starts voice recording into conventional memory.

Entry	BX = 33
	AX = I/O handle
	ES:DI = far pointer to conventional memory buffer
	DX:CX = double-word buffer length in bytes
Exit	AX = 0 if successful
	nonzero if failure

This function starts recording voice source(s) and storing voice data in conventional memory. Recording parameters are established with function 31. After recording begins, control returns to your program, and recording occurs in the background. During recording, the status word is set to 0xFFFF and reset to zero at termination. This function does not create a VOC file header block. Use function 32 in the CTVDSK.DRV driver to automatically create a VOC file header block during input.

Function 34—Input to Extended Memory (Driver V3.00, Sound Blaster 16/16 ASP Only)

Starts voice recording into conventional memory.

Entry	BX = 34
	AX = I/O handle
	DX = extended memory block handle
	DI:SI = extended memory block starting offset
	CX = size of extended memory block in K

Exit   AX = 0   if successful
                  nonzero   if failure

This function starts recording voice source(s) and storing voice data in an extended memory block. Recording parameters are established with function 31. After recording begins, control returns to your program, and recording occurs in the background. During recording, the status word is set to 0xFFFF and reset to zero at termination. This function does not create a VOC file header block. Use function 32 in the CTVDSK.DRV driver to automatically create a VOC file header block during input.

Function 35—Output from Conventional Memory (Driver V3.00, Sound Blaster 16/16 ASP Only)

Starts voice recording into conventional memory.

Entry   BX = 35
                  AX = I/O handle
                  ES:DI = far pointer to conventional memory buffer

Exit   AX = 0   if successful
                  nonzero   if failure

The far pointer to the voice data buffer must point at the start of the data. Once playback of voice data begins, this function returns to your program, and playback continues as a background activity. During playback, the voice status word is set to 0xFFFF and reset to 0 at termination.

Function 36—Output from Extended Memory (Driver V3.00, Sound Blaster 16/16 ASP Only)

Starts voice recording into conventional memory.

Entry   BX = 36
                  AX = I/O handle
                  DX = extended memory block handle
                  DI:SI = extended memory block starting offset

Exit   AX = 0   if successful
                  nonzero   if failure

The contents of DI:SI must point at the start of the playback data. Once playback of voice data begins, this function returns to your program, and playback continues as a background activity. During playback, the voice status word is set to 0xFFFF and reset to 0 at termination.

The Ultimate Sound Blaster Book

Function 37—Stop Voice I/O (Driver V3.00, Sound Blaster 16/16 ASP Only)

Stops voice data input or output.

Entry   BX = 37
                   AX = I/O handle

Exit   AX = 0   if successful
                        nonzero if failure

This function stops voice data recording or playback functions, and resets the status word to zero.

Function 38—Pause Voice Output (Driver V3.00, Sound Blaster 16/16 ASP Only)

Pauses voice data output.

Entry   BX = 38
                   AX = I/O handle

Exit   AX = 0   if successful
                        nonzero if failure

This function pauses voice data output until resumed with function 39 or stopped with function 37. The status word remains unchanged during pause.

Function 39—Continue Voice Output (Driver V3.00, Sound Blaster 16/16 ASP Only)

Continues voice data output.

Entry   BX = 39
                   AX = I/O handle

Exit   AX = 0   if successful
                        nonzero if failure

This function resumes voice data output that has been paused with function 38.

Function 40—Break Voice Output Loop (Driver V3.00, Sound Blaster 16/16 ASP Only)

Exits a repeat loop in voice data.

Entry   BX = 40
                   AX = I/O handle
                   CX = break mode

Exit   AX = 0   if successful
                         nonzero   if failure

This function prematurely exits a repeat block in the VOC file. If CX = 0, the driver completes the current loop before exiting. If CX = 1, the driver exits immediately. In either case, output continues with the next block immediately following the End Repeat Loop block. See Appendix B for VOC file structure.

CTVDSK.DRV

The CTVDSK.DRV uses a double-buffering strategy to allow playback or recording of voice data larger than available memory. As with CT-VOICE.DRV, your application should create a variable named `ct_voice_status` to check progress. This driver must be loaded at offset zero of a segment. All CTVDSK.DRV functions are invoked by a far call to offset zero.

Two contiguous buffers of equal size must be allocated, either by your application or by CTVDSK.DRV. Table 10.8 summarizes the functions available with the CTVDSK driver.

Table 10.8 CTVDSK Driver Functions

Function (BX=)	Description
0	Get Driver Version
1	Set Base I/O Address
2	Set DMA Interrupt
3	Initialize Driver
4	Turn DAC Speaker ON/OFF
5	Set Status Word Address
6	Start Voice Output
7	Start Voice Input
8	Stop Voice I/O
9	Terminate Driver
10	Pause Voice Output
11	Continue Voice Output

continues

Table 10.8 Continued

Function (BX=)	Description
12	Break Voice Output Loop
13	Reserved
14	Get Voice Process Error
15	Set Disk Double Buffer Address
16	Set Recording Mode (SB PRO Only)
17	Set Recording Source (SB PRO Only)
18	Set Recording Filter (SB PRO Only)
19	Set DMA Channel (SB PRO Only)
20	Get Card Type
21	Get Voice Sampling Rate
22	Filter ON/OFF (SB PRO Only)
23	Read Filter Status (SB PRO Only)
26*	Get Environment Settings
27*	Get Parameter
28*	Set Disk Buffer
29*	Set DMA Buffer
30*	Set I/O Parameter
31*	Get I/O Parameter
32*	Input
33*	Output
34*	Stop Voice I/O
35*	Pause Voice Output
36*	Continue Voice Output
37*	Break Voice Output Loop
38*	Initialize Driver

*Note: *Available only with driver V3.00 and later (Sound Blaster 16/16 ASP)*

Function 0—Get Driver Version

Fetches the version number of the loaded driver.

    Entry   BX = 0

    Exit   AH = major version number
                    AL = minor version number

Function 1—Set Base I/O Address

Sets the base I/O address used by the driver. The base I/O address should be captured from the BLASTER environment variable.

    Entry   BX = 1
                    AX = base I/O address

    Exit   none

The default base address is 220H and is assumed if this function is not called. If this function is called, it must be the first function called.

Here are the available I/O addresses:

Card	Address
SBPRO	220H or 240H
SB V2.0	220H or 240H
SB V1.5	210H, 220H, 230H, 240H, 250H, or 260H

Function 2—Set DMA Interrupt

Sets the interrupt number used by the driver. The interrupt is issued by the Sound Blaster card at the end of a DMA transfer.

    Entry   BX = 2
                    AX = DMA interrupt number

    Exit   none

The default interrupt number is 7 and is assumed if this function is not called. If this function is called, it must be called immediately following function 1.

Here are the available interrupts:

Card	Interrupt
SBPRO	2, 5, 7, or 10
SB V2.0	2, 3, 5, or 7
SB V1.5	2, 3, 5, or 7

Function 3—Initialize Driver

Initializes the driver and checks the Sound Blaster card for correct installation and operation.

Entry	BX = 3
	AX = buffer size in 2K/buffer units
Exit	AX = 0 if driver initialized successfully
	nonzero if initialization failure

This function allocates two buffers ranging in size from 2K to 64K per buffer. The value of AX is set from 1 to 32. If your application calls function 15, Set Disk Double Buffer Address, no buffer space is allocated.

Following initialization, output to the Sound Blaster speaker jack is turned on.

This function also intercepts the following interrupts:

INT 8H	Timer Clock
INT 10H	Video
INT 13H	Disk
INT 28H	DOS

These interrupts are released when your application calls function 9, Terminate Driver.

Function 4—Turn DAC Speaker ON/OFF

Following initialization, the Sound Blaster speaker jack is turned on (Sound Blaster only). The speaker must be turned off during voice input and before your application exits.

Entry	BX = 4
	AL = 0 OFF
	nonzero ON
Exit	none

Function 5—Set Status Word Address

Loads the address of ct_voice_status into the driver.

Entry	BX = 5
	DX:AX = ct_voice_status address
Exit	none

The address is a 2-byte value.

Function 6—Start Voice Output

Outputs data contained in a VOC file to the speaker. Your application must open the voice file before calling this function. When this function is called, the value of ct_voice_status is set to 0FFFFH, and control is immediately returned to your application.

Entry	BX = 6
	AX = file handle
Exit	AX = 0 if successful
	nonzero if failure

To monitor transfer progress, check the contents of ct_voice_status. This status location contains one of three values. ct_voice_status is initially set to 0FFFFH and remains nonzero until the end of the voice buffer is reached, or until the transfer process is terminated with a call to function 8, Stop Voice I/O.

At completion, ct_voice_status is set to 0.

If the driver encounters a Marker sub-block, the value of the Marker is loaded into ct_voice_status.

Function 7—Start Voice Input

Begins transfer of voice input to the file specified by AX. When this function is called, the value of ct_voice_status is set to 0FFFFH, and control is returned to your application.

Entry	BX = 7
	AX = file handle
	DX = sampling rate in Hertz
Exit	AX = 0 if successful
	nonzero if failure

The sampling rate values depend on the Sound Blaster card being programmed:

Card	Sample Rate
SBPRO	4000-44100 Hz mono
	22050 or 44100 Hz stereo
SB V2.0	4000-15000 Hz mono
SB V1.5	4000-13000 Hz mono

Voice input is terminated when the disk becomes full or when your application calls function 8, Stop Voice I/O. When either of these conditions occur, ct_voice_status is set to 0.

Only two stereo sample rates are supported by Sound Blaster Pro: 11025 Hz and 22050 Hz. Stereo sampling is started by assigning AX a value twice the desired stereo rate. To record at 11025 Hz, call function 7 with AX = 22020. To record at 22050 Hz, call function 7 with AX = 44100.

Function 8—Stop Voice I/O
Ends any I/O processes and sets ct_voice_status to 0.

Entry   BX = 8

Exit   none

Function 9—Terminate Driver
Terminates the current session and initializes the Sound Blaster card.

Entry   BX = 9

Exit   none

This function turns off the speaker and releases all interrupts. Call function 9 before exiting your application.

Function 10—Pause Voice Output
Pauses voice output. You resume voice output with a call to function 11.

Entry   BX = 10

Exit   none

When function 10 is called, ct_voice_status is not changed.

Function 11—Continue Voice Output
Used with function 10; continues voice output following a pause.

Entry   BX = 11

Exit   none

Function 12—Break Voice Output Loop
Stops voice sub-block repeats. See Appendix B for the file format.

   Entry   BX = 12
                    AX = 0   leave voice loop at end of current cycle
                          1   leave voice loop immediately

   Exit   none

The VOC file format supports sub-block voice data looping. Function 12 can stop looping prior to the embedded looping factor.

Function 14—Get Voice Process Error
Used to determine cause of error in abnormal driver function exit.

   Entry   BX = 14

   Exit   DX = system error code
                    AX = driver error code

If any driver function exits with an error, use this function to determine cause.

Function 15—Set Disk Double Buffer Address
Sets buffer address.

   Entry   BX = 15
                    AX = buffer offset
                    DX = buffer segment
                    CX = buffer size in 2K units/buffer

   Exit   none

If you prefer your application to set the double buffer address, use this function. You must call this function prior to function 3, Initialize Driver.

You may use function 15 to reallocate the disk buffer by specifying a new buffer address in DX:AX.

Function 16—Set Recording Mode (Sound Blaster Pro Only)
Sets stereo or mono recording mode.

   Entry   BX = 16
                    AX = 0   mono
                         1   stereo

   Exit   AX = previous recording mode

Function 17—Set Recording Source (Sound Blaster Pro Only)
Selects the sound source.

Entry	BX = 17	
	AX = 0	microphone (default)
	1	CD
	2	microphone
	3	line-in
Exit	AX = previous source	

Function 18—Set Recording Filter (Sound Blaster Pro Only)
Selects which filter will be used during sampling.

Entry	BX = 18	
	AX = 0	low filter (default)
	1	high filter
Exit	AX = previous filter status	

To avoid having input filtered, use function 22 to turn off the filter.

Function 19—Set DMA Channel (Sound Blaster Pro Only)
Loads the DMA channel number into the driver.

Entry	BX = 19	
	AX = 0	channel 0
	1	channel 1
	3	channel 3
Exit	none	

If you use this function, you must call it after functions 1 and 2.

Function 20—Get Card Type

Entry	BX = 20	
Exit	AX = 1	Sound Blaster V1.5
	2	Sound Blaster Pro
	3	Sound Blaster V1.5

Function 21—Get Voice Sampling Rate

Returns the minimum and maximum sampling rates.

Entry	BX = 21	
	AX = 0	recording
	1	output
	DX = 0	mono
	1	stereo (Sound Blaster Pro only)
Exit	DX:AX = Maximum:Minimum sampling rate	

The values returned in DX:AX must be multiplied by 10 to derive the actual sampling rate.

Function 22—Filter ON/OFF (Sound Blaster Pro Only)

Turns off input and output filtering.

Entry	BX = 22	
	AX = 0	recording
	1	output
	CX = 0	ON
	1	OFF
Exit	AX = previous filter status	

This function uses the AX register to determine whether input or output filtering occurs, and register CX to turn filtering on and off. Use function 23 to determine filter status.

Function 23—Read Filter Status (Sound Blaster Pro Only)

Retrieves the filter status as set by function 22.

Entry	BX = 23	
	AX = 0	recording
	1	output
Exit	AX = 0	ON
	1	OFF

Function 26—Get Environment Settings (Driver V3.00, Sound Blaster 16/16 ASP Only)

Passes the BLASTER environment string to the driver. This function must be used before function 3.

Entry	BX = 26	
	DX:AX = far pointer to BLASTER string	
Exit	AX = 0H	if successful
	1H	far pointer is null or points to empty string
	2H	base I/O address not specified or out of range
	4H	IRQ number not specified or out of range
	8H	8-bit DMA channel not specified or out of range
	10H	16-bit DMA channel not specified or out of range

Error message can be bit-OR combination of exit values.

Function 27—Get Parameter (Driver V3.00, Sound Blaster 16/16 ASP Only)

Retrieves information on the current driver and sound card.

Entry	BX = 27	
	CX = parameter type	
	DX:AX = far pointer to a double-word parameter storage location	
Exit	AX = 0	if successful
	nonzero	if failure

The parameter type must be one of the following constants:

Value	Definition
0x0001	*Driver version*. The driver version word contains the minor version number in byte 0, and the major version number in byte 1.
0x0002	*Card type number*. This value stores the card type number supported by the driver.
0x0003	*Card name*. This value is a far pointer to an ASCIIZ string containing the name of the supported sound card.
0x0004	*Number of input channels*. 1 if mono, 2 if stereo.

Value	Definition
0x0005	*Number of output channels.* 1 if mono, 2 if stereo.
0x0006	*Driver Size, less embedded DMA buffer.* The size in bytes of the driver, less the embedded DMA buffer. Used with 0x0009 and function 30 to create larger external DMA buffer.
0x0007	*Number of I/O handles supported.* The number of I/O handles supported by the driver.
0x0008	*Driver build number.* The least significant word (LSW) contains the build number of the driver. The most signifcant word (MSW) is set to zero.
0x0009	*Size of embedded DMA buffer.* This value is the current size of the embedded DMA buffer. Buffer size is given in units of 2K per half-buffer. For example, a value of 2 means that the embedded DMA buffer is 4K/half-buffer, or 8K total.
0x000A	*Sampling rate limits.* When requesting the sample rate limits, you must specify which limit is to be retrieved by placing a parameter in the double-word location pointed to by ES:DI, according to the following:

Byte 0	Set to 0 to retrieve minimum sampling rate, set to 1 for maximum sampling rate.
Byte 1	Set to 1 to retrieve mono sampling rate, set to 2 to retrieve stereo sampling rate.
Byte 2	Set to 0 to retrieve ADC sampling rate, 1 to retrieve DAC sampling rate.
Byte 3	Always set to zero.

Byte 3 must always be set to zero. On return, the location pointed to by ES:DI will contain the sampling rate limits.

Function 28—Set Disk Buffer (Driver V3.00, Sound Blaster 16/16 ASP Only)

Creates a disk buffer for I/O handle.

Entry	BX = 28
	SI = I/O handle
	DX:AX = far pointer to user allocated disk buffer
	CX = buffer size in units of 2K per half-buffer (value can range from 2 through 32)
Exit	AX = 0 if successful
	nonzero if failure

One DMA buffer per I/O handle is required by the driver, as is a corresponding voice I/O disk buffer. The disk buffer must be at least twice as large as the DMA buffer (see function 29). This function must be called before starting any voice I/O. If the allocated buffer does not start on a 16-byte paragraph boundary, you must allocate an additional 16 bytes.

Function 29—Set DMA Buffer (Driver V3.00, Sound Blaster 16/16 ASP Only)

Allocates a DMA buffer and assigns an I/O handle.

Entry	BX = 29
	SI = I/O handle
	DX:AX = 32-bit linear address of DMA buffer, which must reside in lowest 1M of memory
	CX = buffer size in units of 2K per half-buffer (value can range from 1 through 16)
Exit	AX = 0 if successful
	nonzero if failure

The DMA buffer must not straddle a physical page (64K) boundary. If the buffer does not start on a 16-byte paragraph boundary, you must allocate an additional 16 bytes because the driver will do an internal paragraph adjustment.

The valid range for the buffer size is from 1 through 16. An invalid size causes an error code to be returned.

Function 30—Set I/O Parameter (Driver V3.00, Sound Blaster 16/16 ASP Only)

Sets the value of an I/O parameter.

    Entry   BX = 30
                        SI = I/O handle
                        CX = parameter type
                        DX:AX = parameter value

    Exit   AX = 0   if successful
                        nonzero if failure

The parameter type must be one of the following:

Value	Definition
0x0001	*Voice status word address.* Set this parameter to the far address of the status word. A status word address must be assigned before starting any voice I/O. When the status word is checked, a value of 0 indicates that voice I/O has stopped; any other value indicates that voice I/O is active.
0x0003	*Sampling rate for recording.* Use this parameter to specifiy the recording sampling rate. If no value is assigned, the default rate of 11,025 Hz is used. The acceptable sampling value range is from 4,000 through 44,100 Hz. If an invalid sampling rate is specified, the nearest valid rate is used. Do not double this number for stereo recording.
0x0004	*Mono or stereo.* Use this parameter to set the recording mode. When the parameter is set to 1, record in mono; when set to 2, record in stereo. The default is 1.
0x0005	*Left-channel source.* This parameter selects the source for left channel recording input. The default is the microphone. To select another source, use one or a combination of the following values:

continues

continued

Value	Definition

Value	Definition
0x0003	Microphone
0x0004	CD audio right channel
0x0008	CD audio left channel
0x0010	Line-in right channel
0x0020	Line-in left channel
0x0040	MIDI right channel
0x0080	MIDI left channel

You can mix input sources by performing a logical OR on the required sources. For example, to use both the microphone and MIDI right channel as the left-channel source, set this parameter to 0x0043.

0x0006   *Right-channel source.* This parameter selects the source for right-channel recording input. The default is the microphone. To select another source, use one or a combination of the following values:

Value	Definition
0x0003	Microphone
0x0004	CD audio right channel
0x0008	CD audio left channel
0x0010	Line-in right channel
0x0020	Line-in left channel
0x0040	MIDI right channel
0x0080	MIDI left channel

You can mix input sources by performing a logical OR on the required sources. For example, to use both the microphone and MIDI right channel as the right-channel source, set this parameter to 0x0043.

0x0007   *Recording voice format.* This parameter selects the format in which voice data is recorded:

Value	Definition
	CTVDSK.DRV

Value	Definition
0x0000	8-bit PCM
0x0004	16-bit PCM
0x0006	a-LAW
0x0007	m-LAW
0x0200	Creative ADPCM

CTWDSK.DRV

Value	Definition
0x0001	PCM
0x0006	a-LAW
0x0007	m-LAW
0x0200	Creative ADPCM

The default format is 8-bit PCM. If you select another format, you must also set the bits-per-recorded-sample parameter. Data recorded in a-LAW, m-LAW, or Creative ADPCM is compressed and decompressed in real time on Sound Blaster 16 ASP.

Value	Definition
0x0008	*Bits per recorded sample*. This parameter sets the bits per sample value:

CTVDSK.DRV

Format	Value
8-bit PCM	8
16-bit PCM	16
a-LAW	8
m-LAW	8
Creative ADPCM	4

continues

continued

Value	Definition

CTWDSK.DRV

Format	Value
PCM	8 or 16
a-LAW	8
m-LAW	8
Creative ADPCM	4

Function 31—Get I/O Parameter (Driver V3.00, Sound Blaster 16/16 ASP Only)
Gets the value of an I/O parameter.

Entry	BX = 31
	SI = I/O handle
	CX = parameter type
	DX:AX = far pointer to double-word parameter location
Exit	AX = 0 if successful
	nonzero if failure

The parameter type to be fetched is one of the following:

Value	Parameter
0x0001	Voice status word address
0x0003	Recording sampling rate
0x0004	Mono or stereo
0x0005	Left-channel source
0x0006	Right-channel source
0x0007	Recording voice format
0x0008	Bits per recorded sample

See function 29 for more information regarding the content of the I/O parameters.

Function 32—Input (Driver V3.00, Sound Blaster 16/16 ASP Only)
Starts voice recording into disk file.

Entry	BX = 32
	DX = I/O handle
	AX = file handle
Exit	AX = 0 if successful
	nonzero if failure

This function starts recording voice source(s) and storing voice data in the file specified by AX. Recording parameters are established with function 30. After recording begins, control returns to your program, and recording occurs in the background. During recording, the status word is set to 0xFFFF and reset to zero at termination. This function automatically creates a VOC file header block.

Function 33—Output from Disk (Driver V3.00, Sound Blaster 16/16 ASP Only)
Starts voice output from a disk file.

Entry	BX = 33
	DX = I/O handle
	AX = file handle
Exit	AX = 0 if successful
	nonzero if failure

Once playback of voice data begins, this function returns to your program, and playback continues as a background activity. During playback, the voice status word is set to 0xFFFF and reset to 0 at termination.

Function 34—Stop Voice I/O (Driver V3.00, Sound Blaster 16/16 ASP Only)
Stops voice data input or output.

Entry	BX = 34
	DX = I/O handle
Exit	AX = 0 if successful
	nonzero if failure

This function stops voice data recording or playback functions, and resets the status word to zero.

Function 35—Pause Voice Output (Driver V3.00, Sound Blaster 16/16 ASP Only)

Pauses voice data output.

Entry	BX = 35
	DX = I/O handle
Exit	AX = 0 if successful
	nonzero if failure

This function pauses voice data output until resumed with function 36 or stopped with function 34. The status word remains unchanged during pause.

Function 36—Continue Voice Output (Driver V3.00, Sound Blaster 16/16 ASP Only)

Continues voice data output.

Entry	BX = 36
	DX = I/O handle
Exit	AX = 0 if successful
	nonzero if failure

This function resumes voice data output that has been paused with function 38.

Function 37—Break Voice Output Loop (Driver V3.00, Sound Blaster 16/16 ASP Only)

Exits a repeat loop in voice data.

Entry	BX = 37
	DX = I/O handle
	CX = break mode
Exit	AX = 0 if successful
	nonzero if failure

This function prematurely exits a repeat block in the VOC file. If CX = 0, the driver completes the current loop before exiting. If CX = 1, the driver exits immediately. In either case, output continues with the next block immediately following the End Repeat Loop block. See Appendix B for VOC file structure.

Function 38—Initialize Driver and Sound Card (Driver V3.00, Sound Blaster 16/16 ASP Only)

Initializes the sound card and driver with the environment settings fetched with function 26.

Entry	BX = 38
Exit	AX = 0 if successful
	nonzero if failure

This function hooks the Timer interrupt (INT 8H), Video interrupt (INT 10H), Disk interrupt (INT 13H), and DOS Idle interrupt (INT 28H).

FM Synthesizer

The Sound Blaster FM synthesizer is used to generate the sound for speech synthesis and MIDI instrument output. The FM synthesizers used in the new Sound Blaster 16/16 ASP are the same as those in the Sound Blaster V2.0 and Pro versions, and therefore no special reference is made to the 16/16 ASP in the following descriptions.

The mono FM synthesizer contains 18 operator cells, organized into pairs, with one cell serving as the modulator and the other as the carrier. Furthermore, each cell has three functional blocks, as shown in figure 10.1.

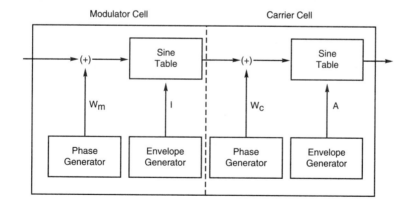

Fig. 10.1

FM chip cell functions.

The modulator cell modulates the carrier cell, which results in an output waveform from the carrier cell. This waveform contains the carrier frequency, as well as whole-number multiples of the modulator frequency. By changing the frequency and amplitude of the modulating waveform, you can change the timbre of the sound output by the carrier cell.

The formula used to express the output of the cell pair is

$$F(t) = A \sin (w_c\, t + I \sin w_m\, t)$$

where

A	= output amplitude
I	= modulation index (amplitude of modulator)
w_c	= carrier frequency
w_m	= modulator frequency
t	= time in seconds

Each synthesizer chip has 18 operator cells, which can be configured in the following modes:

Nine-Channel FM Sound
Each sound uses two operator cells. All nine channels can generate sound simultaneously.

Six-Channel FM Sound + 5 Percussion
Operator cells 1 through 12 generate six FM channels, and operators 13 through 18 produce five percussion instruments (see table 10.9).

Table 10.9 Percussion Instrument Generation

Operator Cell	Instrument
13, 16	Bass Drum
14	Hi Hat
15	Tom Tom
17	Snare Drum
18	Top Cymbal

The synthesizer has 16 preset voices, which can be replaced with voice parameters loaded from disk.

Speech Synthesis
In this mode, each operator is used to produce one sine wave. By combining three to six sine waves of differing pitch and amplitude, you can synthexize an approximation of human speech.

The FM synthesizer chip also contains a vibrato oscillator and an amplitude modulation oscillator, both of which are useful in generating organic sounds.

Sound Blaster Pro contains a pair of FM synthesizer chips and is thereby able to create stereo sound. The V1.0 Pro board used Yamaha OPL-2 chips; the newer V2.0 board uses OPL-3 chips.

FM Synthesizer Registers

The FM synthesizer registers are located at I/O address 388H, and data is written to I/O address 389H.

During write operations to the registers, there is a delay of 3.3 microseconds after register selection, and 23 microseconds after a data write to the selected register.

Table 10.10 lists the FM synthesizer registers.

Table 10.10 FM Synthesizer Register Table

Addr	D7	D6	D5	D4	D3	D2	D1	D0
01				TEST				
02	TIMER - 1							
03	TIMER - 2							
04	IRQ RST	MASK T1	T2				START/STOP T2	T1
08	CSM	SEL						
20-35	AM	VIB	EG	KSR	MULTIPLE			
40-55	KSL		TOTAL LEVEL					
60-75	ATTACK RATE				DECAY RATE			
80-95	SUSTAIN LEVEL				RELEASE RATE			
A0-A8	F-NUMBER(L)							
B0-B8			KEYON	BLOCK			F-NUMBER(H)	
BD	DEPTH AM	VIB	RHYTHM	BASS DRUM	SNARE DRUM	TOM TOM	TOP CYM	HI HAT
C0-C8						FEEDBACK		CON
E0-F5							WAVE SEL	

The addresses of the 18 operators contained in the FM synthesizer do not map directly to the channels. Table 10.11 lists the operator cell and channel numbers, as well as the address offset used. Note that the offsets are not in the order you might expect.

Table 10.11 Operator Cell and Channel Address Mapping

Cell #	1	2	3	4	5	6	7	8	9
Channel	1	2	3	1	2	3	4	5	6
Function	Modulator			Carrier			Modulator		
Offset	00	01	02	03	04	05	08	09	0A
Cell #	10	11	12	13	14	15	16	17	18
Channel	4	5	6	7	8	9	7	8	9
Function	Carrier			Modulator			Carrier		
Offset	0B	0C	0D	10	11	12	13	14	15

The synthesizer status register is read from address 388H and is organized as shown in table 10.12.

Table 10.12 Status Register Contents

D7	D6	D5	D4	D3	D2	D1	D0
IRQ	FLAG						
	T1	T2					

The following text describes each of the registers used in Sound Blaster's synthesizer.

Test (01H)

This register performs an internal test and must be initialized to 0 before using the synthesizer.

Timer –1 (02H)

The synthesizer has two 8-bit presettable counters. Timer –1 has a resolution of 80 microseconds. When loaded with a value of N1, the counter sets the T1 flag in the status bit each time a counter overflow occurs. The following formula is used to load the timer with the N1 value:

$$Toverflow = (256 - N1) * 0.08 \text{ msec}$$

During speech synthesis, this timer is used at overflow to set all cells to KEY ON and then to KEY OFF.

Timer –2 (03H)

This timer is the same as TIMER –1, except that its resolution is 320 microseconds. The following formula is used to load the timer with its N2 value:

$$Toverflow = (256 - N2) * 0.32 \text{ msec}$$

Timer Control (04H)

This register is used to control TIMER –1 and TIMER –2 start, stop, and flag bits in the status register.

D0   *Start/Stop T1.* Set D0 = 1 to start TIMER –1.

D1   *Start/Stop T2.* Set D1 = 1 to start TIMER –2.

D5   *Mask T2.* Set D5 = 1 to mask the TIMER –2 flag in the status register.

D6   *Mask T1.* Set D6 = 1 to mask the TIMER –1 flag in the status register.

D7   *IRQ-RESET.* Set D7 = 1 to reset the IRQ and Timer flags in the status register to 0. Following reset, this bit automatically resets itself to 0.

CMS Mode/Keyboard Split (08H)

This register has two functions. Bit D7 is used to turn on the speech synthesis function, and bit D6 determines in which part of the total frequency spectrum the keyboard will play—the keyboard "split."

D6   *Keyboard Split.* The FM synthesizer is capable of playing eight octaves, referred to by their *block* numbers (blocks 0 through 7). Most standard synthesizer keyboards do not have enough keys to play all eight octaves. The MD-640, for example, has a four-octave keyboard. For this reason, the synthesizer must be programmed to accept where within the frequency range a song is trying to play a note. This problem is illustrated in figure 10.2.

The particular frequency output by an operator pair is governed by the F-number, which is a 10-bit number loaded into the appropriate register set. The F-number registers are at addresses A0 through A8 for the eight lower bits, and B0 through B8 for the two high-order bits. The ninth or tenth bits of the F-number are used to set the keyboard split number.

Bit D6 of the CMS Mode/Keyboard Split register determines whether bit 9 or bit 10 of the F-number sets the keyboard split value. If D6 of the CMS Mode/Keyboard Split register is set to 0, then bit 9 of the F-number switches the keyboard split number. If D6 = 1, then bit 10 of the F-number sets the keyboard split number.

D7   *CMS Mode.* Setting this bit to 1 selects the composite sine-wave speech-synthesis mode. Before you can set composite speech synthesis, all channels must be in the KEY OFF state. See D5 of registers B0-B8.

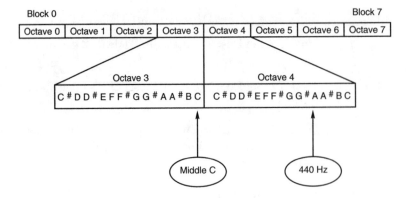

Fig. 10.2

The synthesizer generates eight octaves (blocks) of tones.

Table 10.13 lists the split number generated by either bit 9 or bit 10 of the F-number.

Table 10.13 Keyboard Splits When D6 = 0 and D6 = 1

When D6=0:

Octave (Block #)	0		1		2		3		4		5		6		7	
Bit 9 F-number	0	1	0	1	0	1	0	1	0	1	0	1	0	1	0	1
Split Number	0	1	2	3	4	5	6	7	8	9	10	11	12	13	14	15

When D6=1:

Octave (Block #)	0		1		2		3		4		5		6		7	
Bit 10 F-number	0	1	0	1	0	1	0	1	0	1	0	1	0	1	0	1
Split Number	0	1	2	3	4	5	6	7	8	9	10	11	12	13	14	15

AM/VIB/EG/KSR/Multiple (20H-35H)

This series of registers controls the timbre of each operator cell.

D0-D3 *Multiple.* The multiple is a value that relates to the multiplication factor used in the calculation of a waveform. The formula is

$$F(t) = A \sin (M_c\, w_c\, t + I \sin (M_m\, w_m\, t))$$

where

A = output amplitude

I = modulation index (amplitude of modulation)

w_c = carrier frequency

w_m = modulator frequency

M_c = carrier multiplication factor

M_m = modulator multiplication factor

The multiplication factor is derived from table 10.14.

Table 10.14 Multiplication Factor Derivation

Multiple D0-D3	0	1	2	3	4	5	6	7	8	9	A	B	C	D	E	F
Multiplication Factor	0.5	1	2	3	4	5	6	7	8	9	10	10	12	12	15	15

The multiplication factor determines the kind of harmonics produced from a base frequency, as shown in table 10.15.

Table 10.15 Harmonic Generation by Multiple Bits

Factor	Result
0.5	One octave below
1	At base frequency

continues

Table 10.15 Continued

Factor	Result
2	One octave above
3	One octave + fifth above
4	Two octaves above
5	Two octaves + major third above
6	Two octaves + fifth above
7	Two octaves + major seventh above
8	Three octaves above
9	Three octaves + major second above
10	Three octaves + major third above
12	Three octaves + major fifth above
15	Three octaves + major seventh above

D4   *KSR, Key Scaling Rate*. This bit causes the sound envelope length to be gradually shortened as higher notes are played. The envelope is shortened by increasing the attack, decay, sustain, and release (ADSR) rate. How drastically the ADSR rate is changed depends on the following formula:

$$RATE = 4 * ADSR + KSR_{offset}$$

The ADSR values are set in registers 60 through 95. The KSR_{offset} is defined in table 10.16.

Table 10.16 KSR_{offset} Values

Rate	0	1	2	3	4	5	6	7	8	9	10	11	12	13	14	15
D4=0	0	0	0	0	1	1	1	1	2	2	2	2	3	3	3	3
D4=1	0	1	2	3	4	5	6	7	8	9	10	11	12	13	14	15

As you can see from table 10.16, when D4 = 0, the effect of KSR$_{offset}$ is small. When D4 = 1, bits D0 through D3 of the Sustain Level/Release Rate register are used to set attenuation.

D5   *EG*. This bit determines whether the note is quickly dampened after attack or is sustained until just after key release, as shown in figure 10.3.

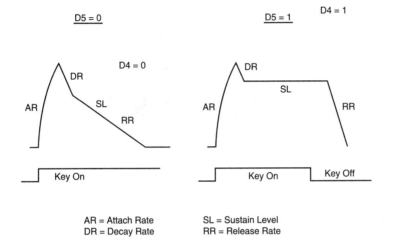

Fig. 10.3

Envelope type is selected by D5.

D6   *VIB, Vibrato*. This bit selects whether a vibrato effect is applied to the operator cell. If D6 = 1, a vibrato frequency of 6.4 Hz is applied. The depth of the vibrato is selected by bit D6 of the register at address BD.

D7   *AM, Amplitude Modulation (Tremolo)*. This bit causes a tremolo effect to be applied to the operator cell. The frequency of the effect is 3.7 Hz. The depth of the tremolo is set by bit D7 of the register at address BD.

KSL/Total Level (40H-55H)

Each operator's output level can be attenuated in one of two ways.

D0-D5   *Total Level*. This 6-bit value attenuates the operator's output level. When a modulator cell's output is attenuated, the frequency spectrum generated by the associated carrier cell is changed. Attenuation is calculated with the following formula:

Attenuation Level = Total Level * 0.75 dB

Maximum attenuation is 47.25 dB.

D6-D7   *KSL, Key Scaling Level.* This 2-bit value adjusts the output of higher-pitch notes downward, simulating the gradual decrease in output levels at higher frequencies by some instruments. Table 10.17 shows the degree of attenuation achieved.

Table 10.17 Attenuation Produced by KSL

Attenuation	D7	D6
0	0	0
1.5 dB/Octave	1	0
3 dB/Octave	0	1
6 dB/Octave	1	1

Attack Rate/Decay Rate (60H-75H)

Attack and decay rates can be set for each operator. The *attack rate* is the rise time for the note. *Decay rate* is the diminishing time following the attack.

D0-D3   *Decay Rate.* Zero is the slowest rate, and 15 is the fastest rate.

D4-D7   *Attack Rate.* Zero is the slowest rate, and 15 is the fastest rate.

Sustain Level/Release Rate (80H-95H)

Each operator's sustain level and release rate are set by these registers.

D0-D3   *Release Rate.* The release rate is the rate at which sound disappears after the key is released. If the sound is diminished by using bit D4 of the AM/VIB/EG/KSR/Multiple register, the release rate is used to select attenuation after the sustain level is reached.

D4-D7   *Sustain Level*. The sustain level follows the sound decay. The sustain level can be set to a maximum of 93 dB by setting all bits to 1. When generating a diminished note using bit D4 of the AM/VIB/EG/KSR/Multiple register at address 20H-35H, set this value to indicate the level at which decay changes to release.

Block/F Number/KEYON (A0H-B8H)

The block and F-number registers are used to select the pitch of the note to be played.

D0-D7   *F-Number L*. These bits are the low-order 8 bits of the 10-bit F-number.

D0-D1   *F-Number H*. These are the high-order 2 bits of the 10-bit F-number.

The output frequency is calculated with the following formula:

$$\text{Frequency} = 50000 * \text{F-number} * 2^{block-20}$$

To demonstrate, assume an F-number of 577 within block (octave) 4. The formula calculates as follows:

$$50000 * 577 * 2^{-16} = 440.216$$

Table 10.18 lists the F-numbers and frequencies within block 4.

Table 10.18 F-Numbers for Block (Octave) 4

F-Number	Frequency	Note
363	277.2	C$\sharp$
385	293.7	D
408	311.1	D$\sharp$
432	329.6	E
458	349.2	F
485	370.0	F$\sharp$
514	392.0	G

continues

Table 10.18 Continued

F-Number	Frequency	Note
544	415.3	G♯
577	440.0	A
611	466.2	A♯
647	493.9	B
686	523.3	C

D2-D4   *Block*. These bits are used to select the octave in which the note plays.

D5   *KEYON*. This bit turns on the operator and sounds the voice. Set to 1 to turn on the voice; set to 0 to turn off the voice.

AM/VIB/Rhythm (BDH)

This register controls depth of amplitude and vibrato and turns on internal rhythm instruments.

D7   *Amplitude Depth*. When set to 1, amplitude depth is 4.8 dB. When D7 = 0, amplitude depth is 1 dB.

D6   *Vibrato Depth*. Set D6 = 1 to select a vibrato depth of 14 cent. D6 = 0 sets depth to 7 cent.

D5   *Rhythm*. When D5 = 1, the synthesizer generates the rhythm sounds available with D0 through D4. D5 = 0 turns off rhythm instruments.

D4   *Bass Drum*. The bass drum sound uses cells 13 and 16.

D3   *Snare Drum*. This instrument uses cell 17.

D2   *Tom Tom*. The tom tom uses cell 15.

D1   *Top Hat*. This cymbal is generated with cell 18.

D0   *Hi Hat*. This cymbal is generated with cell 14.

Feedback/Connection (C0H-C8H)

The feedback registers determine the feedback path and feedback modulation factor for the cell pair.

D0   *CON, Connector.* When D0 = 0, FM modulation is selected. In this mode, shown in figure 10.4, a portion of the output of the modulator is fed back to the input (see D1-D3). This is the mode typically used to generate FM sounds. When D0 = 1, the output of the two operators are electronically added together to create a composite signal. This mode is used to simulate speech.

D1-D3   *Feedback.* These three bits set the level of feedback returned to Operator 1's input. The feedback values are listed in table 10.19.

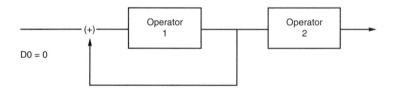

Fig. 10.4

Two feedback methods are available: D = 0 for music, and D = 1 for speech synthesis.

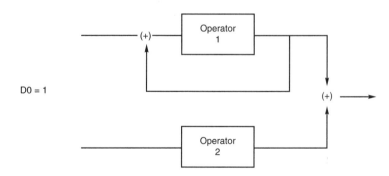

Table 10.19 Feedback Factors

D1-D3	0	1	2	3	4	5	6	7
Feedback	0	Π/16	Π/8	Π/4	Π/2	Π	2Π	2Π

Wave Select (E0H-F5H)

These two bits select the output waveform for each operator, as shown in figure 10.5.

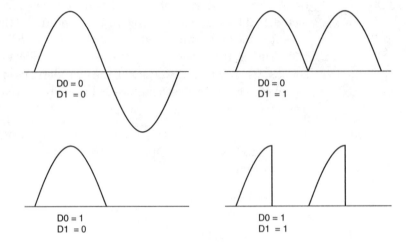

SBFMDRV—FM Driver Functions

Sound Blaster's FM driver, named SBFDRV.DRV, must be resident in memory before any driver functions can be accessed. The driver is loaded by the SBFMDRV.EXE program and is installed at a free interrupt vector between 80H and BFH. The driver resides at segment offset 0.

SBFMDRV can be identified by a five-byte signature string containing "FMDRV" at offset 103H.

SBFMDRV, like CT-VOICE, updates its status into a variable named `ct_music_status`. The `ct_music_status` word will be set to the following values:

- Reset to 0 at initialization.
- Set to FF when the synthesizer starts sound output.
- Set to 0 when the end of a CMF music block is reached.
- Update with the control data value when a control event occurs.
- Not updated when music is paused and then continued.
- Reset to FF if your application calls the Read Status function.

Processor register BX typically contains the driver function number. If a return value exists, it is usually placed in register AX. Long-word values are returned in the DX:AX pair.

All register contents except AX and DX are saved and restored.

Table 10.20 summarizes the functions available with SBFMDRV.

Table 10.20 SBFMDRV Function Summary

Number	Description
0	Get FM Driver Version
1	Set Music Status Byte Address
2	Set Instrument Table
3	Set System Clock Rate
4	Set Driver Clock Rate
5	Transpose Music
6	Play Music
7	Stop Music
8	Reset FM Driver
9	Pause Music
10	Resume Music
11	Set User-Defined Trap for System Exclusive

Function 0—Get FM Driver Version

Returns the major and minor version numbers of the driver.

Entry	BX = 0
Exit	AH = major version number
	AL = minor version number

Function 1—Set Music Status Byte Address

Loads the address of the ct_music_status byte.

Entry	BX = 1
	DX:AX = address of ct_music_status
Exit	none

Your application must provide the address of the status byte.

Function 2—Set Instrument Table

Provides the instrument table's address and number of instruments. See Appendix B for format information.

Entry	BX = 2
	CX = number of instruments (maximum 128)
	DX:AX = instrument table address
Exit	none

Whenever the driver encounters a program change within a music block, the instrument data is read from the instrument table. Sound Blaster has an internal instrument table with 16 instruments. This function is used if you need to supplant the internal table with a larger instrument bank.

Function 3—Set System Clock Rate

Sets the Timer 0 clock rate.

Entry	BX = 3
	AX = 1193180/Timer 0 frequency (Hz)
Exit	none

The default clock rate for Timer 0 is 18.2 Hz. To reset the timer to 18.2 Hz, set AX = 0FFFFH. When music output is complete, the driver restores the clock rate to 18.2 Hz.

Function 4—Set Driver Clock Rate

Used during music playback; defaults to 96 Hz.

Entry	BX = 4
	AX = 1193180/playback frequency (Hz)
Exit	none

Use this function to change the Timer 0 clock rate during music output. A CMF music file contains the correct clock rate value at offset 0CH-0DH in the header block. Use this value to play back the music at the correct rate. You can set AX to a lower or higher value to change the playback rate (tempo) of the music.

Function 5—Transpose Music
Transposes music in semitone steps.

Entry	BX = 5
	AX = semitone offset in positive or negative values
Exit	none

Function 6—Play Music
Loads the music block pointed to by DX:AX and begins playing at the rate determined by function 4.

Entry	BX = 6
	DX:AX = music block address
Exit	AX = 0 no error
	1 error (a music block is already playing)

During play, `cm_music_status` is set to FF.

Function 7—Stop Music
Stops playback and sets `cm_music_status` to 0.

Entry	BX = 7
Exit	AX = 0 no error
	1 error (no music playing)

When the music stops, Timer 0 is set to the clock rate determined by function 3.

Function 8—Reset FM Driver
Resets the driver and instrument table to their defaults.

Entry	BX = 8
Exit	AX = 0 no error
	1 error (music is being played)

This function cannot be called if music is being played. You must use function 7 to stop music before you can use function 8.

Your application must reset the driver before exiting.

Function 9—Pause Music
When function 9 is called, the music file currently being played is paused.

Entry	BX = 9
Exit	AX = 0 no error
	1 error (no music is being played)

The cm_music_status word is not changed. Music is resumed by calling function 10 or is stopped by calling function 7.

Function 10—Resume Music
Resumes playing music paused by function 9.

Entry	BX = 10
Exit	AX = 0 no error
	1 error (music was not paused)

Function 11—Set User-Defined Trap
Sets up a trap to handle system-exclusive commands.

Entry	BX = 11
	DX:AX = trap routine address
Exit	none

When the driver encounters a system-exclusive command within the music block, this function is called. The driver performs an intersegment call to the trap-routine address pointed to by DX:AX. Your trap routine must save all registers and return via an RETF instruction.

On entry, registers ES:DI point to the byte within the music block just following the system-exclusive command. On return, the driver passes over the system-exclusive block and resumes playing music.

On program exit, disable the trap routine. To disable the trap, call function 11 with AX and DX set to 0.

Mixer

Sound Blaster Pro was the first Sound Blaster to include a mixer chip that allowed sound sources to be mixed. The primary differences between the Pro and 16/16 ASP mixers are shown in table 10.21.

Table 10.21 Sound Blaster Pro and 16/16 ASP Mixer Differences

	SB Pro	SB 16/16 ASP
Microphone volume	8-level	32-level
Other source volume	16-level	32-level
PC speaker line volume	1-level	4-level
Recording sources	Single	Multiple
Tone control	None	16-level bass and treble
Filter control	Passive	Dynamic

The new 16/16 ASP mixer is not totally backward-compatible with the Pro mixer. The 16/16 ASP has no filter controls or VSTC bit for stereo playback, and the microphone volume control adjusts incoming signal amplitude.

Sound Blaster Pro Mixer

The mixer chip used in Sound Blaster Pro is accessed at I/O addresses 2x4H and 2x5H, depending on whether you have set the base address to be 220H or 240H. The address port is at 2x4H, and data is written to or read from port 2x5H.

Register Map and Descriptions

Table 10.22 lists the mixer chip registers.

Table 10.22 Sound Blaster Pro Mixer Register Summary

Addr	D7	D6	D5	D4	D3	D2	D1	D0
00H	DATA RESET							
02H	RESERVED							
04H	VOICE VOLUME LEFT				VOICE VOLUME RIGHT			
06H	RESERVED							
08H	RESERVED							
0AH							MIC MIXING	
0CH			IN FILTER			ADC		
0EH		DNFI				VSTC		
20H	RESERVED							
22H	MASTER VOLUME LEFT				MASTER VOLUME RIGHT			
24H	RESERVED							
26H	FM VOLUME LEFT				FM VOLUME RIGHT			
28H	CD VOLUME LEFT				CD VOLUME RIGHT			
2AH	RESERVED							
2CH	RESERVED							
2EH	LINE VOLUME LEFT				LINE VOLUME RIGHT			

Reset Register (00H)

Any write to this register causes the mixer chip to be reset, regardless of data. At reset, all registers are set to their default values.

Voice Volume Register (04H)

This 4-bit value controls the volume for sampled voice data playback. Volume values range from 0 through 15, with 0 silence. Level 9 is the default.

Microphone Mixing Register (0AH)

These three bits are used to mix microphone input and one other active input. The default value is 0.

In Filter/ADC (0CH)

Input source and filtering to Sound Blaster's analog-to-digital converter is selected using this register.

D1-D2   *ADC.* These two bits select one of the following input sources:

D2	D1	Source
0	0	Microphone (Default)
0	1	CD audio

1	0	Microphone
1	1	Line-in

D3-D5   *In Filter.* Bits D3-D5 select input filtering:

D5	D4	D3	*Filter*
0	X	0	Low Filter (default)
0	X	1	High Filter
1	X	X	No Filter

DNFI/VSTC (0EH)

These two registers specify output filtering and mode.

D1   *VSTC.* This bit switches between mono and stereo output: D1 = 0 for mono and D1 = 1 for stereo.

D5   *DNFI.* This bit controls the output filter: D5 = 0 to turn on the filter and D5 = 1 to turn off the filter.

Master Volume (22H)

These two 4-bit values set master volume output. The minimum (silence) value is 0, and the default value is 9.

FM Volume (26H)

These two 4-bit values set FM synthesizer volume output. The minimum (silence) value is 0, and the default value is 9.

CD Volume (28H)

These two 4-bit values set CD input volume output. The minimum (silence) value is 0, and the default value is 9.

Line-In Volume (2EH)

These two 4-bit values set line-in volume output. The minimum (silence) value is 0, and the default value is 9.

Sound Blaster 16/16 ASP Mixer

The mixer chip used in Sound Blaster 16/16 ASP is accessed at I/O addresses 2x4H and 2x5H, depending on whether you have set the base address. The address port is at 2x4H, and data is written to or read from port 2x5H.

Register Map and Descriptions

Table 10.23 lists the mixer chip registers.

Table 10.23 Sound Blaster 16/16 ASP Mixer Register Summary

Addr	D7	D6	D5	D4	D3	D2	D1	D0
00H	DATA RESET							
04H	VOICE VOLUME LEFT				VOICE VOLUME RIGHT			
0AH							MIC VOLUME	
22H	MASTER VOLUME LEFT				MASTER VOLUME RIGHT			
26H	MIDI VOLUME LEFT				MIDI VOLUME RIGHT			
28H	CD VOLUME LEFT				CD VOLUME RIGHT			
2EH	LINE VOLUME LEFT				LINE VOLUME RIGHT			
30H	MASTER VOLUME LEFT							
31H	MASTER VOLUME RIGHT							
32H	VOICE VOLUME LEFT							
33H	VOICE VOLUME RIGHT							
34H	MIDI VOLUME LEFT							
35H	MIDI VOLUME RIGHT							
36H	CD VOLUME LEFT							
37H	CD VOLUME RIGHT							
38H	LINE VOLUME LEFT							
39H	LINE VOLUME RIGHT							
3AH	MICROPHONE VOLUME							
3BH	PC SPKR VOLUME							
3CH				LINE L.	LINE R.	CD L.	CD R.	MIC
3DH		MIDI L.	MIDI R.	LINE L.	LINE R.	CD L.	CD R.	MIC
3EH		MIDI L.	MIDI R.	LINE L.	LINE R.	CD L.	CD R.	MIC
3F	INPUT GAIN L.							
40H	INPUT GAIN R.							
41H	OUTPUT GAIN L.							
42H	OUTPUT GAIN R.							
43h								AGC
44h	TREBLE LEFT							
45H	TREBLE RIGHT							
46H	BASS LEFT							
47H	BASS RIGHT							

Reset Register (00H)

Any write to this register causes the mixer chip to be reset, regardless of data. At reset, all registers are set to their default values.

SP Pro-Compatible Volume Registers (04H-2EH)

These registers offer some compatibility to the Sound Blaster Pro volume registers. These registers are actually mapped to the new volume registers (30H-3BH), and the default values are as described for the new volume registers.

Master/Voice/MIDI Volume (30H-35H)

These five-bit registers control volume with 32 levels. Values are 0 (–62 dB) through 31 (0 dB), in 2 dB steps. The default value is 24 (–14 dB).

CD/Line/MIC Volume (36H-3AH)

These five-bit registers control volume with 32 levels. Values are 0 (–62 dB) through 31 (0 dB), in 2 dB steps. The default value is 0 (–62 dB).

Speaker Volume (3BH)

This register adjusts the speaker line input from the PC motherboard. Values are 0 (–18 dB) through 3 (0 dB). The default value is 0 (–18 dB).

Output Mixer Switches (3CH)

These bits control whether a signal is output (closed = 1) or not (open = 0).

Input Mixer Switches (3DH-3EH)

These bits control whether a signal is input (closed = 1) or not (open = 0). When you record in mono, samples are taken from the left input only by default.

Input/Output Gain (3FH-42H)

These bits set the input and output gain value. Values range from 0 (0 dB) through 3 (18 dB). Default is 0 (0 dB).

Microphone Automatic Gain Control (43H)

Set D0 = 1 to turn on AGC; use D0 = 0 to set a fixed gain of 20 dB.

Treble/Bass (44H-47H)

These registers provide 16 levels of tone control. Values range from 0 (–14 dB) through 15 (14 dB) in 2 dB steps. Default is 8 (0 dB).

AUXDRV—The Mixer Driver

The mixer driver, AUXDRV.DRV, has a number of functions that can be called by your application program to control mixer actions. AUXDRV 3.00 is backward-compatible with previous versions of the driver for Sound Blaster Pro. AUXDRV must be loaded into offset zero of a segment. Your application can verify that the driver is correctly loaded by checking for the existence of the text string "CT-AUXDRV" starting at offset 03. Functions are invoked by a far call to the offset zero of this segment. Table 10.24 lists the function numbers and descriptions.

Table 10.24 AUXDRV Function Summary

Number	Description
0	Get Driver Version
1	Set Base I/O Address
2	Set Fade Status Word Address
3	Set Pan Status Word Address
4	Initialize Driver
5	Terminate Driver
6	Set Volume
7	Get Volume
8	Setup Fade
9	Setup Pan
10	Start Pan and Fade
11	Stop Pan and Fade
12	Pause Pan and Fade
13	Clear Source
14	Set Pan Position
15	Get Pan Position
17*	Reset Mixer
21*	Set Gain
22*	Get Gain

Number	Description
23*	Set Tone
24*	Get Tone
25*	Set AGC
26*	Get AGC
27*	Set Mixer Switches
28*	Get Mixer Switches
29*	Get Environment Settings

*Note: *Available only with driver V3.00 and later (Sound Blaster 16/16 ASP)*

AUXDRV updates two status variables: CTFadeStatus and CTPanStatus. Each variable is reset to 0 during initialization. Only the first five bits of the variables are used and are set to 1 when a source's fade or pan starts. At the end of the fade or pan, the corresponding bit is set to 0. Note the following bits and their sources:

Bit	Source
0	Master
1	Voice
2	FM
3	CD
4	Line-in

Once a source begins a pan or fade, no change is allowed in effect, volume, or pan position until the effect is either finished or cleared. In addition, no other source may be set up for pan or fade until the first source is completed.

Function 0—Get Driver Version

Returns the major and minor version numbers of AUXDRV.

Entry	BX = 0
Exit	AH = major version number
	AL = minor version number

Function 1—Set Base I/O Address

Loads the Sound Blaster base address into AUXDRV.

Entry   BX = 1
         AX = base I/O address

Exit   none

You do not have to call this function if you are using the default address of 220H.

Function 2—Set Fade Status Word Address

Loads the address of CTFadeStatus into the driver.

Entry   BX = 2
         ES:DI = address of CTFadeStatus

Exit   none

Function 3—Set Pan Status Word Address

Loads the address of CTPanStatus into the driver.

Entry   BX = 3
         ES:DI = address of CTPanStatus

Exit   none

Function 4—Initialize Driver

Used to initialize AUXDRV; must be called once before calling any other driver functions excluding functions 0 and 1.

Entry   BX = 4

Exit   none

Function 5—Terminate Driver

Ends the current session.

Entry   BX = 5

Exit   none

When function 5 is called, the pan and fade status words are set to 0.

Function 6—Set Volume

Sets source volume.

Entry	BX = 6
	AX = volume source
	0 = Master
	1 = Voice
	2 = FM
	3 = CD
	4 = Line-in
	5 = Microphone mixing
	6 = PC speaker (16/16 ASP only)
	DX = mic mixing volume level (0-255)
	DH = left volume (0-255, Pro only)
	DL = right volume (0-255, Pro only)
Exit	AX = 0 if successful
	1 if failure

In V3.00, the high byte of AX holds the left volume, and the low byte holds the right volume. For mono sources, the entire word holds the volume level.

The DX register is used to mix microphone input with another selected source. DH and DL set stereo volume levels for the source selected in AX (SB Pro only).

Function 7—Get Volume

Reads the incoming volume level of the source selected in function 6.

Entry	BX = 7
	AX = volume source
	0 = Master
	1 = Voice
	2 = FM
	3 = CD
	4 = Line-in
	5 = Microphone mixing
	6 = PC speaker (16/16 ASP only)
Exit	AX = microphone mixing volume level (0-255)
	AH = left volume level (0-255, SB Pro only)
	AL = right volume level (0-255, SB Pro only)

In V3.00, the high byte of AX holds the left volume, and the low byte holds the right volume. For mono sources, the entire word holds the volume level.

Function 8—Set Up Fade

Sets up a fade effect. The effect is processed with function 10, Start Pan and Fade.

Entry	BX = 8
	AL = fade source
	0 = Master
	1 = Voice
	2 = FM
	3 = CD
	4 = Line-in
	5 = Microphone
	AH = fade mode
	0 = fade in OR fade out
	1 = fade in or out then loop back
	CX = fade time per cycle in milliseconds (0-65535)
	DX = repeat count (0-65535)
	DI = target volume level (0-255)
Exit	AX = 0 if successful
	1 if failure

Fade begins from the initial volume level and proceeds to the target volume level. If AH is set to 1, a cyclic fade occurs. In other words, in mode 1 a fade in will immediately be followed by a fade out. Likewise, a fade out will immediately be followed by a fade in.

To repeat the fade process, load a repeat value into DX.

Function 9—Set Up Pan

Sets up a pan effect. The effect is processed with function 10, Start Pan and Fade.

Entry	BX = 9
	AL = pan source
	0 = Master
	1 = Voice
	2 = FM
	3 = CD
	4 = Line-in
	5 = Microphone mixing

AH = pan mode
    0 = pan left or pan right
    1 = pan left or right, and then loop back
CX = pan time per cycle in milliseconds (0-65535)
DX = repeat count (0-65535)
SI = initial position (0-255)
DI = target position (0-255)

Exit   AX = 0   if successful
                   1   if failure

Pan shifts audio between left and right speakers. Position 0 is extreme left, and position 255 is extreme right. If AH is set to 1, a cyclic pan occurs. In other words, in mode 1, a pan left is immediately followed by a fade right. Likewise, a pan right is immediately followed by a pan left.

To repeat the pan process, load a repeat value into DX.

Function 10—Start Pan and Fade

Once a pan or fade is set up with functions 8 and 9, function 10 triggers the effect. This function is also called to resume a pan or fade that has been paused by function 12.

Entry   BX = 10

Exit   AX = 0   if successful
                   1   if failure

Function 11—Stop Pan and Fade

Stops the current pan or fade, and sets the `pan` and `fade` status words to 0.

Entry   BX = 11

Exit   AX = 0   if successful
                   1   if failure

Function 12—Pause Pan and Fade

Pauses the current pan or fade process.

Entry   BX = 12

Exit   AX = 0   if successful
                   1   if failure

The relevant status word is not changed during a pause. To continue, call function 10.

Function 13—Clear Source

Clears a pan or fade source. This function can be called before or after function 10.

Entry	BX = 13
	AX = source
	0 = Master
	1 = Voice
	2 = FM
	3 = CD
	4 = Line-in
	5 = Microphone
	DX = control mode
	0 = fade
	1 = pan
Exit	AX = 0 if successful
	1 if failure

Function 14—Set Pan Position

Establishes the pan position for a source.

Entry	BX = 14
	AX = source
	0 = Master
	1 = Voice
	2 = FM
	3 = CD
	4 = Line-in
	5 = Microphone
	DX = position (0-255)
Exit	AX = 0 if successful
	1 if failure

If the source has already been set up for a pan using function 9, this function has no effect.

Function 15—Get Pan Position
Reads the pan position of the source.

Entry   BX = 15

AX = source

0 = Master

1 = Voice

2 = FM

3 = CD

4 = Line-in

5 = Microphone

Exit   AX = position (0-255)

−1   if failure

If the source has not been set up to perform a pan effect, a −1 value is returned in AX.

Function 17—Reset Mixer
Resets the mixer to its default state.

Entry   BX = 17

Exit   none

Function 21—Set Gain
Sets gain of input or output mixer.

Entry   BX = 21

AX = mixer

0 = input

1 = output

DX = gain

Exit   AX = 0   if successful

1   if failure

The high byte of DX sets left-channel gain, and the low-order byte sets right-channel gain. The range for each channel is from 0 through 3.

Function 22—Get Gain
Gets gain settings of input or output mixer.

Entry	BX = 22
	AX = mixer
	0 = input
	1 = output
Exit	AX = gain

Function 23—Set Tone
Sets treble or base tone.

Entry	BX = 23
	AX = tone
	0 = treble
	1 = bass
	DX = level
Exit	AX = 0 if successful
	1 if failure

The high byte of DX sets left-channel tone, and the low-order byte sets right-channel tone. The range for each channel is from 0 through 255.

Function 24—Get Tone
Gets treble or bass tone settings.

Entry	BX = 24
	AX = tone
	0 = treble
	1 = bass
Exit	AX = level

Function 25—Set Automatic Gain Control
Turns microphone AGC on and off.

Entry	BX = 25
	AX = on/off
	0 = off
	1 = on
Exit	AX = 0 if successful
	1 if failure

Function 26—Get Automatic Gain Control Setting

    Entry   BX = 26

    Exit   AX = on/off

                   0 = off

                   1 = on

Function 27—Set Mixer Switches

Sets the input and output mixer switch positions.

    Entry   BX = 27

                   CX = mixer

                       0 = input

                       1 = output

                   DX:AX = switches

    Exit   AX = 0   if successful

                       1   if failure

The switches can be any bit-OR combination of the following:

Value	Definition
0x0003	Microphone
0x0004	CD audio right channel
0x0008	CD audio left channel
0x0010	Line-in right channel
0x0020	Line-in left channel
0x0040	MIDI right channel
0x0080	MIDI left channel

The output mixer does not provide left- and right-channel control. Only the low word of DX:AX is used on output.

Function 28—Get Mixer Switches

Gets the input or output mixer switch positions.

    Entry   BX = 28

                   CX = mixer

                       0 = input

                       1 = output

    Exit   AX = switch value

Function 29—Get Environment Settings

Loads the BLASTER environment string into the driver.

Entry	BX = 29	
	ES:DI =	far pointer to the BLASTER environment string
Exit	AX = 0	if successful
	1	if string is null or points to empty string
	2	if base I/O address not specified or out of range

BLASTER.DRV—Speech Synthesis

The BLASTER driver converts ASCII text to synthesized human speech. BLASTER.DRV is a DOS TSR program—a terminate-and-stay-resident program—that is installed in memory with the SBTALKER.EXE program. Another program named REMOVE.EXE will remove BLASTER from memory if BLASTER is the last TSR loaded.

BLASTER links to the multiplex interrupt vector 2FH. To access the driver after it is loaded, your application must do the following:

1. Call DOS INT21H, function 35H to get the interrupt vector for 2FH:

    AX = 352FH

    The service routine will return the segment address of INT 2FH in register ES. If ES = 0, no driver is installed at this vector, and your program should abort.

2. If a TSR is installed (ES = nonzero), invoke INT 21H again, this time with the AX register set as follows:

    AX = 0FBFBH

On return, register AX should be set to 0 if the BLASTER driver is installed, or set to nonzero if a different driver is installed.

When the second call to INT 21H is successfully completed, an address pointer is contained in ES:BX. The fourth offset from the address pointed to by ES:BX contains the far call address to the driver. ES:BX+4 contains the offset address, and ES:BX+6 contains the segment address. Function calls to the driver must do a far call to this location.

The function number is loaded into register AL. Parameters are passed between the application and the driver by using a Speech Record, which is located at ES:BX+20H:

ES:BX+4	Offset Address
ES:BX+6	Segment Address
ES:BX+20H	Speech Record

To speak a string, the appropriate speech characteristics and the text string itself are loaded into the Speech Record. Then a call is made to set the speech parameters, followed by another call to speak the text.

Speech Record

The Speech Record is used to contain the string to be spoken, as well as the speech parameters for the driver. Although the default values for each parameter may be changed, they are generally satisfactory, and alteration may make speech difficult to understand. The structure of the Speech Record is shown in Table 10.25.

Table 10.25 SBTALKER Speech Record

Label	Length (Bytes)	Description
INPUT_STR	255+1 maximum	This is the string to be spoken. The first byte in the string must contain the length of the string in bytes. Therefore, a maximum string length of 255 bytes is allowed.
OUTPUT_STR	255+1 maximum	This location is used by the driver. It is exactly the same size as INPUT_STR. To calculate the location of the remaining records, assume that INPUT_STR is duplicated.
GENDER	2	0 = male, 1 = female. Not functional. At this writing, the gender of the simulated speech is male and cannot be changed to female.

continues

Table 10.25 Continued

Label	Length (Bytes)	Description
TONE	2	0 = bass (default), 1 = treble
VOLUME	2	Value = 0-9, default = 5
PITCH	2	Value = 0-9, default = 5. This is used to set speech inflection.
SPEED	2	Value = 0-9, default = 5. This is the playback speed of the text. Speed may be increased without increasing the tone or pitch.

Function 2—Set Speech Parameters

After the speech parameters have been loaded into the Speech Record (ES:BX+20H), this function loads the parameters into the driver.

> Entry   Far call to ES:BX+4 (address), ES:BX+6 (segment)
> AL = 2

> Exit   none

Values for all parameters are updated each time; therefore, your application must provide correct values each time function 2 is called.

Function 7—Speak Text String

Speaks the text string loaded into the Speech Record.

> Entry   Far call to ES:BX+4 (address), ES:BX+6 (segment)
> AL = 7

> Exit   none

The string contained in the INPUT_STR field of the Speech Record is compared with a phonetic dictionary, and the phonetic version of the text is output to Sound Blaster.

CHAPTER 11

Sources and Shareware

Since the introduction of the Sound Blaster card, a wealth of software and music has been produced. This chapter briefly describes the software included with this book. The software is divided into three areas: DOS applications, Windows applications, and Multimedia applications. The multimedia applications actually run from within DOS instead of within the Windows multimedia environment, but they certainly demonstrate what can be done, even from DOS.

Sources of Software, Music, and Information

Getting access to software, music, and information is very easy. Most computer bulletin boards carry sound software and music these days. Your favorite shareware catalog undoubtedly has both.

The CompuServe service is among the leading purveyors of sound-related information. Among the forums worth checking out are these:

MIDI Vendors

MIDI/Music

Sight and Sound

Music/Arts

Multimedia Vendor

Pacific Vendor

The Pacific Vendor forum has a subforum on Sound Blaster, and that is where you can find information on Sound Blaster hardware and software, as well as share ideas with other Sound Blaster users.

Another source of information about Sound Blaster is *The WAFFER! Multimedia Digest*, published monthly by Brad Barclay in Brampton, Ontario, Canada. *The WAFFER!* is distributed through a select number of bulletin boards and on CompuServe. A copy of the latest version for Windows is included in the file WMD002.EXE on the disks that come with this book. If you want to reach the publisher directly, write to the publisher at the following address:

> Brad Barclay, Publisher
> *The WAFFER! Multimedia Digest*
> c/o WAFFER! MultiMedia Productions
> 36 Sutter Avenue
> Brampton, Ontario, Canada L6Z 1G7
> (416) 840-0104

It would be safe to say that millions of bytes of sampled sound and MIDI files are racing across the electronic network at any one moment. Finding sounds will not be a problem.

DOS Applications

The DOS-based programs that use the Sound Blaster card generally cannot be run from Windows simply because Windows is using the card and will not share. The file-conversion utilities listed in Chapter 5, "Saving Sound," are described in that chapter and will not be covered again in these pages.

Silly String

This discussion starts with the least helpful but probably the most entertaining use of Sound Blaster I have seen, and I hope the developer of Silly String takes that as a compliment. It is.

Silly String, shown in figure 11.1, displays sound as image.

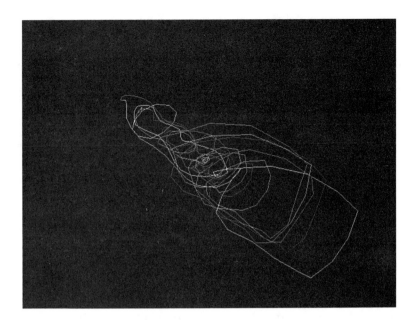

Fig. 11.1

Silly String displaying a voice pattern on the monitor.

When you speak into the microphone connected to Sound Blaster, Silly String converts the sound patterns into lines on the monitor, in much the same way a digital oscilloscope displays waveforms. It's interesting to try to make as circular a sound as possible, hinting at the chance that a pure tone will generate a perfect circle.

Silly String is produced in Massachusetts by the following company:

> Sound Applications
> 20 Fellows Road
> Ipswich, MA 01938
> CompuServe ID 73760,1242

This is not serious software, but who said that all software had to be serious?

BLASTER Master

The BLASTER Master program is one of the most popular sound applications available through the shareware network.

BLASTER Master, shown in figure 11.2, is a sound file editor that edits VOC, WAV, and SND files.

Fig. 11.2

BLASTER Master
editing a VOC file.

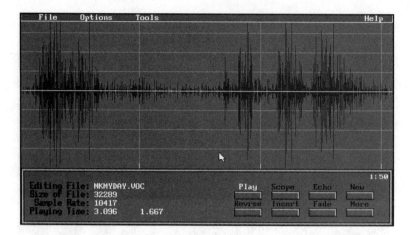

The BLASTER Master program is a highly professional sound-editing package. It is capable of editing files stored in the Creative Labs VOC format, Microsoft's WAV format, and the ever-popular SND format. BLASTER Master serves as a serious sound editor and is capable of cutting, copying, pasting chunks of sound within a file, and adding echoes and other effects. The shareware version of BLASTER Master works only on sound files of 25 seconds or less.

Here is the developer of BLASTER Master:

> Gary Maddox
> 1901 Spring Creek #315
> Plano, TX 75023

Gary provides excellent support for his program, as well as useful documentation. Give BLASTER Master a try!

SBTimbre

The SBTimbre program is an impressive application that lets you access the Sound Blaster FM chips directly. One of the many functions that SBTimbre offers is shown in figure 11.3. This window enables you to control the synthesis elements of the FM synthesizer chip.

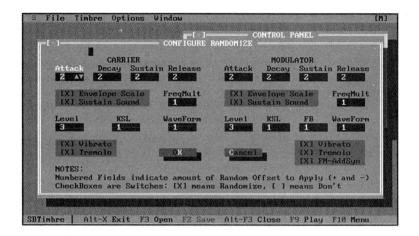

Fig. 11.3

The SBTimbre window in which you can modify existing instruments or create new ones.

SBTimbre, developed by Jamie O'Connell, enables you to see and hear the register settings for the FM synthesizer chip. With Chapter 10 of this book in hand and SBTimbre, you get a real sense of how changing a bit in a register can radically alter the sound produced by the chip.

You can create new sound bank files in the Sound Blaster IBK format. Provided with SBTimbre is a file-conversion utility called SBANK. SBANK converts the AdLib INS, SBI, and BNK files into the IBK format.

You can obtain both programs from Jamie O'Connell at the following address:

> Jamie O'Connell
> 191 Park Dr. #44
> Boston, MA 02215

The SBTimbre program alone will, if given the chance, consume a lot of your time.

Visual Player

The last program in the DOS collection is used to play MOD files originally recorded for play on Amiga computers. The Visual Player program, shown in figure 11.4, is one of the most fascinating sequencer players I have had the pleasure of using.

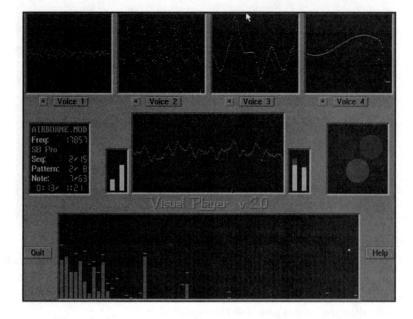

Fig. 11.4

Visual Player
playing an Amiga
MOD file on the
PC.

Without a doubt, the developers of this program from Spain gave far more thought to the appearance of their software than do most designers. Its smooth-scrolling display and highly active windows are as entertaining as the MOD files the program plays.

For information about Visual Player, contact Luis Crespo at FidoNet 2:343/108.21. The latest version of Visual Player is always available on the programmers' BBS, ST-Telecos, which can be accessed via FidoNet 2:343/108 or by phone at 34-3-4017068.

Visual Player supports a number of sound cards and will even play MOD files over the PC speaker.

Windows Applications

The Windows-based programs cover a wide spectrum of functionality. Some of the programs can simply be uncompressed and run; others need a second installation step.

WinJammer

WinJammer, shown in figure 11.5, is a sophisticated MIDI sequencer, comparable to the Cakewalk Apprentice program, provided with the Sound Blaster MIDI Kit, and Wave Blaster. As you can see in the figure, WinJammer has the now-standard pushbutton user interface to record and play back MIDI songs.

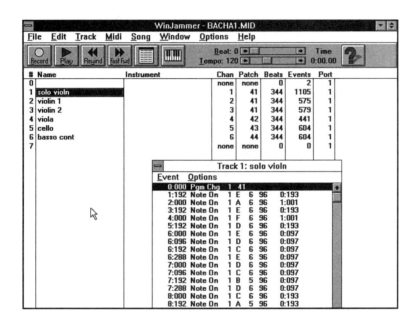

Fig. 11.5

A WinJammer screen.

WinJammer has an extraordinarily rich set of commands and options. In figure 11.5, for example, you can see that a track can be selected, and then a scrolling list of all the events that happen on that track can be shown. This figure shows the solo violin events. At six seconds into the song, the solo violin is playing an E note on port 1 (Sound Blaster) with a duration of 0:097 seconds. You can also edit the events, as shown in figure 11.6.

The WinJammer program can read AdLib ROL files and record through Sound Blaster's MIDI port.

WinJammer comes from the following source:

> Dan McKee
> WinJammer Software Limited
> 69 Rancliffe Road
> Oakville, Ontario, Canada L6H 1B1

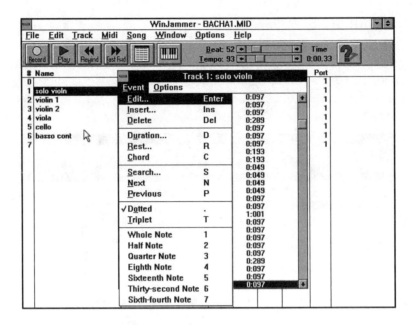

This is a highly professional MIDI package and well worth the registration fee.

InCube

The InCube package is a working voice-recognition system for Windows, using Sound Blaster's voice-sampling capabilities. InCube, shown in figure 11.7, samples your voice command and then converts your speech into a specific Windows command.

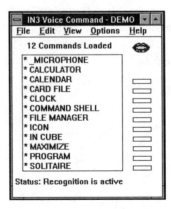

In its shareware version, InCube is capable of learning to obey 11 different Windows commands as you speak them, including InCube itself.

To use InCube, you must go through a training exercise to teach the software how to recognize your spoken commands. You select which Windows program you want to use—for example, the calculator—and then you speak the word *calculator* into the microphone a couple of times at InCube's prompting until it has learned your particular way of saying "calculator." Then, whenever InCube is active (and it can always be active if you copy it into your Startup window), you simply say "calculator" into an active microphone, and InCube will start the Windows calculator program.

Actually, you could say any word you like as long as you can repeat it reliably. After all, InCube recognizes your speech as a series of 1s and 0s (zeros); it doesn't really *understand* what you are saying. Therefore, if you wanted to start the calculator program by saying "kumquat," you could do that.

The InCube program is provided by the following company:

> Command Corp. Inc.
> 3675 Crestwood Parkway
> Duluth, GA 30136
> (404)925-7950

If you want to use voice recognition in a Windows environment without getting Sound Blaster 16/16 ASP, InCube is the way to go.

Wave Editor

Although you can perform a certain amount of editing on WAV files with Windows' Sound Recorder, Wave Editor is much more sophisticated and useful. Shown in figure 11.8, Wave Editor gives you a great deal of control over the way your sampled files sound.

In addition to providing an excellent waveform display, which you can use to chop bits of sound out and move them around, Wave Editor can apply a unique set of filters to your sound, including a Fourier transform, which is a way of looking at sound in terms of frequency instead of time.

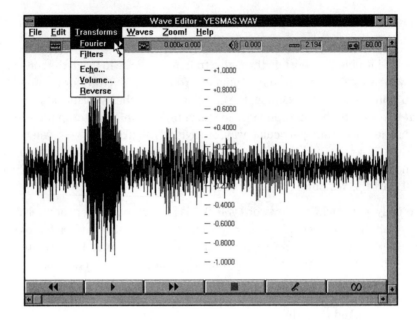

Fig. 11.8

Using Wave
Editor to perform
significant
transformations
on your sound file.

Wave Editor, as the program tells you when you start it, comes from the following source:

Keith W. Boone
ASG Inc.
11900 Grant Place
Des Peres, MO 63131

Version 2.0 of Wave Editor has a few bugs fixed and a large number of new features.

A Multimedia Application

One of the most exciting possibilities that Sound Blaster brings to the computing world is that of multimedia presentations. The capability to produce CD-quality sound, as well as animation and full-motion video, opens the door wide for the future of multimedia. The multimedia demo program is a DOS-based program, proving that you can do very impressive multimedia work without relying on Windows.

The actual name of the program is John & Rob's Multimedia Kaleidoscope. The Kaleidoscope is sort of an electronic fireplace with nice music. Songs have been written specifically for this piece of electronic art. The songs are accompanied by visual imagery that is fun to watch, consisting of photographs that are bent and twisted, seemingly with the wind, and floating glass spheres and rings. And best of all, you get to control how everything moves.

If you're interested in the Kaleidoscope, you can contact John Ratcliff at the following address:

John W. Ratcliff
Wallace Music & Sound
6210 West Pershing Avenue
Glendale, AZ 85304
CompuServe ID: 70253,3237

Some people struggle with this kind of presentation—this use of a computer. When the Kaleidoscope was demonstrated to one person, she asked, "Very pretty, but what do you do with it?" To those people, I can only answer, "Nothing at all." But the rest of you know what to do with it. Enjoy!

APPENDIX A

Note Frequencies and Scales

The following table lists the frequencies of one octave, starting with middle C:

Note	Frequency (Hertz)
Middle C	261.6
C#	277.2
D	293.7
D#	311.1
E	329.6
F	349.2
F#	370.0
G	392.0
G#	415.3
A	440.0
A#	466.2
B	493.9
C	523.3

The frequency differences between the notes in this table are based on the idea of the equal- or even-tempered scale. There are many other ways of tuning or establishing the difference between one note and its nearest neighbors. Western music is generally based on equal temperament, proposed in the 1500s and standardized during the late 1700s, where an octave is divided into 12 equally spaced tone intervals. The ratio between a tone and its next higher neighbor is 1.05946 (multiply by 0.943877 to go the other way).

You can readily see that some rounding takes place in the table and in our ears and brains. The distance between any two adjacent tones is called a half step, or a *semitone*. For example, it's a half step between A and A#, and a half step between B and C. A whole step is, of course, an interval equal to two half steps. The interval between A and B is a whole step, as is the interval between A# and C.

Many tuning systems and common understandings of how tones go together exist. When tones are arranged in an ascending or descending order, they are collectively called a *scale*. The Greeks came up with a scale of seven tones, called a *diatonic* scale. The diatonic scale can be played today on the white keys of the piano and consists of a pattern of tones that contains five whole steps and two half steps.

There are scales, and there are scales, however. If you play the pattern of notes shown in figure A.1 on your piano keyboard (or on the FM Organ, if you like), you will be playing in the Ionian mode.

Fig. A.1

A diatonic scale in the Ionian mode.

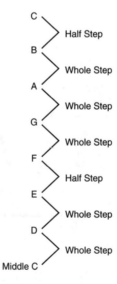

C
Half Step
B
Whole Step
A
Whole Step
G
Whole Step
F
Half Step
E
Whole Step
D
Whole Step
Middle C

You can see that the pattern of five whole steps and two half steps indicates a diatonic scale. If you were to start playing the scale on the A note, using the same pattern of steps, you would be playing the Aeolian mode, which is called the A minor scale today.

Any number of scales are possible and are used around the world in various societies. The chromatic scale consists of all the notes in the octave. Microtonic scales divide the octave into even smaller tone intervals.

File Formats

This appendix details the file formats used to store sound information in the VOC, CMF, SBI, and IBK formats. The first of these formats is used for voice recording, and the other three are used for music.

VOC Files

The Sound Blaster VOC file format is relatively straightforward. The file is divided into two main blocks: the header block and the data block. The data block is further divided into eight sub-blocks.

Header Block

The header block contains an identifier, a version number, and a pointer to the start of the data block. The offsets listed in the following table are in hexadecimal:

Offset	Description
0-13	*File type descriptor.* The descriptor contains the following message: "Creative Voice File", 1AH.
14-15	*Offset of data block.* This two-byte word points to the offset of the data block from the start of the voice file.
16-17	*Voice file format number.* This word contains the version number of the voice file format. The low byte contains the minor version number, and the high byte contains the major version number. The current version number at this printing is 1.10.

continues

continued

Offset	Description
18-19	*Voice file identification code.* This word contains the complement of the file format version number plus the value 1234H. For the current version (1.10), this word contains 010AH + 1234H = 1129H.

Data Block

The data block is divided into eight sub-blocks. Each sub-block has its own header information:

Byte	Definition
0	*BLKTYPE.* The first byte of each sub-block defines the data type held in the sub-block.
1-3	*BLKLEN.* The next three bytes define the sub-block length, excluding the first four bytes that contain BLKTYPE and BLKLEN. Only the Terminator sub-block does not have a BLKLEN field.

The rest of the data in the sub-block may contain voice data, attributes, and information.

Sub-Block Type 0—Terminator Block

The Terminator sub-block marks the end of the entire data block. This block type indicates that there are no other sub-blocks to follow.

The Terminator sub-block is one byte wide and is not followed by a BLKLEN word.

Sub-Block Type 1—Voice Data

01	BLKLEN	TC	PACK	VOICE DATA

The Voice Data block contains a set of voice data. VOC files can contain multiple Voice Data sub-blocks. The BLKLEN value must include the one-byte

TC value, the one-byte PACK value, and the length in bytes of the voice data itself.

The TC field is one byte wide and contains the value TIME_CONSTANT. TC is defined as follows:

TC = 256 − (1000000/sampling rate)

For example, if the sampling rate is 44.1 kHz, TC is set to the nearest integer value, which is 256 − (1000000/44100) or 233.

The PACK byte defines the packing method for this sub-block of voice data:

Value	Definition
0	8-bit raw or unpacked
1	4-bit packed
2	2.6-bit packed
3	2-bit packed

Each Voice Data sub-block can use a different packing method.

Sub-Block Type 2—Voice Continuation

02	BLKLEN	VOICE DATA

The Voice Continuation sub-block continues the voice data from the previous voice Data sub-block. In this sub-block type, the value of BLKLEN is just the length of the voice data.

Sub-Block Type 3—Silence

03	BLKLEN	PERIOD	TC

The Silence sub-block defines a silent period before, between, or after Voice Data sub-blocks.

The PERIOD value is two bytes long and is set in units of the sampling cycle minus 1. The TC byte is defined as follows:

TC = 256 − (1000000/sampling rate)

The BLKLEN value for this sub-block type is always 3.

Sub-Block Type 4—Marker

04	BLKLEN	Marker

The Marker sub-block allows a two-byte marker value to be embedded in a voice file. The marker value must be between 0001H and FFFEH. Values 0000H and FFFFH are reserved.

When you use the Creative Labs CT-VOICE driver and CTVDSK driver, the status word `ct_voice_status` is updated with the marker value.

The BLKLEN value is always set to 2.

Sub-Block Type 5—ASCII Text

05	BLKLEN	ASCII DATA	NULL

The ASCII Text sub-block is used to insert ASCII strings into a voice file. The ASCII data is terminated by an ASCII NULL. The value of BLKLEN includes the length of the ASCII data in bytes as well as the NULL byte.

Sub-Block Type 6—Repeat Loop

06	BLKLEN	COUNT

The Repeat Loop sub-block specifies the beginning of a repeat loop of the next Voice Data sub-block(s). All voice data between this sub-block and the End Repeat Loop sub-block is to be repeated COUNT+1 times.

COUNT is a two-byte value between 0001H and FFFEH. If COUNT = FFFFH, an endless loop occurs.

Sub-Block Type 7—End Repeat Loop

07	BLKLEN	COUNT

The End Repeat Loop sub-block follows the last voice data to be repeated. BLKLEN = 0.

Sub-Block Type 8—Extended Block

08	BLKLEN	TC	PACK	MODE

When used, the Extended Block sub-block always precedes Type 1 Voice Data sub-blocks. This sub-block carries additional attribute information for the Voice Data sub-block that follows. The attribute information in this sub-block supersedes the information carried in the Type 1 Voice Data sub-block that follows.

The Extended Block sub-block can usually be found preceding stereo or high-speed voice data.

The TIME CONSTANT (TC) field is defined in two ways, depending on whether the voice data is mono or stereo. If the voice data is mono, TC is as follows:

TC = 65532 − (256,000,000/sampling rate)

If the voice data is stereo, TC is as follows:

TC = 65532 − (256,000,000/(2*sampling rate))

The PACK byte is set to the packing method used:

Value	Definition
0	8-bit raw or unpacked
1	4-bit packed
2	2.6-bit packed
3	2-bit packed

The MODE byte specifies the sampling method used: mono (0) or stereo (1).

Music File Formats

Sound Blaster works with three different file types from Creative Labs for storing musical instructions: CMF files, which store both instrument and song data; SBI instrument files, which contain data on only one instrument; and IBK files, which are instrument bank files that store data on multiple instruments.

CMF File Format

The CMF file is a slightly modified MIDI file structure. CMF files are made up of three block types:

Header block   Contains version, timing, and offset information.

Instrument block   Contains instrument definitions. The number of instruments defined is contained within the header block.

Music block   The music block contains music data in the standard MIDI format.

Header Block

The header block contains the following information:

Offset	Description
00-03	*File ID.* This offset contains the string "CTMF".
04-05	*File format version.* The MSB contains the major version number, and the LSB contains the minor version number. At this printing, the current version number is 1.10.
06-07	*Instrument block offset.* The offset is calculated from the start of the file.
08-09	*Music block offset.*
0A-0B	*Ticks/Quarter note.* This word contains the number of timer ticks equivalent to a quarter note. This value defaults to 48.
0C-0D	*Clock ticks/second.* This value is equivalent to the frequency of Timer 0 in Hz. The default value is 96, which means that the driver will interrupt 96 times/second. The recommended range for this value is 20-160.
0E-0F	*Music title offset.* The title is a null-terminated ASCII string. If the offset is set to zero, there is no title.
10-11	*Composer name offset.* The name is a null-terminated ASCII string. If the offset is set to zero, there is no composer name.
12-13	*Remarks offset.* The header block can contain remarks in a null-terminated ASCII string. The remarks field supports a maximum of 32 characters, including the null. If the offset is zero, no remarks are contained in the file.

Offset	Description
14-23	*Channel-in-use-table.* This is a 16-byte table that indicates which of the 16 possible channels are used by the music. If a channel is used in the song, its corresponding byte is set to 1.
24-25	*Number of instruments.* This value is the number of instruments used in the file.
26-27	*Basic tempo.*
28-	Space for title, composer, and remark strings.

Instrument Block

The instrument block contains the description of each instrument. Each instrument record is a 16-byte image of the FM synthesizer register sets. The format is identical to that used in an SBI file and is described there.

Music Block

The music block mostly adheres to MIDI specifications and is essentially a Standard MIDI File (SMF), with the exceptions described in the following sections.

Events

Sound Blaster CMF files use only MIDI events. System Exclusive and Meta events are not used. The MIDI events are described in the following table:

MIDI Control Number	Data
66H	*1-127.* These are used as markers in the music.
67H	*0 = melody and 1 = rhythm.* This control number is used to set either melody or rhythm mode for the FM chips. See Chapter 10, "Programming Sound Blaster."
68H	*0-127.* This raises the pitch of all notes that follow this event by the specified number of 1/128 semitone.
69H	*0-127.* This lowers the pitch of all notes that follow this event by the specified number of 1/128 semitone.

Delta Time

A delta time delay precedes every event. The delay is variable in length. In SMF, the delta time for a music timing value does not change when the tempo changes. The timer frequency does change, however.

In CMF, the delta time does change when the tempo changes. The following table illustrates the change:

Timer Frequency	Delta Time	Tempo
96 Hz	48 Ticks	120
96 Hz	24 Ticks	240

Instrument File (SBI) Format

The SBI file contains the specifications for one instrument. You use the IBK instrument bank format to store more than one instrument. The contents of the SBI file relate directly to the register set used by the FM synthesizer chips. See Chapter 10, "Programming Sound Blaster," for more information on these registers. The following list shows the offsets for each file element:

Offset (Hex)	Description
00-03	File ID. This is the ASCII string "SBI", ending with 1AH.
04-23	Instrument name. This is a null-terminated ASCII string.
24	Modular sound characteristic. This byte defines the sound characteristics for the modulator cell:

Bit	Characteristic
7	AM - Pitch Vibrato
6	VIB - Amplitude Vibrato
5	EG - Sustaining Sound Type
4	KSR - Envelope modification
0-3	MULTIPLE - Frequency Multiplier value

Offset (Hex)	Description
26	Modulator scaling/output level.

Bit	Characteristic
6-7	KSL - Level Scaling
0-5	TL - Output Level

Offset (Hex)	Description
27	Carrier scaling/output level.

Bit	Characteristic
6-7	KSL - Level Scaling
0-5	TL - Output Level

Offset (Hex)	Description
28	Modulator attack/decay.

Bit	Characteristic
4-7	AR - Attack Rate
0-3	DR - Decay Rate

Offset (Hex)	Description
29	Carrier attack/decay.

Bit	Characteristic
4-7	AR - Attack Rate
0-3	DR - Decay Rate

Offset (Hex)	Description
2A	Modulator sustain level/release rate.

Bit	Characteristic
4-7	SL - Sustain Level
0-3	RR - Release Rate

Offset (Hex)	Description
2B	Carrier sustain level/release rate.

Bit	Characteristic
4-7	SL - Sustain Level
0-3	RR - Release Rate

Offset (Hex)	Description
2C	Modulator wave select.

Bit	Characteristic
0-1	WS - Waveform Select

continues

continued

Offset (Hex)	Description
2D	Carrier wave select.

Bit	Characteristic
0-1	WS - Waveform Select

Offset (Hex)	Description
2E	Feedback/Connection.

Bit	Characteristic
1-3	Modulator Feedback
0	Connection

Offset (Hex)	Description
2F-33	Reserved.

Instrument Bank (IBK) Format

The IBK file contains multiple instrument definitions. Each IBK can define up to 128 instruments. This file has the following format:

Offset	Description
00-03	*File ID*. This contains the ASCII string "IBK" and ends with 1AH.
04-803	*Instrument parameters*. These are the definitions for up to 128 instruments. Each definition consumes 16 bytes.
804-C83	*Instrument names*. Each name is a 9-byte, null-terminated ASCII string.

APPENDIX C

Sound Blaster MIDI Cable

The connection between Sound Blaster and any MIDI instrument must be made with active circuitry that isolates and correctly directs the signals between the two units. If you buy the MIDI Kit from Creative Labs, the kit contains an active cable. That is, the end of the cable that plugs into the Sound Blaster card contains electronic circuitry. You cannot simply connect wires between the Sound Blaster MIDI port and a MIDI instrument.

The Sound Blaster MIDI port is a non-MIDI standard connector that contains the standard MIDI port electronic signals. If you want to build your own MIDI interface circuitry, you may use the schematic shown in figure C.1.

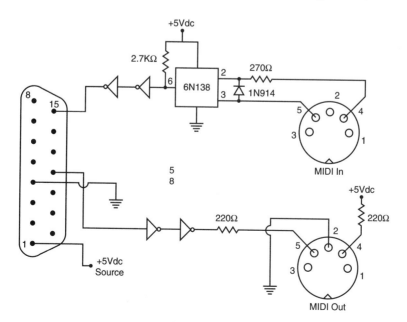

Fig. C.1

MIDI interface between Sound Blaster and MIDI connectors.

If you want to build your own MIDI interface cable for Sound Blaster, you would need the following components:

1	6N138 Opto_Isolator
1	74LS04 Inverter
1	2.7K ohm resistor
1	270 ohm resistor
2	220 ohm resistors
1	DB-15M D connector
2	5-pin DIN connectors

Use shielded cable to prevent EMI problems.

CAUTION

Please do not attempt to build this circuit unless you have successfully built such circuitry in the past. Neither the author nor the publisher of this book assumes any liability for damage that might be done to you, Sound Blaster, or any other equipment.

Installing the Software

The two disks included with this book are packed with some of the best sound and multimedia software available. Some of the software is shareware, and other programs are demonstration versions of commercial packages. All the software is provided in compressed format, allowing more programs on each disk. The files are self-extracting (you don't need any additional program to decompress them), and this appendix shows you how to extract the files you want. But before that, you should understand what shareware is.

What Is Shareware?

Shareware is software you can try before you buy. It is *not* free software, but it *is* a neat idea.

Shareware utilities are written by talented, creative individuals. Their software, quite often, provides the same power as programs you can purchase at your local computer or software store. However, you have the advantage of knowing what you are getting before you buy it.

Each program on these disks has with it a text file that shows you how to register the software. You are obligated to register any software that you like and plan to use regularly.

What benefits do you gain by registering the shareware? First of all, you have a clean conscience, knowing that you have paid the author for the many hours spent in creating such a useful program.

Second, registering the software gives you technical support from the author. The author will provide you with a way to get help for any questions you have while using the software.

Finally, registering the software enables you to keep informed about updates the author makes to the software. Registering the software is important because you benefit from increased features with new versions, and you remain compatible with new versions of DOS.

Copying and Extracting the Software

All the files on the disks are contained in self-extracting, compressed files. (The exception is BADMARY.MID, which is not compressed and is ready to use as is.) Before using any of the software, follow these steps:

1. Make a backup copy of each disk that comes with the book. Store the original disks in a safe place and use the backup copies.

2. Create a directory on your hard drive for the program you are going to use.

3. Copy the file from the directory on the floppy disk to the directory on the hard drive.

4. At the DOS prompt for your hard drive's directory that contains the program, type the program name and press Enter. For example, if you copied JROBMULT.EXE from the JROBMULT directory on disk 2 to C:\JROBMULT, type

    JROBMULT

    at the `c:\JROBMULT>` prompt and press Enter. This step extracts all the files associated with this program.

5. Before using the software, read any text, documentation, or README files for any directions on using or installing that particular program.

6. After you have extracted the files, you can delete from your hard drive the files they were extracted from. In this example, you would delete C:\JROBMULT\JROBMULT.EXE. Be careful not to delete the wrong file because the compressed versions have names similar to the extracted names in some cases. If you delete the wrong file, you can redo these steps to extract the software again.

> **NOTE**
>
> It is a good idea to create a different directory for each program you plan to install. That way, you won't get the files for one program mixed up with those for another.

Disk 1 contains the following software:

Directory	Program Subdirectory	Software Name
DOS	BMSTR5	BLASTER Master
	IFFVOC	IFF2VOC
	MODMID	MOD2MIDI
	SBANKQ	SBANK
	SBTIMB	SBTIMBRE
	SILSTR	Silly String
	SNDCONVQ	Sound Converter
	SUNVOC	SUN2VOC
	UNSTUF	UnStufit
	VPQ	Visual Player
MUSIC	AIRBORNE	AIRBORNE
	MIDIMUS	A collection of MIDI format music
	ROMEO	More music files
SNOOPR		Snooper
WMD		*The Waffer! Multimedia Digest* (There are two compressed files in this directory. Extract them both to use this software.)

Disk 2 contains the following software:

Directory	Program Software	Software Name
JROBMULT		Kaleidoscope Multimedia Demo
WINDOWS	IN3	IN3 Demo
	WAVEDIT	Waveedit
	WINSPK	WINSPEAK
	WNJMR22	WinJammer

Index

Q-R

S

X-Z